The National Capitol, Washington, D.C.
Lambert Photo

Fundamental
USINESS LAW

by Jay F. Christ

A.B. (Morningside College)
J.D. (University of Chicago)

Illustrated • 1945
AMERICAN TECHNICAL SOCIETY
CHICAGO, U.S.A.

PREFACE

The field of commercial law is vast, and the principles involved in it are numerous and complex. Therefore, any textbook on commercial law can consist of no more than a skeleton outline of principles and a limited number of illustrations of those principles. The illustrations are necessary because a statement of principles alone can be of very little use to the practical man. The illustrations given in this book are, for the greater part, digested or adapted directly from actual court decisions, so that they may safely be regarded as authoritative and as indicative of prevailing rules of law. This book is presented as a reliable summary of the most important and most frequently encountered principles of the law in relation to common business transactions.

It is necessary to warn the student (and, perhaps, to remind the teacher) that "sweeping" generalizations, in the field of law as elsewhere, are certain to be more or less inaccurate because nearly all such generalizations are subject to modifications, qualifications, limitations and exceptions. Such modifications and the like as are given should be closely studied and remembered. Some of them are almost, if not quite, as important as the principles to which they belong.

The student should also keep in mind that an introductory book can present only basic common law principles. The extensive and voluminous changes which have been made by statute are almost entirely omitted, except for the Statute of Frauds, the Uniform Sales Act, the Statutes of Limitations, the Uniform Negotiable Instruments Law, and a few others. As an example of a branch of law which is no more than mentioned in the book, there is the law of limited partnership. This branch of the law is based entirely upon statutes. No limited partnership may exist at all unless there is a valid statute which permits such organization. Since the law of limited partnership differs somewhat in different states, it is believed that the subject is too technical and difficult to lend itself to a brief statement of principles. It has therefore been omitted from the book. The student may occasionally come upon some other omission of the same general character. Such omissions are due to the fact that this book is intended for use in a first course in commercial law, and as such it is confined to basic principles of general application, together with the more important modifications of those principles.

Likewise, the student may be somewhat puzzled by the failure of the book to discuss some, at least, of the great mass of modern legislation which regulates business. These omissions are intentional due to the belief that they have no place in a book of basic principles. The numerous and complicated regulatory measures with which business is just now afflicted are largely of an emergency character and, it is hoped, temporary. We shall need many regulatory measures for a long time, to be sure; but they are likely to be changed frequently as we find out more about what kinds of regulation we need.

In addition to the fact that the illustrations are practical ones, as far as it has been possible to make them so, an effort has been made to make the book useful in another way. The book contains more than statements about what the law is; it contains many instances in which the law is uncertain, or in which it varies in different states, or where, for one reason or another, the services of an expert are required. The cases in which one should consult legal counsel are indicated in the book. The student will find that the ability to recognize problems and situations in which he needs advice is just about as important as knowledge of the law itself. Such ability enables one to call for help *before* he gets into trouble; an ounce of prevention is worth a pound of cure.

There are some questions in the book which cannot be answered by mere reasoning. For example, question 1 on page 199, question 2 on page 200, and some others are of this kind. Such questions require specific information which cannot be produced by any amount of reasoning. In a few cases, such as question 3 on page 200, information is necessary as a basis for an adequate answer; but the answer can be inferred from basic information. In this particular case, a correct understanding of the nature of bailment will enable the student to work out a satisfactory answer.

Teachers and students alike should pay special attention to Chapter XII, which outlines two important subjects usually omitted from introductory books in this field; namely, the chief rules which guide the courts in the process of interpreting the language used in contracts, and the basic principles by which the courts determine *how much* money damages can be recovered for breach of contract. Both of these subjects are of extreme importance; they are, of course, technical in their remoter aspects, but the general principles of both are such that they are neither too difficult for the student to grasp, nor too complex for him to remember easily. It is hoped that this chapter may prove to be one of the most valuable features of the book.

Special pains have been taken to provide a complete index. If properly used, an adequate index can be extremely valuable. Every student should learn to use indexes and should look up cross references whenever they are encountered.

Whatever effectiveness this book may possess will in considerable part be due to certain extracts and adaptations taken from two other books by the same author. One of the books is *Modern Business Law,* published by MacMillan & Co., New York, and the other is *Law of Contracts and Sales,* published by Longmans, Green & Co., also of New York. These two publishers have permitted use of certain tables, cuts, extracts, and adaptations. Specific acknowledgments will be found at appropriate places in the book. The author is also grateful to Mr. O. Peterson of the Chicago office of the United States Secret Service for his generous aid with the preparation of the material for the chapter on counterfeit money.

JAY F. CHRIST

Chicago, 1944

United States Supreme Court Building, Washington, D.C.

Underwood & Underwood

A Courtroom

CONTENTS

CONTENTS

JUSTICES OF THE SUPREME COURT, 1944

Left to right, seated, Associate Justices Stanley F. Reed and Owen J. Roberts, Chief Justice Harlan F. Stone and Associate Justices Hugo L. Black and Felix Frankfurter; *standing,* Associate Justices Robert H. Jackson, William O. Douglas, Frank Murphy, Wiley B. Rutledge

CHAPTER I

THE FORMATION OF CONTRACTS

THE NATURE OF CONTRACTS

Every contract is a business agreement which has been made in legal form, by legally competent parties, for valuable consideration, and for some object or purpose not contrary to law or public policy.

The above statement should not be regarded as a definition in the usual sense of the word. Rather, it is a statement which, first, indicates that there are certain legal prerequisites to the making of any contract, and which, second, furnishes a list of those requisites. When you have learned the meaning of all the terms used in the above statement, you will know what a contract is. The statement also is a sort of inventory of things to be learned, and you can check back to this list from time to time in order to take account of your progress.

Consider, first, what is meant by the term *business agreement.* No precise definition is possible, but the usual engagements of business men are characterized by two things. For one thing, they are promissory in character because business men typically make bargains depending on the future conduct of the parties with whom they deal. They make agreements about the payment of money in the future, the erection of buildings, the fabrication of machines, the rendering of services, the delivery of goods—all in the future. In fact, the prime function of contracts is to reduce as much as possible the uncertainties of the future, whether for supplies and materials and labor coming into a business establishment, or for goods and services going out from it. These engagements, since they consider the future conduct of the parties to the agreements, are *promissory* in character. In the second place, business agreements are characterized by the element of *exchange*. The worker's promise to work is exchanged for the employer's promise to pay, in the future; the contracting builder's promise is exchanged for the promise of the owner of the land to pay in the future, whether by installments or in a lump sum; the promise to deliver goods from a factory is exchanged for a promise to buy the material when it is finished. Similarly, it is found that all business agreements show this *exchange* element.

From these facts there follow naturally these elementary rules.

Rule 1. *Gratuitous promises are not usually enforcible as contracts.* If a rich uncle promises to set his nephew up in a business when the latter has completed his education, and the young man expresses his assent, there is surely an agreement; but since nothing is to be given or promised by the nephew, there is no exchange, and the agreement is not a business agreement. The uncle's promise in such a case is gratuitous, and gratuitous promises are not enforcible, as a general rule.[1]

Rule 2. *Wagering agreements are not enforcible.* A wager of ten dollars on a football game is an agreement, of course; and it also consists of an exchange of promises. If Grant bets twenty dollars with Hale on the election of a certain candidate, Grant clearly promises that if his candidate loses, Grant will pay Hale twenty dollars; and Hale, on his side, promises that if the candidate wins, Hale will pay twenty dollars to Grant. But this is not a business agreement, since it is not the kind of agreement which is typical of business transactions; and such an agreement is not enforcible in most states.[2] The wager differs from a business agreement in that while the business agreement is designed to make the future somewhat more certain, a wager does not in the least affect the outcome of the subject of the wager.[3]

---

[1] Some gratuitous promises, in the form of subscriptions to churches, schools, or other charitable or semicharitable institutions, are enforcible in some states under certain conditions. Such cases are considered in a later part of this chapter, in connection with the discussion of consideration in contracts.

[2] Some kinds of betting have been legalized by statutes—for example, the *pari mutuel* system.

[3] Contracts of insurance were once regarded as wagers, but they are essentially different from wagers because (a) the premiums are payable whether or not losses occur (b) insurance actually reduces the probability of losses by rais-

Rule 3. *Social agreements are not enforcible.* If Kent and Wilson promise each other that they will play golf together on a certain day, this is an agreement. It contains an exchange of promises, but it is not a business agreement; and if Wilson did not show up at the appointed time and place, no matter how much inconvenience or loss may have been occasioned to Kent, the courts would not award damages to Kent for breach of contract.[4] This would be designated a *social agreement,* which is not properly to be regarded as a *business transaction.*

Rule 4. *Business agreements are enforcible in the courts.* Subject to the limits mentioned (though still to be discussed in detail in this book), business agreements are enforcible. On May 10, Graham promises to paint Campbell's house before the ensuing July 1, and Campbell promises that, if the house is properly painted by the agreed date, he will pay Graham $250 on August 1 of the same year. Here, again, is an exchange of promises, and thus far it is similar to the other illustrations discussed; but in this case the subject matter of the agreement is precisely the same as that with which business men deal. There is the promise of a more or less definite service on the one side, and the promise of money to be paid for the service on the other side. There is an exchange of promises, as in the other cases, but there is an exchange of assurances about a second exchange to take place in the future. This second exchange is to be an exchange of *business values* or *economic values,* of the kind with which business transactions are commonly concerned. This, then, is what distinguishes a business agreement from other agreements: the subsequent exchange of *business* or *economic* values *in the future—* after the making of the agreement.

Thus the typical business agreement is made by an exchange of promises—by an exchange of nothing of any tangible character. At the time the business agreement was made between Graham and Campbell, no money was paid and no work had

---

ing standards of insurability, and (c) insurance reduces the loss if damage does occur.

[4] No actual reported case is precisely like this, because we do not have lawsuits about such frivolous matters; but legal authorities have long held and expressed the belief that this and other similar agreements are not enforcible.

been done. The substance of the agreement was to be performed at a later time, and the things to be exchanged were of *economic* or *business* value. The typical business agreement, then, is an agreement because it consists of an exchange of promises; it is a business agreement, because it involves *business* values.

As indicated earlier, business men enter into such agreements because they wish to have some positive assurances as to the future conduct of those with whom they deal. They wish to assure themselves, as far as possible, of continuous supplies of fuel, materials, and labor, and to be as sure as they can that the products of their work, or their factories, or their transportation facilities, will be taken by customers. To obtain these assurances (and many others, like bank credit, insurance, bank deposits, etc.), they enter into engagements in which, in exchange for the promises of others, they in turn make promises to the others. The results are business agreements. Such agreements have become so important a part of the structure of our financial order, that they are enforcible in the courts, subject to the limitations that have already been suggested, and which we shall study in detail.

Before that is done, however, it is desirable to consider carefully certain rules of law relative to the actual processes by which enforcible business agreements are made. In order to do that, it is necessary to discuss the legal concepts of the terms *offer* and *acceptance*. These must be regarded as technical terms; they cannot be adequately understood by the mere process of defining the words. It is necessary to develop an understanding of the concepts underlying them. When that has been done, the student will have gone a long way toward an understanding of contracts and contract law.

THE MAKING OF CONTRACTUAL OFFERS

From what has already been stated, it should be fairly clear that contracts—agreements which the courts will enforce—are the result of *expressions*. It is worth while emphasizing at this point that contracts are not the result of the *intent* of the parties to agreements; contracts are the result of *expressions of intent*.

Therefore, when one encounters in law books the terms *mutual assent, meeting of the minds,* and other similar terms, it is necessary to remember that these terms do not mean what they seem to mean. Such terms signify there has been (or there has not been), in the given case, the proper kind of *exchange of expression* for the formation of an enforcible agreement—a contract.

Since an agreement, to be enforcible, must consist of an exchange of promises,[5] it follows that before any such exchange can take place, some person must make some positive, promissory statement to some other person. In order to become a part of an agreement, such a statement must not only promise something definite, it must also indicate that this promise will be exchanged for some other promise, and it must also state clearly just what is desired in exchange for the initial promise. In the language of the law of contracts, the person who makes an initial, positive promise such as that just described, is said to make an *offer;* and if the person to whom such a promise is *offered* (he is called the *offeree*) makes the required response, he is said to *accept* the *offer*. These terms, it must be repeated, are merely the names given to the concepts underlying the legal idea of contract; and it is necessary to study in some detail the concepts which these words denote. To repeat once more: mere word definitions of *offer* and *acceptance* are not enough; the student should realize that he is in search of an understanding of the underlying ideas.

One effective way to make clear the meaning of the concept underlying *offer* is to set forth certain rules of law which affect the making of offers. These rules may appear in different forms, but essentially there are three fundamental ideas involved in the rules. Two of these rules already have been stated in this chapter, but these matters are of such far-reaching importance that they will bear some repetition.

Rule 5. *Every offer for a contract must contain a promise.* Suppose that Smith said to Jones, "Will you sell your house to

---

[5] It is true that some contracts are formed by the exchange of acts for promises, but for the present it seems best to ignore those. They will be discussed in another chapter. Just now, consider only those contracts with promises on both sides.

me for $10,000?" Such a statement cannot possibly be an offer, and no kind of reply will result in an agreement without further expression from Smith. Why is this? It is because Smith has asked a question; he has not made any promise; he has not made any positive expression of his willingness to do (or not to do) anything whatever.

Rule 6. *Every offer must propose an exchange of a business character.* An offer must not only contain a promise; it must also propose to exchange that promise for something (typically another promise, as stated before), and the something must be of a business character. Note, once more, that this proposal characteristically proposes two exchanges: there must be in the offer a proposal to exchange the promise (in the offer) for another promise, and there is also the proposal to exchange goods for money, or the like, at some later time. The first exchange (of the promises), if it is made, will constitute the agreement; the second exchange, if made, will normally constitute the performance of the agreement.

If the word (and idea) of exchange appear to be used rather often, consider the following simple case: Bell said to Gates, "I will pay you fifty dollars for your watch," and Gates replied, "All right; I will take it." This is a business agreement. The offer is the promise of Bell: and the precise meaning of the promise is: "I hereby propose to give you my promise to give you my fifty dollars for your watch, if you will give me your promise to give me the watch for fifty dollars." Bell proposes first to exchange promises as indicated, and second, if the promises are exchanged, to exchange the money for the watch at some later time. So, if Gates replies, "All right," we have an agreement, although the seller still has the watch and the buyer still has his money.[6]

Rule 7. *Every offer must seem reasonably serious from the viewpoint of the offeree.* It is not enough that an offer (to be capable of being turned into an agreement or contract) should contain a promise and that it should propose exchanges as just shown. Many promises involve proposals to make exchanges of some business character, without being offers in the legal sense.

---

[6] See footnote 4 on page 3.

This is because the courts insist that any proposal, in order to be capable of becoming an element in a contract, must be made in such a way and under such circumstances as to make it reasonable for the offeree to believe that the offerer is sincere in his statement—that he means what he says.

Some illustrations should help to clear up this point. Carter owned an old horse, worth perhaps twenty-five dollars. One cold winter morning the horse was gone from its stall, and Carter ran to the nearest police station to report the theft. Without hat or coat, obviously much excited, he shouted, "I will give a thousand dollars to discover the thief." Now, this might sound as though he meant to say, "I hereby give my promise to pay one thousand dollars in exchange for information as to the identity of the thief"; but, in view of all the facts, it probably would not be reasonable to believe that he expected to be taken seriously. The low value of the horse, his obvious excitement, the relatively large amount mentioned—all these would make a reasonable person reluctant to rely upon such an expression.[7] This kind of situation is covered by the statement of **Rule 7.** The same thing is sometimes expressed by the saying: An offer must be made with apparent seriousness. It is also important to notice that it is not the real state of mind of Carter with which we are concerned; we are concerned with the question: Would it be reasonable to rely upon the expression as an offer, in view of all of the attendant circumstances? In the illustration given, it seems that the answer should be *no.*

Another illustration is of a kind rather frequently encountered in everyday transactions. Ulster owned a fifty-foot city lot in a block in which the valuation was about $300 per front foot. Ulster wrote to Kane, offering the lot for sale for $1,500. This looks, on the surface, like an offer to sell the lot for $1,500, so far as the wording goes, but if Kane knows that the current value of lots in the vicinity is much higher, he is not entitled, legally, to regard this expression as an offer. Under the circumstances, a reasonable man with the knowledge possessed by Kane, would probably

---

[7] This does not mean that Carter could not make an offer of this kind with relation to this kind of horse and this kind of situation. It means only that we cannot take such an expression at its face value without further confirmation which would make it reasonable for us to rely on the expression.

regard the figure as an error and could not treat the letter as a valid offer unless other circumstances made it reasonably probable that Ulster actually did mean what he said in the letter.

Rule 8. *An offer must be received and understood by the offeree.* This rule is in fact no more than a corollary of what has gone before. Suppose Richards said to Hale, "I would like to sell my launch to Wilson. I would take $600 for it." Suppose that Wilson, without having heard of this statement, told Richards that he (Wilson) would give $600 for the launch. This would not be an acceptance, and Richards would be legally free to reject or accept the proposal made by Wilson. The statement of Richards to Hale is not an offer to Wilson, and can never be an offer until the offeree receives and understands it, for a man cannot reasonably rely upon what he has never heard. Another application of this rule is as follows: Suppose that Gardner wrote out a statement of his willingness to buy Keen's radio transmitter for $250. Suppose that Gardner mailed this letter, but that the mailbox was destroyed by fire while the letter was in the box. This could not be an offer since it was not received. Again, suppose that Lewis wrote a letter to Beck, offering to buy Beck's chicken farm for $3,600. Suppose that Beck, before he opened the letter, lost it and never found it. Here, again, there was no offer in the legal sense, for the same reason that was given in **Rule 8.**

Rule 9. *An offer may be made only by authority of the offerer.* Take the first illustration in the preceding paragraph. Now suppose that Hale reported to Wilson this statement of Richards. This statement still would not be an offer, unless Richards had authorized Hale to make the proposal to Wilson for Richards. Any proposal, to be an offer, must come either directly from the offerer or by definite authority from him; otherwise the offeree cannot rely upon the statement as an offer.

Rule 10. *Offers may be made in different forms.* Since an offer is an expression of willingness to enter into a business agreement, it follows naturally that an offer may consist of any kind of conduct which constitutes such an expression. An offer may be made orally, by letter or telegram, by informal writing, by actions, signs, or conduct of any kind, just so long as the conduct expresses a willingness to exchange promises, and so long as the conduct makes reliance upon it seem reasonable. Parties to bargains most often use words, of course, but that is merely because words are the symbols most commonly in use and the most easily used and understood; but many offers are made in boards of trade, for example, or at auction sales, by making signs or gestures which are well understood in the trades where they are used. In fact, one may make an offer in a very simple manner. Suppose that you walk into a store where you have an account. You are in a hurry, and you pick up two packages of cereal from a rack and hold them up so that a clerk can see them. The clerk nods his head, and you go away with the cereal. Your conduct says, as plainly as any words could say, "I promise to pay for these when the bill is rendered in the due course of business." This is an offer, because there is only one meaning which the clerk can reasonably attach to your conduct.[8]

Some Exceptional Cases. There are a few cases in which the decisions of the courts do not conform to the above rules. Such cases constitute a minority of all the decisions, but since these exceptional cases do not conform to the general principles so far set forth, it is necessary to describe them; however, it must be remembered that they are exceptional.

Rule 11. *At auction sales, the offer is said to come from the bidder, and not from the auctioneer.* When an auctioneer promises to sell to the highest bidder, this is a promise, without any doubt. Furthermore, most persons would agree that the bidder who makes the highest bid at a sale would be reasonable in believing that the auctioneer would be bound by law to sell to such highest bidder. In the case of an ordinary auction sale, however, this is not the case. The courts hold uniformly that an announcement of an auction sale, or even a specific promise to sell to the highest bidder, is not an offer. Therefore, the auctioneer is legally entitled to reject any bid, for any reason, and the bidder, also, is entitled to withdraw his bid at any time before the hammer falls. This rule may seem to be an arbitrary one, and perhaps

---

[8] The clerk's nod, of course, was an acceptance, which we shall consider subsequently.

it is, but the rule is universally applied to ordinary auction sales.

In about thirty states, where the Uniform Sales Act is in effect, an auctioneer who promises to sell to the highest bidder without reserve, is held to be bound to sell to such highest bidder. This obligation, it must be noted, is the result of the statute in the form of the Sales Act. It is not a part of the general law of contracts.[9]

Rule 12. *Advertisements and displays of goods for sale, even with an announcement of specified prices, are not treated as offers.* In spite of the fact that persons who see goods on display with price tags affixed might reasonably suppose that, if they signified their willingness to buy, the dealer or person responsible for the display would be legally obligated to sell the goods to such buyer, this is not true. Such displays, as well as advertisements expressing willingness to sell, are not regarded as offers. They are regarded as *invitations to deal,* and the offers in such cases are regarded as coming from the prospective buyer; the *seller* may accept or reject, as he likes, just as he may accept or reject other offers. Here, again, it must be remembered that while this rule may seem arbitrary, it is the result of long experience, and it must be remembered as an exception to the general principles of the law of offers.

Rule 13. *Price quotations are not regarded as offers.* Duke wrote to B. & Co. asking their price on certain canvas and when delivery could be made. In reply, B. & Co. wrote, stating that the price was two and one-half cents per yard, and that delivery could be made in five or six weeks. Duke then sent an order for the quantity specified in his first letter. B. & Co. declined to fill the order because the price had gone up. Duke thought that the letter was an offer, and that his order was an acceptance. In his suit for breach of contract, the court declared that this letter of B. & Co. was not an offer, but a *quotation.* It is impossible to state precisely the meaning of this term *quotation,* but it is at least safe to say that a mere statement of a price at which a thing will be, or would be, sold is likely to be regarded as a quotation and not as an offer, in spite of the fact that a buyer in the

[9] See page 91 for a list of the states where the Sales Act is in effect.

position of Duke might well be reasonable in regarding the letter as an offer. This is another case in which the rule appears to be arbitrary; but whether it is or not, the possibility that a statement of price will be regarded as a quotation must always be kept in mind. Note that this rule does not apply to all statements of price, and it does not mean that a seller cannot make an offer. These three exceptions, relative to auction sales, displays and advertisements, and quotations, represent certain exceptions to the general rules about offers. The first two are easy enough to distinguish, but the third one—quotation—is very hard to handle. About all one can do is to remember that there is such a thing, and that it may be encountered unexpectedly, but not very often.

Rule 14. *Offers of rewards are treated differently in different states.* Hinton's horse strayed or was stolen. Hinton published a notice of a reward for the return of his horse. Jackson found the horse and returned it to Hinton before Jackson had any knowledge of the offer of the reward. When he learned of the reward, Jackson demanded it, but Hinton declined to pay it, and Jackson brought suit. In such a case, if the courts followed the *reasonable* theory, or if they followed the rule that an offer must be received and understood before it can be turned into a contract by acceptance, they would decide that Jackson could not recover the reward, because he did not know of it. This is the rule which is followed in the states of Alabama, California, Illinois, Kansas, Minnesota, Missouri, New Jersey, New York, North Dakota, and Texas. But in the states of Delaware, Indiana, Kentucky, Massachusetts, and Vermont, the opposite rule is followed: in the case of a published offer of reward for information, or the recovery of lost or stolen goods, or the like, knowledge of the existence of the offer is not necessary to make binding the promise to pay the reward to the person who performs the act requested in the offer. In the latter states, therefore, offers of rewards are treated in an exceptional way. In those states which have not been named here, no such cases have been reported, so we do not know what the courts would do in such cases; but it seems probable that most of them would follow the first theory, and not treat these offers as exceptions.

The substance of the law of offers is this: In order that a business proposal can be considered an offer in the legal sense (and, therefore, can be developed into a contract), the proposal must be an expression of willingness to enter into some more or less definite[10] business agreement; and the expression must be made under such circumstances that it is reasonable for the offeree to believe that, if he does what the offer requests him to do, the maker of the offer will be bound by contract to carry out his promise. In addition to this general principle, it is necessary to remember the several exceptional cases which have been discussed, in which there may be no offer in spite of the fact that the proposals seem to illustrate the general principle.

THE TERMINATION OF OFFERS

Once an offer has been made, the question may arise in some form or other: Are there any events, the occurrence of which will put an end to the possibility of accepting the offer? And the further question may arise: If there are such events, what are they? The answers to these questions may be determined by one who is familiar with certain rules of the law of contracts. In general, an offer may be regarded as still in effect, and therefore capable of being turned into a contract, as long as it remains reasonable for the offeree to believe that the offer exists. To put this in another way: Every offer must create a reasonable belief in the mind of the offeree that the offerer has made the proposition in earnest; but when some event occurs, of such a nature that the offeree no longer can reasonably believe that the offerer still intends to carry out the bargain (if one should be made), then the possibility of accepting the offer will come to an end. There are several kinds of events which may bring about the termination of offers. Some of them, it will be noticed, have the effect of ending the offer because the reasonable expectation of the offeree is ended, but other events terminate offers for different reasons. These events are enumerated and explained in connection with the following rules of law.

---

[10] The matter of definiteness—how far an agreement must be definite in order to become a contract—will be discussed in another chapter.

Rule 15. *An offer may be terminated by revocation on the part of the offerer, before acceptance by the offeree.* A revocation, or a withdrawal, is an expression by the offerer to the offeree, stating that the offer is no longer open. Take as an illustration a case in which Hart had advertised an auction sale. Jensen made a bid on a team of horses; but while the auctioneer was trying to get a higher bid, Jensen decided that he did not want to buy the horses. Jensen called to the auctioneer, "I withdraw my bid." The auctioneer did not receive any higher bids, and announced that the team had been sold to Jensen at his bid. Jensen refused to take or pay for the horses when the auctioneer's hammer fell, and Hart brought a suit for breach of contract. In the discussion of **Rule 11** it was pointed out that at an ordinary auction sale the offer is said to come from the bidder. In the case before us, the court took this view and decided that since the bid was an offer, and since an offer can be withdrawn before acceptance, the bid could be withdrawn, and that the falling of the hammer did not form a contract.

In another case, Gregg, a farmer, signed an order for a silo. On the printed form was the statement, "No order can be revoked," while in another place appeared the words, "No order is binding upon the seller until his acceptance." After signing this order, but before the seller accepted it, Gregg notified the seller that he wished to cancel the order. He refused to take the silo or permit installation of it. When he was sued for breach of contract, the court said that even a promise by an offerer not to revoke his offer does not take away his legal right to do so. The promise not to revoke, in such a case, is a gratuitous promise and not enforcible under **Rule 1.**[11]

Rule 16. *A revocation does not terminate an offer until the revocation is received.* In the auction case, under **Rule 15** if the hammer had fallen before the auctioneer heard the withdrawal, the withdrawal would not have been effective, and the falling of the hammer would have been an acceptance. Similarly, in the silo case, if the company had signified its acceptance of

[11] A paid-for promise not to revoke—a paid option—is treated otherwise; this is discussed under **Rule 17.**

the offer before it received the revocation, the contract would have been operative and binding upon both buyer and seller. Thus, in the silo case, if the withdrawal had been mailed, and if the letter of withdrawal had been lost in the mail, when the acceptance was completed the contract would have become valid. A revocation is not effective to terminate an offer until the revocation is received by the offeree. This is in keeping with **Rule 7,** for, when an offer has been made, it is reasonable for the offeree to consider that it is still in effect until something happens to make this belief unreasonable. If the event which occurs is a withdrawal, it cannot affect his reasonable belief until he receives the withdrawal.

Rule 17. *Paid-for options are not revocable at all.* Glenn offered to sell his lot to Hill for $500, and, in exchange for a payment of ten dollars, Glenn promised to keep the offer open until noon on the following Wednesday. Within a couple of days, and before Wednesday, Glenn offered to return the money to Hill and said that the offer was no longer open. Before noon on Wednesday, Hill sent a proper acceptance to Glenn, but the latter refused to sell. Hill then sued for breach of contract. Under such circumstances, Hill was entitled to judgment. The promise not to revoke is regarded as a contract because that promise was paid for, and it is a breach of contract not to carry out the promise to hold the offer open. The proper meaning of the rule stated above, then, is that it is not lawful to revoke a paid-for option. An attempt to do so is a breach of contract, if the original offer is accepted.

Rule 18. *An offer may be terminated by the lapse of time.* Of course, if the offer stipulates a time for its own duration, as was done in the option case referred to in the last preceding paragraph, the offer certainly will come to an end with the lapse of the stipulated time, if it has not been accepted previously to that time. No offeree could reasonably believe that an offer was still open after the passage of time named in the offer itself, and this is true whether the option is paid for or not. Even when the offer does not set any time limit for acceptance, yet there is such a limit. An offer does not continue in existence forever. Williams offered certain stocks for sale to Miller in October, 1936.

Miller did not reply until November of 1940. It is quite clear that no reasonable man could suppose that this offer was still open, after all that time.

Just how long is a reasonable time for the offeree to wait is a question to which no definite answer can be given. If the goods in question are such as fluctuate rapidly in price, the time for acceptance will be shorter than it would be if the price of the goods were more stable. The matter goes back to the basic question: At the time when the offeree tried to accept, was it reasonable in view of all the circumstances for him to think that the offer was still open? Or had he waited so long that he could not reasonably hold this belief? If it is reasonable for him so to believe, he can accept; if it is not reasonable for him so to believe, he cannot accept.

Rule 19. *Any revocable offer is terminated by death or insanity of the offerer, whether known to the offeree or not.* Fisher made an offer to Bushnell, in which Fisher agreed to sell certain machinery to Bushnell, provided the latter's acceptance and check should reach Fisher at or before 10 A.M., December 1, 1938. Bushnell sent a proper acceptance which reached Fisher's address on November 25, 1938. Fisher had died suddenly on November 22, but this fact was unknown to Bushnell until about December 3. Bushnell demanded the delivery of the machinery, but the administrator of Fisher's estate returned Bushnell's check and refused to deliver the machinery. In a suit for breach of contract, it was held that the death of Fisher had terminated the offer automatically, even without the knowledge of Bushnell as to the death of Fisher. This rule may seem somewhat arbitrary. Certainly it does not seem to coincide with the *reasonable expectation* idea discussed under **Rules 7** and **8,** and it has been severely criticized by leading authorities in this field of law. There is a contrary decision in Alabama, but the rule stated in this paragraph is the rule generally followed. The same rule is followed when the offerer becomes insane before acceptance of the offer is completed. The death of the offeree before acceptance will terminate most offers, too, for an offer is not regarded as inheritable by the heirs of the offeree, unless specifically made so by the offerer itself.

Rule 20. *An offer may be terminated by rejection, which is regarded as effective when sent, whether or not it is ever received.* Rejection consists of a statement by an offeree, directed to the offerer, to the effect that he does not intend to accept the offer. A mere failure to reply is not a rejection. Moss offered a used car for sale to Peters, at a stated price. Peters replied that this was too much. This was a rejection. Some hours later (within a reasonable time), Peters told Moss that he would take the car at the price named. Moss, however, said that he had changed his mind, and would not sell it at that price. Peters thought he had accepted an offer, but he was mistaken. His rejection had put an end to the offer, and that particular offer could not thereafter be accepted.

This rule is sometimes important in a case like the following one: Wells sent to Bates, by mail, an offer to sell a certain machine to him for $200. Bates wrote and mailed at once a reply, stating that he did not want the machine at that price. Within a few hours, Bates encountered a customer who wanted such a machine and was willing to pay $250 for it. Bates at once telegraphed Wells, "I accept your offer. Send machine at once." The telegram reached Wells before the letter reached him, but before he had sent the machine, the letter of rejection reached him. The letter's postmark showed that the letter had been mailed before the time of the filing of the telegram. Wells had another customer for the machine at $225, and wished to know whether he was bound by the telegram of acceptance, which reached him before the letter reached him, or whether the offer was terminated by the sending of the letter, which took place before the telegram was sent. The answer was that the offer was terminated by the letter of rejection, which was operative to end the offer, at the moment when the rejection was dispatched. Since this ended the offer, there was no offer at the time when the telegram was sent (or when it arrived), and there was, therefore, no contract between Wells and Bates.

Rule 21. *A counteroffer operates as a rejection.* The following situation is one which is very common, and which is usually misunderstood by the parties concerned. Suppose that Healy sent to Nash an offer to buy a large amount of scrap iron at eight dollars per ton, and that Nash replied, "Your price is rather low, isn't it? You can have this scrap for ten dollars a ton." Healy did not raise his bid, and Nash finally sent a letter stating, "I wish now to accept your offer." This, of course, Healy supposed to be an acceptance of the original offer, but he was mistaken. A counter-offer is treated by the courts precisely the same as a rejection, and a counteroffer therefore terminates the original offer, and there can be no subsequent acceptance unless the original offer is renewed by the original offerer. This rule is important because of the frequency of the occurrence of counteroffers of the sort discussed. The result is the same whether the original offer is written or oral.

Rule 22. *Continuing offers are treated just as other offers by the courts.* Sometimes an offer contains an assurance of such a kind that acceptance may consist of a series of acts, and those acceptances may result in a series of contracts. Holly wrote the G. Mfg. Co. to the effect that if the G. Mfg. Co. would fill certain orders submitted by Belden, he would endeavor to see that the goods were paid for by Belden, and that if Belden did not pay, then the G. Mfg. Co. could look to Holly for payment. This offer constitutes a continuing sort of promise. Every time Belden submits an order which is filled by the G. Mfg. Co., there is a new contract of guaranty between Holly and the G. Mfg. Co. If there are forty separate transactions, then there will be forty separate contracts of guaranty. This kind of offer is called a continuing offer, and acceptances can be made with the result of binding obligations upon the guarantor (Holly), just as long as the offer remains in effect—that is, so long as the offer has not been withdrawn, or rejected, or lapsed due to the passage of time. One who makes a guaranty of this continuing sort, therefore, should stipulate some time limit. If renewal seems desirable, renewal is easy, but revocation of such an offer may sometimes be difficult.

SOME PRACTICAL SUGGESTIONS

Options. If an offeree wishes an offer to be held open on any important matter, he should insist on an option, and he should insist upon paying something for the option. Under such an agreement, there is no obligation to accept, but there is an obligation

to leave the offer open. Also, one who takes an option should see
to it that the terms of the option provide that, if the offer is accepted, the amount paid for the option shall be applied on the
purchase price, or, if the seller has an option, that the amount paid
for the option should be returned upon acceptance of the offer.
In this way, the amount of the option-payment is forfeited if the
offer is not accepted, but it is applied to the contract if the offer
is accepted. The option, therefore, is a protection to the offeree
before acceptance.

Duplicate Offers Covering the Same Subject Matter.
Clay was desirous of selling a secondhand mimeograph machine.
He wrote a personal letter to Smith, describing the machine and
saying that, as he knew Smith to be in the market, he was offering the machine for sixty dollars. Within a couple of days, not
having heard from Smith, Clay wrote an identical letter, offering
the machine to Brown. Before the lapse of sufficient time to terminate either offer, both Smith and Brown sent letters of acceptance, with checks. Now, the natural opinion about this situation
might be that the first one to accept has a right to the machine.
The fact, however, is that Clay had made two contracts. He sent
an offer to Smith, which was accepted, and he sent another to
Brown, which was accepted. He may give the machine to either,
but he then will break his contract with the other. Every person
who makes more offers than one, regarding the same subject matter, should keep this in mind; and he should be very careful not
to have two outstanding offers at the same time, regarding the same
subject matter. There is a real danger here, and one who does not
avoid that danger will be obliged to charge his mistake only to his
own ignorance or carelessness.

ACCEPTANCE OF OFFERS

The acceptance, of course, is the offeree's expression of his
willingness to enter into the agreement proposed by the offerer. If
there is an expression in the proper way, the acceptance will result
in the formation of a contract. What the proper mode of expression is, is governed by certain rules which are summarized as
follows:

Rule 23. *An acceptance must be an expression.* The acceptance is the expression of the offeree, stating his willingness to enter
into the agreement proposed by the offerer. The acceptance must
be some kind of expression, which may be made in any manner
not inconsistent with the terms of the offer. An owner of a building negotiated with a carpenter for some alterations. After the
carpenter had made an estimate, the owner wrote a note, saying,
"You may begin work as soon as you are ready, on the basis of
our last estimate." This was an offer, but the carpenter, instead
of making some kind of reply, merely bought a quantity of material with which to do the work. Before the carpenter gave any
expression of his acceptance, the offer was withdrawn. The carpenter was naturally disappointed and brought suit for breach of
contract, but it was held by a court that there was no contract
because the carpenter had performed no act of an expressive
character. The mere fact that he bought some lumber was not the
kind of fact which would ordinarily become known to the other
party, and even if it had become known, such a purchase would
not necessarily mean that the material was bought for that particular job. The carpenter should have sent some word, indicating
his acceptance.

Rule 24. *An acceptance must conform to the terms of the
offer.* A steel mill offered to sell from 2500 to 7500 tons of rails
at a certain price per ton. The offeree ordered 1800 tons at this
price. The company refused to fill the order, and the offeree, think-
ing that his reply had been an acceptance, brought suit for breach
of contract. He was mistaken, however, since it is a universal rule
that the terms of acceptance must conform strictly to the terms
of the offer. If an offer stated that the offerer was willing to sell
his car for $400, but also stated that he would do so provided the
acceptance be made by sounding the fire alarm at the corner of
Spruce and Main Streets, then there would be no other way in
which the offer could be accepted. Of course, persons who make
offers do not ordinarily make such absurd provisions. An extreme
illustration has been used to emphasize the importance of this rule.

Again, what seems absurd may not really be absurd. A South
American dealer agreed to take and pay for certain machines,

provided the packages were marked with green stripes. These instructions were disregarded, and when the dealer refused to accept the goods, there was no contract. The provisions seemed absurd to the seller, but the buyer had a good reason: certain men who were to handle the packages were unable to read and could identify the packages only by some color device, such as the one suggested.

Rule 25. *Any reasonable manner of acceptance is sufficient if not contrary to the conditions of the offer.* Suppose an offerer said, "I will sell you 600 barrels of sugar at five dollars per hundred, provided your acceptance reaches me before noon on March 31, 1942." Any mode of communication which actually reaches the offerer will be sufficient to make a contract, but if the acceptance does not reach the offerer within the stipulated time, there will be no acceptance because that is what the offerer required.

A word of caution is needed here. Sometimes, offers contain phrases which appear to be directions for modes of reply, but which in reality are merely formal phrases. Typical of this kind of language are the phrases *answer by return mail, answer by wire, wire at once,* and other similar phrases. The courts do not usually consider that such language is to be taken literally. These and many similar expressions are usually construed by the courts to mean that the offerer wants a somewhat prompt reply, but he does not expect that the offeree will suddenly drop what he is doing and *immediately* send a reply. As a general rule, unless the mode of acceptance is clearly and definitely specified, the acceptance may be sent in any manner which is reasonable. This is not so important when the offer stipulates that the acceptance must be received, in order to make a contract, but it may become very important in connection with cases discussed in connection with **Rule 26.**

Rule 26. *An acceptance need not be received in order to become effective, unless the offer so stipulates.* Hall sent by mail to Kelly an offer to buy Kelly's house and lot at a stated price, asking for a prompt reply, but not making any stipulation beyond that. Kelly at once mailed a letter, stating that the offer was accepted. This letter was destroyed in the wreck of a plane carrying it with other mail. After ten days or so, Hall bought another lot. Kelly, not having heard from Hall, but expecting further communication at any time, took no further steps until the eleventh day. He wrote Hall again, and when Hall explained that he had not received any reply, Kelly claimed that a contract had been made, under which contract Hall was obligated to buy Kelly's lot or pay damages for breach of contract. The courts are in agreement on the rule, that when an offer does not stipulate for receipt of the acceptance, the acceptance is regarded as completing the making of the contract at the moment when the letter of acceptance is properly stamped and addressed and put into the mail. In the case of telegraphic replies, the acceptance is regarded as effective when the telegram of acceptance is filed.

All of this, of course, must be understood to depend upon whether or not the acceptance was in the proper form, considering the circumstances of the particular case. Where the offer does not stipulate clearly the mode of reply, and where the offer does not require that the acceptance must be received to make a contract, any reasonable mode of acceptance is sufficient, and the acceptance will be effective to make the contract binding at the moment when the acceptance is properly dispatched.

A combination of **Rules 25** and **26** becomes important in a case like the following one. Nelson mailed a letter to Platt, offering to sell a certain lot for a stated price. The letter was a valid legal offer. Platt sent a telegraphic reply, accepting the offer. Platt used the telegraph because it was then too late to get a letter into the mail that day in Platt's town. The telegram was filed on the day when the offer was received. The telegraph company delayed the transmission of the telegram for several hours, however, and by the time it reached Nelson, he had sold the lot to another party. If the telegram were a proper mode in which to reply, then the contract was accepted at the moment when the telegram was filed, and a contract was formed. On the other hand, if it were not proper to use the telegraph in reply to an offer received by mail, the reply was not a valid acceptance, and there was no contract. Most courts would agree that this mode of reply was proper, in view of the circumstance that there was no mail out of Platt's town on that day. This made it reasonable for him to reply by telegram. The answer to the question of the sufficiency of such acceptances always depends upon whether or not the mode of reply was reasonable under the circumstances. There is not a complete agreement among all of the state courts in all cases, as to the reasonableness of the modes of replies to offers; and, in order to avoid this troublesome question, if there is any doubt at all in the mind of the offeree as to the mode of his acceptance, he can protect himself by doing two things. For one thing, he should select the mode which will normally reach the offerer in the shortest time, and then he should reply by the same means used in the communication of the offer, if that is possible.[12]

Rule 27. *Mere silence cannot be a valid acceptance of an offer.* Suppose an offer were made in the following terms: "I will pay you ten thousand dollars for your house and lot, Link's subdivision. If you do not reply to the contrary before noon on next Tuesday, the 24th, I shall assume that you have decided to accept my offer." (Signed) W. F. Gilmore. A failure of the addressee to reply would not be considered an acceptance. Some years ago, it was common practice for insurance companies to make proposals of this kind. Their letters said, in effect, "Your policy will expire on February 27. If we do not hear from you to the contrary before that date, we will renew the policy." In one of such cases, the policyholder wanted the renewal, and did not reply. In another case, a building was destroyed after the expiration date of the old policy and before any further steps had been taken regarding the new one. In such cases, the courts have uniformly held that there was no contract.

This may seem somewhat harsh upon the offeree in such cases, but it should be remembered, first, that failure to reply may be due to one or more of several reasons, and, therefore, mere silence is not a mode of expression. Since that is true, **Rule 23,** stated previously, has not been complied with, and there is no acceptance. Second, if contracts could be made in this way, sellers of goods might cause considerable inconvenience to offerees, because such offerees would be bound to buy all sorts of goods offered them,

---

[12] Since not many replies are lost, and since any expressive communication which reaches the offerer will be sufficient, this kind of question does not arise very frequently; but since it may arise at any time, the principle set out here should be kept in mind.

unless they took the trouble to reply, and such offers might become very numerous. The rule that mere silence cannot constitute an acceptance is a sound rule and one of general application. Insurance companies do not use this mode of communication any more, as a usual practice.

A word of caution is desirable in connection with a type of case which is no longer very common, but which is sometimes encountered even yet. A publisher sent to Greer certain books along with a letter to the effect that if Greer did not want the books he might return them, but that if he did not return them, the publisher would assume that he wanted them and would bill him for the price. Greer did not want the books, nor had he ordered nor requested them. In most states, if the books have not been used, the recipient is under no obligation to pay for them, nor even to return them. In fact, though no authority has been found, it seems probable that the recipient of unsolicited merchandise could not be held liable if he tossed it into the nearest garbage can. Certainly, he is not under any legal obligation to return the goods. On the other hand, if he makes any use of them and that use can be proved against him, then his use will become an act of acceptance. In the latter case, we would have more than mere silence: we would have silence plus use.

Rule 28. *Silence may constitute an acceptance if it is expressive.* Sometimes, because of the background of a transaction, it is reasonable for an offerer to assume that silence is an expression of assent. Suppose, for example, that Price offered his radio set to Welch for fifty dollars, and that Welch replied, "Give me time to think it over. If you do not hear from me to the contrary by noon tomorrow, I will take the set and pay you for it the first of the month." In such a case, there is more than mere silence. The offeree himself has stated that his own silence will be his means of expressing assent, and the background of the transaction gives meaning to the silence which has, by this means (of preliminary assent) become expressive. In reality, in such cases as this, there is a preliminary agreement to the effect that silence is to have a special meaning in this case. Welch said, in reality, "I will buy the set unless I notify you to the contrary." Of course, a sensible person having knowledge of these rules of the law of contracts, will always see to it that he himself does not rely on the silence of others as assent, and he will also make sure, so far as he can, that others do not rely on his silence to indicate his consent.

Rule 29. *Silence may sometimes operate as a waiver.* Certain goods were delivered to Bates as the result of an order. The goods were defective, but Bates did not make any protest or other report. He did not pay any attention to the statements sent him in due course, and then, some months later, when suit was threatened to collect the amount of the bill, Bates finally lodged his complaint as to the defect of the goods. In such cases, the courts usually hold that, while silence is not an acceptance of an offer, yet it does operate as a waiver of the right to object to the character of the goods, shortage, or other defects in the transaction. Therefore, one should lodge his complaints promptly, since failure to do so may result in the loss of any right to expect an adjustment.

CONSIDERATION IN CONTRACTS

Rule 30. *In general, consideration is required in every contract.* In reality, this rule is merely a restatement of **Rule 1** and **Rule 4.** But it is necessary to use the word consideration in discussion of some other rules of law, because some of those rules are commonly stated by using the word. It is necessary that one should know not only that consideration is required, but also what the meaning of the term is. Some writers give this meaning by stating a verbal definition of consideration; but for practical purposes, it seems better to show the extensive meaning of the term by a series of illustrations of its use. See illustrations with **Rules 31** to **35.**

Rule 31. *Some gratuitous promises are enforcible as contracts.* In connection with the discussion of **Rule 1,** it was pointed out that in some exceptional cases gratuitous promises are enforcible. In general, these enforcible gratuitous promises take one of two forms. One form in which they occur is the commonly known subscription to funds for colleges, churches, or similar institutions. In fact, such promises are usually promises to make gifts, and they are purely gratuitous. But, under either of two conditions, the courts usually enforce such promises. Clark promised to give $50,000 to B college, upon condition that the college should get promises of an equal amount from other subscribers. If the other subscribers are secured in the stated amount, all of the promises, including Clark's, are enforcible. It is said that each promise was given in reliance upon the promises of other donors, and such consideration is sufficient to make them all enforcible.

In another kind of situation, Kennedy promised to give $1000 to M church at a certain date, making no conditions. In reliance upon this promise, the church authorities bought coal and other supplies on credit. Kennedy died before the given date, but it was held that his estate was bound to make good the promise. Most courts agree, in similar cases, that the consideration for the promise is found in the fact that the donee has contracted debts in reliance upon the promise. Not many such suits arise, but when they do, subscription promises, even though gratuitous in the general sense, are held to be enforcible, if the promises have been made or relied upon, as indicated in these two illustrations. As a rule, other charitable subscriptions, which do not meet these conditions, are held not enforcible.

Rule 32. *A promise, to be consideration in a contract, must be certain.* This rule means merely that the form of the promise must be such that what is to be done is clearly determinable, either at the time when the promise is made, or at the time of performance. If either of these things is true, then the promise is regarded as sufficiently certain so that it may be adequate consideration in a contract. It is not necessary that there be a certainty that the promise can be performed; it must merely be certain in the sense that the meaning of it is clear. For example, Gates promised Mary Ellen, his niece, that if she would keep house for him as long as he lived, he would leave her some land in his will. He did not say what land it was to be, nor how much. After his death, it was found that his will made no mention of Mary Ellen. Now, if the promise had been certain, it could have been enforced as a contract against the estate, but since it was uncertain (what he was to do was not clear), it could not be enforced as a contract.[13]

---

[13] Mary Ellen's right to recover reasonable pay for her work is indicated in connection with **Rule 83.**

On the other hand, Willis agreed to sell and Cline agreed to buy Willis's crop of peaches, at the market price. When the crop was ripe, Willis claimed that the agreement was not enforcible because the price was not named and because the amount of the crop was uncertain. Such an agreement, however, is certain enough for the purposes of the law of contracts. The amount of the crop and the price, while not named specifically in the agreement, can be readily ascertained when the time for performance arrives, and such an agreement can be enforced.

Rule 33. *Consideration must be adequate.* This rule is apt to be somewhat confusing, because it sounds as though the law requires some kind of equality between the values to be exchanged; but this is not true. The meaning of this rule is that there must be some value to be exchanged on each side. So long as there is a genuine expression of willingness to exchange values, the courts never inquire into the relative values on each side. All of this means merely that there must be a business agreement; there must be a consideration. It does not mean adequate in value; it means adequate to make a real exchange. Thus, the courts do not refuse to enforce foolish or unequal bargains, merely because those bargains are foolish or unequal. David agreed to sell and Phillips agreed to buy a certain patent right. When the articles were manufactured they proved to be unmarketable, and Phillips refused to pay, claiming that the value he received was inadequate; but the contract was valid because the exchange was genuine. Similarly, the courts would enforce an agreement to pay $5000 for a certain used postage stamp, whether it was worth that much or not (as long as there was a real bargain and no fraud).

However, the value promised on one side is sometimes so small that it is clear that there is no real bargain, and the agreement is not enforcible. Schnell promised his niece that he would give her $600 in exchange for one cent. This agreement was not a real agreement at all; it was a gratuitous promise. To be sure, it was fixed up to look like a contract, but it was not a real bargain, and so the promise was not enforcible.

Rule 34. *Past consideration is not consideration.* Wilson's son was injured in an accident and taken to a hospital where the care given him was of an extraordinary kind, and Wilson was so grateful that he promised to give the hospital a new X-ray machine. This promise was not given in exchange for the treatment of his son. It was not a part of the agreed price for the treatment. It was a promise given because of a benefit received, but not in exchange for it. The treatment would be regarded as past consideration, which is no consideration at all in the law of contracts, and the promise to give the machine would not be enforcible as a contract. It was merely a gratuitous promise for which there was a good reason, but there was no consideration and no contract.

Rule 35. *The performance of a legal duty, owed to the promissor or to the public, cannot be consideration for a contract.* There are several kinds of cases in which persons try to exact pay for performing duties which they already owe. Here are some examples:

a) McDevitt was a jockey employed by Stokes. Before a certain race, Stokes promised McDevitt a reward of $1000 if McDevitt's mount, owned by Stokes, should win the race. The horse did win the race, but Stokes did not pay the reward. In a suit by McDevitt, a Kentucky court decided that there was no contract. The court pointed out that under his contract as a jockey, it was McDevitt's duty to win every race if he could. Therefore, in winning this race he did no more than perform what was his duty without regard to the promise. In such cases as the one where an advertiser offered a prize to every ball player who should hit a home run, not many suits arise because advertisers usually perform such promises; but such promises are probably not enforcible as contracts, for reasons similar to those given in the McDevitt case.

b) Wain was under contract to erect a building for Lang. While the work was in progress, Wain threatened to stop work unless Lang would agree to pay him an extra $500 when the work was finished. Lang did promise, but when the work was finished and the extra $500 was not paid, it was held that this promise (to pay the extra $500) was not enforcible, because there was no consideration for it. In finishing the work, Wain was merely doing what was required by his original agreement.[14]

  c) Nelson's car was stolen. He offered a reward for its recovery. The car was recovered by Gilbert, a police officer detailed
to the special duty of recovering stolen cars. If Gilbert recovered
the car and if the reward were not paid, he would not be entitled
to recover the reward in a suit, since he was only performing his
sworn legal duty in recovering it. It would be lawful for Nelson
to pay the reward and lawful for Gilbert to receive it, but it is
not enforcible as a contract under the circumstances given here.

  d) Mays owed a debt of $500 to Johns. The debt was due
on May 1, 1938. In March of 1941, the debt was still unpaid.
Johns told Mays that, if Mays would raise $400 in a week, he
(Johns) would give a receipt in full for the whole debt. Mays
did pay the $400 and was given the receipt in full. Sometime
later, Johns brought suit for the remaining $100. This he was
entitled to recover. In paying the $400 after the debt was due,
Mays was doing only a part of what he was already obligated
to do, and this kind of act, in accordance with **Rule 35,** is not
legal consideration for the promise to discharge the remainder.
If this same arrangement had been made in March of 1938, then
the promise to discharge the balance would have been enforcible,
because, in that case, Mays would have paid the $400 at a time
earlier than required by his contract. Such payment would not
have been required by his original contract, and would have been
valid consideration for the promise to discharge the balance.[15]

  e) Pelton agreed to pay $250 for some dental work to be
done. After the work was done, Pelton thought that the price
was too high, though he did not criticize the work. He sent a
check to the dentist for $175, marking it *In full of account.* If the
dentist cashed this check, he would still be able to collect the balance, because, first, he did not promise to discharge the balance,

---

[14] Most courts agree with this view, in such case, but a small number does
not. It is a matter of local law upon which a local lawyer should be consulted.
[15] If there had been a genuine dispute about the amount of the claim or
about its validity in the 1941 case, the promise would have been enforcible, and
the whole of the debt would have been discharged by the payment of part in
exchange for the receipt in full; or, if, in either the 1938 case or the 1941 case,
Mays had given a valid negotiable instrument, such as a note, for the part of
the debt, the promise to discharge the whole would have been good.

and second, even if he had so promised, Pelton was paying only a part of his debt, the amount of which was not in dispute. But suppose that when the work was done, no price had been agreed upon. Then, if the amount of the bill were genuinely regarded by Pelton as too high, and if the check, marked *In full of account,* were cashed by the dentist, the latter could not recover any more for his work. When the case involves a genuine dispute, acceptance of any amount as payment in full is regarded as a compromise which is enforcible as a contract. The cases which fall under **Rule 35** are often of a very difficult character, and the advice of competent attorneys should always be sought in connection with such problems.

PARTIES TO CONTRACTS

At the beginning of this chapter, there is a general statement somewhat descriptive of contracts. Among other things, that statement declares that only competent parties can make valid contracts. Parties may be incompetent because of their age, or for other reasons, but since most questions of incompetency arise because of the matter of immature age, most of the present discussion is confined to incompetency arising from that cause. Persons who are under age are known in legal terminology as infants, or, sometimes, as minors. An infant is said to reach his majority at the first moment of the day preceding the twenty-first anniversary of his birth. In thirty-one states, this is true of both men and women; in the other seventeen states, women reach their full contractual capacity on their eighteenth birthdays.[16] With regard to agreements made by infants, the following rules are applied:

Rule 36. *An infant may avoid an executory agreement if he does not affirm it after he reaches his majority.* An infant's executory agreement is an agreement made by the infant, but not yet performed by him. Any purchase of goods on account, or borrowing of money, or other agreement made by an infant, is executory but may not be enforced against the infant unless he

---

[16] The seventeen states are Arkansas, California, South Dakota, Idaho, Illinois, Iowa, Kansas, Maryland, Minnesota, Missouri, Nebraska, Nevada, Oregon, Ohio, Vermont and Washington.

affirms this agreement after he has reached his majority. This rule is literally interpreted by the courts; it means just exactly what it says. The infant cannot be held on such agreement without his affirmance after his majority, even though the party who deals with him does not know he is an infant; and even if the infant misrepresents his age, he still cannot be held liable on the agreement. Thus, if an infant buys a car on credit, he cannot be held liable for the price unless he affirms the agreement after his majority. The affirmance need not be made in words; any act which indicates willingness to take the benefits of the transaction, if such acts are performed after the majority of the infant, will be sufficient affirmance. So, should the infant in the above case continue to use the car after he reaches majority, this probably would be regarded as an affirmance.

An infant can be held liable for his torts, however, such as fraud, negligence, assault, trespass to land, and the like. For that reason, if an infant misrepresents his age, and some person suffers a loss in reliance thereon, the infant can be held liable to the extent of the loss, but not for breach of the agreement which may have been based on his fraud.

Rule 37. *An infant's executed agreement may be avoided by him.* An infant's executed agreement is one which has been made by an infant and which has been performed by him. Under **Rule 36,** it was stated that an infant's executory agreement is not valid unless affirmed by him after his majority; but an infant's executed agreement is regarded as valid unless the infant disaffirms it. If an infant, in executing his agreement, has transferred money or other personal property, he may disaffirm the agreement and become entitled to recover his consideration, either before majority or within a reasonable time after his majority; but, if he has conveyed real estate in executing his agreement, he cannot disaffirm and recover the land before majority, but may do so within a reasonable time after his majority. Again, it makes no difference, in the application of this rule, whether or not the other party knew he was dealing with an infant.[17]

---

[17] There are some questions, relative to the legal obligation of an infant to restore what he has received under an agreement which he seeks to disaffirm.

Rule 38. *A few infants' agreements are wholly void.* An appointment of an attorney by an infant is entirely void, and cannot be affirmed even after the infant reaches majority. The same is true of his appointment of an agent. In nearly all states, an infant cannot be held liable as a principal, nor can an adult be held liable as principal for an agent whom he appointed while the principal was an infant, even though the appointment was affirmed after majority of the infant.

Rule 39. *Some infants' promises are enforcible, although not as contractual obligations.* A few infants' agreements are enforcible because of public policy. Enlistment of an infant in the armed forces of the United States cannot be avoided by the infant, and a recognizance bond by which an infant warrants his appearance in court is enforcible. These promises, however, are not contracts. In addition, obligations arising from tort claims are enforcible. For example, Trent, an infant, damaged Young's car by negligent driving. In satisfaction of the claim for damages, Trent signed a note, which was not paid but could be enforced in spite of the fact that the maker was an infant. The basis of the enforcement was the liability for the tort.

Rule 40. *An infant may be held liable for the reasonable value of necessaries actually received by him.* This rule is a special case of **Rule 39,** but **Rule 40** is construed very strictly. It must be kept in mind that the liability is limited to necessaries, to the

---

The common law rule in effect in most states is to the effect that if the infant does not have the consideration which he received, he is not obligated to restore anything when he disaffirms or avoids his agreement. This rule is modified somewhat by statutes in Maryland, Minnesota, Mississippi, Montana, New York, and Texas. There is some conflict of authority among the states as to whether an infant who has the consideration must return it before he can disaffirm, or whether he can disaffirm and then merely be liable to return it. On the groups of questions suggested in this footnote, there is some confusion, and one who deals with infants runs the risk that he may not be able to enforce anything at all against the infants. Of course, the practical thing to do is to refrain from dealing with infants, unless there is some way of inducing them to perform apart from legal procedure ; or, if dealings with infants seem desirable, a guaranty should be taken from some responsible adult. Such a guaranty must be in writing to be enforcible. On the question of guaranty, as well as on the questions concerning the restoration of consideration by an infant, local rules differ to such a degree that practical problems of these kinds should be submitted to attorneys familiar with local law.

reasonable value of those necessaries, and only to such necessaries as have actually been received by the infant. Necessaries include only food, clothing, shelter, medical attendance, and common school education, but these are regarded as necessaries only so far as reasonably necessary for the support of the infant in his customary station in life, and he may be held for only the reasonable value of those necessaries actually received by him. Here, again, the safest thing to do is to demand pay in advance or to require a written guaranty by an adult. Of course, most infants do meet their obligations without any regard to their legal excuses for avoiding them, but since there is always the risk that this might not be so, persons who deal with infants should know the outlines of this branch of law, so that they may judge for themselves whether they wish to take such risks.

Rule 41. *The liabilities of insane and drunken persons are similar to those of infants, in a general way.* A person is regarded as insane, relative to his capacity to make contracts, if he has been declared incompetent by a court, or if his mind is so deranged that he does not understand what he is doing when he makes a particular agreement, but his subsequent insanity (after making an agreement) does not affect his liability on such agreement. Agreements of insane persons are treated much the same as those of infants, but there is a tendency among the courts to decide that an insane person's agreement may be enforced against him if the agreement is fair and reasonable and if he has received the consideration from the other party. Local law differs in this regard, however, and there is considerable statutory law[18] about it. In cases involving such matters, the advice of an attorney is usually necessary if the question of legal rights is involved.

Drunken persons are treated in much the same way. However, if a person has been adjudged a habitual drunkard, contractual dealings with him are unsafe. They should be carried on, if at all, through his legal guardian or other official representative.

Rule 42. *The contractual capacity of corporations is limited.* Corporations have implied powers to make contracts within the

---

[18] Statutory law is a name given to laws enacted by legislative bodies.

scope of the general powers granted them in their charters, but not beyond such powers. For example the ordinary business corporation cannot, in most instances, make a valid contract guaranteeing the performance of some other person's contract; nor can the usual industrial or commercial corporation make valid accommodation indorsements of commercial paper. The questions relative to the contractual powers of corporations are technical in character, and the legal distinctions are such that they should always be submitted to attorneys competent in the field of corporation law.[19]

Rule 43. *Agreements of married women are enforcible, as a general rule.* Under the common law[20] rules of contract, married women were held to be without capacity to make valid contracts in their own names. This rule has been either abolished or greatly modified in every state in this country. Under existing law, married women have full and complete contractual capacity and their agreements are dealt with precisely as those of men or those of unmarried women, with the following exceptions:

Alabama: Contracts of surety and guaranty are invalid.

Florida: No general power to contract without consent of a court. The law in Florida is complicated in this field.

Georgia: Same as Alabama, with some difference of detail.

Idaho: Some obscure limitations, apparently limiting the contractual powers of women to their own personal property. Local attorney should be consulted.

Indiana: Wife cannot sell or mortgage her land without husband's consent.

Kansas: Similar to Idaho.

Kentucky: Same as Indiana, but also same as Alabama with some difference in details.

Maine: No specific laws enabling women to make contracts,

---

[19] Another class of legally incompetent persons consists of aliens. In general, aliens are permitted to carry on business in this country just as citizens do. There are, however, some important restrictions upon land ownership by aliens, so that dealings in real estate should be supervised by competent legal counsel whenever aliens are involved on one side or the other of such transactions.

[20] Common law is a name given to a vast body of rules worked out by the courts without reference to any acts of legislative bodies.

but most authorities seem to agree that there are no important restrictions upon them as the law is actually administered.

Michigan: Women's surety agreements are probably not valid, but this and other provisions are not at all clear. There is no specific enabling statute.

Nebraska: Similar to Idaho.

New Hampshire: Same as Alabama with some difference of detail.

North Carolina: Same as Idaho with some difference of detail.

Oregon: Similar to Maine.

Pennsylvania: No valid contracts of guaranty, surety, or indorsement for accommodation.

Texas: A woman cannot make a binding agreement upon community property of husband and wife, nor convey real estate without husband's consent, nor make a valid joint note or act as surety without husband's consent, and is not bound by her agreements in her separate business unless there is a court order to that effect. Somewhat like Florida, in regard to the last.

Vermont: Some uncertainty about wife's guaranty of husband's debts.

Washington: Agreements not binding upon community property of husband and wife.

In a few cases, contracts with the husband as the other party are not valid.

LEGAL REQUIREMENTS OF FORM

In general, there are no rules of law which require that any particular form must be followed in order to make valid contracts. So long as the expressions are clear and unambiguous, so that the parties show that their understandings of the subject matter are similar, the form of the language used is not important. Of course, in the making of land contracts, leases, negotiable instruments, and the like, certain language has become standardized as being expressive of certain meanings; but (aside from negotiable instruments, which are discussed later in this book) if the meanings can be expressed without using these standardized phrases, the validity of contracts will not be affected by the type of language used.

Rule 44. *There is no general requirement of law that contracts must be in writing to be enforcible.* Excepting certain agreements which come within the Statute of Frauds, and a few contracts covered by some other rather rare statutes, agreements need not be in writing in order to be enforcible. To be sure, written evidence of the terms of agreements is better than oral evidence, but the law does not require written evidence, as a rule.

Rule 45. *Writing is required by law if the parties express their intent that they shall not be bound without written evidence.* Nearly all life insurance companies make plain upon their applications for life insurance that the applications are to be regarded as offers, that only written applications will be accepted, and that no contract shall result from an application without the written expression of the approval of the home office. Different terminology may be used in different applications to say about the same thing, but most life insurance applications are based upon this kind of provision. It must be noted, however, that the reason that writing is required in such cases is that one of the parties has clearly indicated that he will not be bound to a contract until his written approval has been given. In connection with most fire insurance policies, as a rule, no such requirement is made. Many fire insurance policies are made over the telephone. The applicant for insurance describes the property and indicates the amount of the insurance, and the agent states that he is covered from that time forward. It may be that the bill for the premium will not be sent for several days, and it may be payable even in thirty days, or possibly later. The contract of fire insurance is very commonly made in this way. Life insurance contracts could be made in this way if the companies should agree to it. A considerable amount of automobile insurance is made orally, too, although some companies require applications in writing for automobile insurance. But, again, it is not a legal requirement that such contracts be in writing; the requirement is due to the choice of the parties.[21]

---

[21] See Chapter X.

Rule 46. *The Statute of Frauds requires that some kinds of contracts must be in writing to be enforcible.* The Statute of Frauds is a legislative act first adopted in England in 1676, and since then enacted in some form or other in every state in this country. The language used in the Illinois Act in Sections 1 and 2 is as follows: [22]

STATUTE OF FRAUDS
Section 1 of the Act of February 16, 1874

Be it enacted by the People of the State of Illinois, represented in the General Assembly, That no action shall be brought;

(a) Whereby to charge any executor or administrator upon any special promise to answer any debt or damages out of his own estates; or

(b) Whereby to charge the defendant upon any special promise to answer for the debt, default or miscarriage of another person; or

(c) To charge any person upon any agreement made in consideration of marriage; or

(d) Upon any agreement that is not to be performed within the space of one year from the making thereof;

Unless the promise or agreement upon which such action shall be brought, or some memorandum or note thereof, shall be in writing, and signed by the party to be charged therewith, or some other person thereunto by him lawfully authorized.

Section 2 (part of Section 4 of the English Statute) reads:

No action shall be brought to charge any person upon any contract for the sale of lands, tenements, or hereditaments or any interest in or concerning them, for a longer term than one year, unless such contract or some memorandum or note thereof shall be in writing and signed by the party to be charged therewith, or some other person thereunto by him lawfully authorized in writing,[23] signed by such party. This section shall not apply to sales upon execution or by any officer or person pursuant to a decree or order of any court of record in this state.

The following points should be emphasized:

The requirements of the statute are strictly enforced.

---

[22] These two sections comprise what is generally referred to as the Fourth Section of the Statute of Frauds, because that was the number of the section in the original act.

[23] The words, in writing, are omitted at this point in most states. Where they are omitted, the agent's authority need not be written, but as a matter of good practice it should be written.

Since it is impossible to know in advance who will be the party to be charged (the defendant in a suit under the contract), both should sign it.

The written memorandum may be in the form of letters, telegrams, or any other kind of writing which makes clear the terms of the agreement.

Many difficult questions have arisen, and will continue to arise, as to whether or not a given contract is one which the Statute of Frauds requires to be in writing, but all of these troublesome questions can be avoided by the use of written memoranda in every case where there is the least suspicion that the statute might be applicable. Better still, perhaps, all important agreements should be in writing for this reason and for other reasons to be stated later.

Some provisions of the Statute of Frauds are more important to the business man than others, and there is a great difference of opinion among lawyers as to what some of the provisions mean; but a few illustrations of the way in which the statute has been applied will give an idea of the way it works.

In Section 1 of the Illinois Act, there are four classes of contracts upon which the courts will give no relief unless there is a written memorandum of the agreement. (Of course, all other requirements for the formation of contracts must also be met.)

The most casual reading of this statute should disclose some of the difficulties of interpretation of it, and it should be remembered that these technical questions cannot be adequately solved by the layman for himself. As already suggested, the best practice is to avoid all such questions by seeing to it that all important contracts are in writing and properly signed.

In addition to this, there are two other good reasons for putting contracts into written form. For one thing, with the contract in written form, each party may tell with reasonable certainty, not only what he may require of the other party, but also what the other party may require of him. It is most convenient to be able to turn to a written instrument in order to determine one's obligations. It is almost impossible to keep clearly in mind all of the details of a complicated transaction, and a written memorandum makes it unnecessary to do so. For another thing, written evidence is usually the very best kind of evidence, if a dispute comes to a law suit. For that matter, the possession of a clear memorandum with signatures is very often the means of avoiding litigation because each party knows that, so far as the terms of the agreement are concerned, the courts regard a written instrument as practically conclusive.

Rule 47. *The standard fire insurance policy laws are not requirements of form.* In a number of states, so-called standard policy laws have been enacted, relative to contracts of fire insurance. These statutes do not require that fire insurance policies be in writing to be binding; they state merely that every contract of fire insurance (in a state where the statute is in effect), shall contain the terms of the standard fire policy. If agreements are made contrary to these terms, the courts do not hold that such agreements are invalid; the courts hold that a contract exists between the parties, and that its terms are those of the standard policy, no matter what the parties intended, and no matter what their agreement said about it. Thus, the standard policy laws do not merely state that policies must conform to the terms of the act; as they are interpreted, those statutes provide that all contracts of fire insurance do in fact conform to the standard terms if such contracts are valid in other respects.[24]

QUESTIONS AND PROBLEMS

1. Give an illustration, other than one in the book, showing that in the ordinary agreement, there are two exchanges. Point out in your illustration exactly what these two exchanges are. **Rule 6.**

2. Why was it that the promise to pay the reward of one thousand dollars for the return of the stolen horse was not enforcible? Be sure you make this answer clear to yourself. **Rule 7.**

3. Smith lost a valuable set of drawing instruments. He offered a reward of twenty dollars for their return. The set was found by Glass and returned to Smith without knowledge (of Glass) that the reward had been offered. (A small card in the case gave Smith's address.) Smith thanked Glass but did not pay him any reward. Some time later, Glass learned that a reward had been offered, and, after his request for it had been refused by Smith, he brought suit for the

---

[24] See **Rule 324,** also.

reward. What, in your opinion, would the courts in your state do with this suit? **Rules 8** and **14.**

4. Give an illustration, from your experience or general reading, of the making of an offer without spoken or written words. Explain carefully why you think your illustration contains an offer. **Rule 10.**

5. Gates put up certain goods for sale at auction, acting as auctioneer. On a certain antique table the highest bid was made by Clifford, who was a responsible person both financially and morally. Gates, however, did not like Clifford and did not want to sell him the table. Gates ignored Clifford's bid and sold the table to Wells, who had bid five dollars less than Clifford. Clifford, on the ground that he had accepted an offer by making the highest bid, brought suit for breach of contract since he was a dealer in antiques and could have sold the table at a good profit to Mills. What would be the result of the suit? **Rule 11.**

6. If you saw in a store window a radio set of a kind difficult to obtain, and if you went into the store and tendered the exact price named on the tag, but the store-keeper refused to sell the set to you because your necktie did not match your suit, would you have any legal right to do anything at all about the matter? Be sure you have a satisfactory reason for your answer. **Rule 12.**

7. What is the most significant thing with regard to quotations in the law of contracts? **Rule 13.**

8. In the case in the last paragraph of **Rule 15,** Gregg promised that he would not withdraw his order. Now, why is it that this promise, which seemed to be part of a contract, is not enforcible; why would the courts permit him to withdraw his offer in spite of the promise? **Rule 15.**

9. Ames wrote an offer to Beale and soon afterward he sent a letter revoking the offer. While the letter of revocation was on its way, Ames received an acceptance of the offer from Beale. Ames claims that there is no contract, while Beale claims there is one. Which is correct? **Rule 16.**

10. **Rule 17** states that a paid-for option is not revocable. Do you infer from this that if an option is not paid for, it can be revoked without penalty? If so, give an illustration and state why you believe as you do. If you do not think that a gratuitous (unpaid for) option can be revoked at will, state the reason for your belief.

11. In the last paragraph of **Rule 18,** it is said that if an offer concerns goods which fluctuate rapidly in price, the time for acceptance will usually be shorter than it would be for an offer of goods with more stable prices. Explain why this should be true.

12. State the rule generally followed in a case like that which is discussed in connection with **Rule 19.** Is this rule consistent with the ideas underlying **Rules 7** and **8?**   Give a reason for your answer.

13. Lynch offered a used car for sale to Hill for $350. Hill replied that he thought this was too much and that he would give $300. After looking around for several hours, he came to the conclusion that he could not do any better, so he called Lynch and advised him that he would take the car at $350. However, Lynch refused to sell at that price. Hill supposed that he had accepted an offer and made a contract. Does this seem to you to be a reasonable assumption by Hill? Is it in accordance with the law? Is the law unreasonable, or would it be a mistake to think that Hill was reasonable in his belief that the offer still existed after his counter offer? **Rules 20** and **21.**

14. Read the paragraph regarding duplicate offers. If you wanted to offer a lot for sale to more than one party at the same time, how would you proceed in order to avoid the difficulty which is pointed out there? You will not find the whole of the answer in the book. You will have to think it out.

15. State in your own words the meaning of **Rule 33.** Give an illustration other than those in the book.

16. Under **Rule 35,** five kinds of cases are discussed. Do any of the results in those cases seem unreasonable to you? Give a reason for your answer if it is in the affirmative. In case any of them seem unreasonable to you (and some of them may very well appear so), read again very carefully the paragraph which concerns that particular case. See if you can find where your trouble lies if you have any.

17. In your opinion, could **Rule 36** be stated in the following terms and still be accurate? An infant can never be held liable upon any executory promise unless he affirms such promise sometime after he reaches his majority. Give a good reason for your answer.

18. So far as the infant's ability to avoid his agreements is concerned, does it make any difference at all whether or not the other party to the transaction knows that he is dealing with an infant? **Rule 37.**

19. State accurately the rule regarding liability of infants for necessaries. **Rule 40.**

20. Is there any rule of law which requires contracts to be in writing, as a general rule, in order to be enforcible? **Rule 44.**

21. What is the Statute of Frauds? What is the most important thing about the formation of contracts which you learned from the study of **Rule 46?**

Alabama State Capitol, Montgomery
Underwood & Underwood

Arizona State Capitol at Phoenix
Phoenix Chamber of Commerce

Arkansas State Capitol at Little Rock
Courtesy of Information Division, State of Arkansas Planning Board, Little Rock, Ark.

Colorado State Capitol at Denver
O. Roach Photograph—Courtesy of Denver Chamber of Commerce

CHAPTER II

UNENFORCIBLE AGREEMENTS
OF COMPETENT PARTIES

In addition to agreements which are unenforcible because the Statute of Frauds has not been complied with, or because they have been made by parties who are legally incompetent, there are two other important classes of agreements which are also unenforcible. These two classes of agreements are unenforcible in spite of the fact that they have been made by legally competent parties. and in conformity with the requirements of the Statute of Frauds. In one class, agreements are unenforcible because of the character of the acts which the parties agree to perform, and, in the other class, agreements are unenforcible due to some defect in the relationship of the parties while making the agreement.

ILLEGALITY OF OBJECT OF AGREEMENTS

In the preliminary statement about the nature of contracts, it was said that an agreement, to be enforcible, must not be contrary to law or public policy. Agreements of this kind are treated by the courts, as a general rule, in accordance with the ensuing rules.[1]

Rule 48. *An agreement to commit a crime is not enforcible.* This rule needs no more than a simple illustration. In some instances, during the Civil War, draft-dodgers agreed to pay certain fees to surgeons for amputations of fingers or toes. The fees so agreed upon were not collectible because such operations were (and still are) unlawful. Similarly, an agreement to pay

---

[1] It must be kept in mind that in a brief textbook it is possible to draw merely the general outlines of the law. The instances and rules discussed here are therefore selected as typical, and the list is not to be regarded as exhaustive.

for the burning of one's house, in order to collect insurance, is unenforcible for the same reason.

Rule 49. *An agreement in violation of a state or federal statute is not enforcible.* Illustrations of this principle are very numerous. Among the common ones are the following:

Sunday Laws. In many states, the making of contracts on Sunday is forbidden, and where such laws are in force, contracts made then are not enforcible. In a few states, such as Illinois, there are no such laws, and in most of the states where such laws are in effect, there is a tendency on the part of the courts to construe such statutes very narrowly, so as to make them inapplicable if possible.

Usury Statutes. In nearly all of the states, as shown by the table of rates,[2] statutes prohibit the making of agreements for the payment of interest at rates above those stipulated in such statutes. Such agreements are called usurious. Under such laws, in most of the states, the creditor can recover his principal, but no interest; in some states, he can recover principal and interest up to the lawful rate; in a few states, he can recover neither principal nor interest. There are no common law limits upon interest rates; all usury laws in this country are statutory.

Antitrust Laws. Agreements made in violation of the federal or state antitrust laws are unenforcible. In some instances, especially under the federal antitrust laws, the making of such agreements is punishable as a criminal offense because the statutes so provide. Usually, unless the statutes do so provide, the making of such agreements is not criminal; the agreements are merely unenforcible.

Licensing Laws. Where a state statute requires the licensing of any business, as, for example, a hotel, agreements with customers may or may not be enforcible without the license. In general, if the measure is regarded by the courts as a revenue law, the making of agreements, without the required license, does not affect the customer's liability to pay under the agreement; but if the license statute is regarded as a regulatory measure, the customer cannot be held liable for the services rendered.

---

[2] See Chapter IV for table.

Rule 50. *Agreements in violation of city ordinances are usually unenforcible.* An ordinance of the city of Chicago forbade all persons to act as real estate brokers for pay without a license from the city to carry on such business. Humason promised to pay Buckley a commission for selling a lot in Chicago. Buckley sold the lot, but when he brought suit for the commission, it was shown that the transaction was completed in the city of Chicago, and that Buckley had no license. It was held that he could not enforce the promise to pay the commission. The agreement was held void because of violation of the ordinance. Here, as it was pointed out in connection with the discussion of state statutes above, if the license ordinance were a revenue measure, it is probable that most courts would enforce the agreement; but they would not enforce the agreement, if the ordinance were a regulatory measure, as it was in the Chicago case.

Rule 51. *Agreements merely incidental to unlawful conduct are not necessarily unlawful agreements.* There are a vast number of cases in which agreements are collateral to the performance of some unlawful act, by one of the parties to the agreement. In some of these cases, the agreements have been held unlawful and so unenforcible, while in other cases such collateral agreements have been held enforcible. In general, the distinction is made upon the ground of the remoteness or proximity of the collateral agreement to the unlawful act. For instance, if a hardware dealer knew that the purchaser of a gun intended to use the gun in violation of the game laws, such knowledge would not invalidate the promise to pay for the gun unless there were a statute which specifically made such a provision. Thus, in a New York case, a contract of lease was held invalid and unenforcible on the ground that the lessor knew that the premises were to be used for an unlawful purpose when the statute specifically forbade the making of leases for that purpose. Again, there was a lawful sale of liquor in New York, the seller having knowledge of the buyer's intent to sell the liquor in Maine in violation of the laws of the latter state. The sale in New York was held valid. In some states and in some cases, the courts adopt a test suggested in the New York sale case just referred to. It is said that if the contemplated unlawful acts are of extreme gravity, this will render the agreement unenforcible; for example, if the hardware dealer sold a gun to a customer with knowledge that the customer expected to commit murder with the gun, the promise to pay for the gun might not be enforcible.[3]

Rule 52. *An agreement may be lawful for one purpose and not for another purpose.* In such a case as the New York-Maine liquor case, previously mentioned, the seller was able to recover the price agreed upon. The agreement was lawful in this respect. However, if the seller had refused to deliver the liquor, most courts would not permit a recovery of damages by the buyer for breach of contract. That is, while the contract was valid for the purpose of enabling the seller to collect the price if the goods were delivered, the same agreement was not enforcible on behalf of the buyer if the goods were not delivered at all. It is again necessary to emphasize the difficulty of reaching a sound determination of the questions raised by such cases. The prudent business man will consult counsel in such cases before such agreements are made if he makes such agreements at all.[4]

AGREEMENTS CONTRARY TO PUBLIC POLICY

There are many kinds of agreements which are of such character that the courts refuse to enforce them on the grounds of *public policy,* though they do not contemplate the violation of any specific rules of law. This means that the courts believe that such agreements are apt to produce socially undesirable effects, and therefore, they will not enforce such agreements. The term, *contrary to public policy,* is an extremely vague term. It cannot be precisely defined, but a few illustrations should serve to indicate the variety and the specific character of some of the cases in which this concept, public policy, is applied by the courts.

Rule 53. *Agreements tending to unreasonably restrain competition may be held unenforcible.* This principle is effective not only under state and federal antitrust laws but also under common

---

[3] This subject is extremely difficult. Competent counsel should be consulted in relation to any such cases.

[4] Compare this with discussion of **Rule 58.**

law principles. The principle is very extensive in its applications since it includes several types of agreements, the most important of which are indicated by the examples given in the ensuing subsidiary rules. The qualification *unreasonably* must be kept in mind since not all agreements which actually restrain competition are invalid.

Rule 53A. *Monopolistic agreements are usually invalid.* In some of the early cases in which restraints of trade were held invalid the agreements were monopolistic. For example, a group of ship-owners operating between two geographical areas formed an association. By the rules of this association, it was agreed that no member would transport any goods for shippers who gave any patronage at all to persons who were not members of the association, and that the net profits of the operations of the members should be pooled and distributed from time to time among themselves. After a time, one of the members claimed that he had not been given an adequate share of the pool under the agreement, but his suit for an accounting, in accordance with the agreement, was dismissed by the courts. The agreement was held to be an attempt to establish a monopolistic control of trade, and as such, it was held contrary to public policy and invalid. It was agreements and pools of this kind at which the federal antitrust laws were originally aimed, so far as such agreements affected interstate and foreign commerce.

Rule 53B. *Price maintenance agreements are usually invalid.* Many agreements by which the parties are obligated to maintain certain established price levels are made either between competing manufacturers or distributors, or between distributors and their customers. There is a great deal of confusion in the law as to the enforcibility of such agreements. The general rule is often stated to be that such agreements are invalid if, in their necessary or contemplated operation upon the actions of the parties to them, they tend to restrain natural rivalry and competition. While this principle seems to be fairly clear-cut, it is necessary to keep in mind the conflict of opinions as to the application of the principle, and any such agreements and their probable effects as well should be carefully analyzed by experienced and competent counsel. In many instances, such agreements are not only unenforcible, but the making of them may be punishable. For that reason, persons who contemplate making such agreements will usually find it advisable to consult law-enforcing officers before such agreements are made or carried out.

Rule 54. *Many agreements, actually restrictive of trade or competition, are nevertheless enforcible if the restraints are reasonable.* Since restraint of trade may be fairly regarded, in many instances, as a legitimate result of the conduct of business, and since many such restraints do not necessarily contribute to the establishment or maintenance of monopolistic combinations, a considerable number of agreements are enforcible in spite of the fact that they actually restrict competition. Sometimes the restriction is quite extensive, as some of the following illustrations indicate.

Rule 54A. *Agreements for protecting patent rights and copyrights are generally enforcible.* The owner of patent rights is the owner of a series of monopolistic rights conferred upon him by government itself. Agreements for the sale of such rights and agreements for the protection of such rights are, therefore, generally enforcible. But a monopolistic agreement between the owners or two or more competing holders of different patents will not be enforced. Also, agreements by the holder of a patent, imposed by him upon his customers and restricting their rights of resale, are valid and enforcible only if such agreements do not extend the monopolistic rights beyond the limits of the monopoly given by the patent. The patent laws, in general, do not afford protection for price maintenance agreements nor other monopolistic agreements. In general, similar principles govern agreements relative to copyrights.

Rule 54B. *Partial restraints of trade are valid.* In some cases, the question, whether or not the restraint of trade is reasonable (as a result of a particular agreement), is answered in terms of the extent of the restraint which may be measured either in respect to the time during which the restraint is to operate, or in respect to the extent of the territory in which the agreement is to be effective. This was once summarized by Judge Taft of the United States Circuit Court of Appeals. He said,

Covenants in partial restraint of trade are generally upheld as valid when they are agreements (1) by the seller of property or business not to compete with the buyer in such a way as to derogate from the value of the property or business sold; (2) by a retiring partner not to compete with the firm; (3) by a partner pending the partnership not to do anything to interfere, by competition or otherwise, with the business of the firm; (4) by the buyer of property not to use the same in competition with the business retained by the seller; and (5) by an assistant, servant, or agent not to compete with his master or employer after the expiration of his time of service. Before such agreements are upheld, however, the court must find that the restraints attempted thereby are reasonably necessary (1, 2) to the enjoyment by the buyer of the property, of good will, or interest in the property sold; or (3) to the legitimate ends of the existing partnership; or (4) to the prevention of possible injury to the business of the seller from use by the buyer of the thing sold; or (5) to protection from the danger of loss to the employer's business caused by the unjust use on the part of the employee of the confidential knowledge acquired in such business.

It would be stating it too strongly to say that these five classes of covenants in restraint of trade include all those upheld as valid at the common law; but it would certainly seem to follow from the tests laid down for determining the validity of such an agreement that no conventional restraint of trade can be enforced unless the covenant embodying it is merely auxiliary to the main purpose of a lawful contract, and necessary to protect the covenantee in the enjoyment of the legitimate fruits of the contract, or to protect him from the dangers of an unjust use of those fruits by the other party.

This probably is one of the best summaries of this branch of law to be found anywhere. The following five rules with their accompanying case descriptions are intended to be briefly illustrative of the specific applications of the principles announced by Judge Taft.

Rule 54C. *Restrictive sale of a business is usually valid.* When the owner of a shoe-repair shop sold his shop, he agreed not to set up a similar shop anywhere within two miles nor within six months of the time of the sale. Such an agreement is valid and enforcible, in line with the principles set out previously, only if the court is convinced that the time is not unreasonably long and that the area affected is not unduly large. In addition to this, some difference might be found in two cases, otherwise similar, if in one case the business were sold to one who was already a competitor, while in the other case the buyer was not already a competitor. The matters to be watched in such cases are, in the main, two: Does the restraint tend to establish or foster a monopoly (as might be true if the buyer were already a competitor of the seller), and is the restraint to cover a very broad area and operate for a very long time? Within these limits, a restrictive agreement, made as part of the sale of a business, is enforcible.

Rule 54D. *The sale of a business with good will is valid.* As a corollary of **Rule 54C,** it follows naturally that when a business is sold *with good will* the buyer should be protected against some competition by the seller. The meaning of good will is the probability that customers will continue to come to a place of business, merely because they have become accustomed to come there. This probability usually is a part of the reason the buyer is willing to pay the price for the business, and an agreement on the part of the seller to respect this good will certainly is not an unreasonable restraint of trade. In fact, this attitude is so wide-spread on the part of the courts that when a business is sold, there is an implication of the sale of good will, even when the agreement is silent about it. In cases of the latter sort, while it is lawful for the seller to enter at once into competition, it is not lawful for him to solicit his former customers to follow him to his new place of business.

Rule 54E. *Agreements not to divulge trade secrets are valid.* Many years ago, an employee of a kodak company agreed, upon accepting employment, that any discoveries which he might make should belong to the employer and that he would hold confidential all trade information he acquired while employed there. Some years after this agreement was made, the employee left the company, started a rival company, and made use of some formulas which he had discovered or learned while in the employment of the company. He also advertised that he was in possession of certain secret formulas. In a proceeding to enjoin this use of the information, the agreement was held valid as a proper restraint of competition. There have been many instances of this sort, but some of the questions are extremely difficult because it is very hard to decide just which information is to be regarded as secret. For example, the driver of a milk-delivery wagon makes many contacts with the customers of his employer. Suppose he quits this employer and takes a job of the same kind with a rival of his first employer. Is it unlawful for him to solicit the customers whose names and addresses he can scarcely fail to remember? Is it lawful for him even to mention to such customers that he is now working for the rival employer? The difficulty of such questions is further complicated by reason of the fact that, in not a few cases, there is considerable probability that some of the good will of the first employer may attach to the driver personally. On such questions, the advice of competent counsel should be sought.

Rule 54F. *Sales or leases of property with restrictions upon its use or resale are valid if the restraints are reasonable.* The seller of real estate may reserve to himself an easement, or he may require the buyer to agree that the land will not be used for certain purposes (such as operating saloons), or that when the property no longer is used for a certain purpose (for example, a street), that the property shall revert to the seller. Such agreements are nearly always regarded as valid because the restraints are usually regarded as reasonable. Here, again, of course, one may encounter the question whether such restriction in a given agreement is likely to be held contrary to public policy, and, for that reason, counsel should be consulted if there is the slightest doubt of the enforcibility of such an agreement. The lease of certain machines, with restrictive covenants as to the use of them and with tying agreements requiring the purchase of repairs and parts from the lessor, has offered some very difficult problems in this field. In general, they are upheld, but sometimes they are not, and the advice of an expert should be sought before such agreements are entered into.

Rule 54G. *Agreements for exclusive dealing are usually held valid.* The courts usually hold valid agreements by which sales agencies are granted exclusive territory, agreements by which a manufacturer agrees to sell the whole of his output to a single buyer, and agreements by which a buyer promises to buy from only one seller or distributor. In any case of these types, however, it must always be remembered that such agreements will not be enforced (a) if they are monopolistic, (b) if they tend to seriously restrain competition, and (c) if they violate specific provisions of the federal or state antitrust laws. Since state antitrust laws differ in the details of their provisions in this respect, and since the other questions involved are difficult and technical, it is once more necessary to keep in mind the need for consulting competent advice in this field. In fact, in the whole field of restrictive agreements the same thing is true.

Rule 55. *Agreements incidental to employment may be invalid.* Many years ago, some employers desired to free themselves from the risk that they might become liable for injuries to their employees, especially in those cases in which it might be possible to prove that an employee's injury was legally chargeable to the employer's negligence. Many employers required all of their employees to agree, upon accepting employment, that they would not attempt to hold the employers liable for any injuries incurred while acting in their employment. This kind of agreement was declared, a long time ago, to be contrary to public policy and unenforcible.[5] Thus, the employer could not by agreement evade his liability for negligence. To be sure, workmen's compensation acts have superseded this rule in most industrial employments, but there are many kinds of employments even yet which are not subject to workmen's compensation acts, and to these, the common law, as just stated, is still applicable. Again, agreements by which an employee promised to refrain from joining or supporting a labor union were valid under common law rules. This rule, too, has been almost entirely superseded by modern legislation, but there are still some instances to which modern legislation is held to be inapplicable and in which the common law rule still is applied.

Rule 56. *Agreements not to bid at an auction are invalid.* Regarding such agreements, a Massachusetts court once said: "An agreement between two or more persons that one shall bid for

---

[5] See **Rule 347.**

the benefit of all upon property about to be sold at public auction, which they desire to purchase together * * * none of them desiring the whole, or for any similar honest or reasonable purpose, is legal in its character and will be enforced"; "but such agreement, if made for the purpose of preventing competition and reducing the price of the property to be sold below its fair value, is against public policy and in fraud of the just rights of the party offering it, and, therefore, illegal."

Rule 57. *Agreements in fraud of creditors are unenforcible.* It is probably unnecessary to do more than remind ourselves of the principle involved in this rule. When a debtor attempts by agreement, concealment, or otherwise to manipulate the disposal of his assets in such a way as to deprive his creditors of their just dues, such devices cannot well be regarded as valid, and agreements made for such purposes are not usually enforcible. But this branch of the law, like some others previously mentioned, is technical and characterized by difficult and delicate distinctions between lawful and unlawful. Here, too, the advice of counsel should be sought by the debtor. However, a note of warning is necessary here because of the high probability that, if the debtor's affairs are already approaching insolvency, lawyers' fees may even further reduce them. For that reason, it is often advisable to put all of the facts before the creditors and let them have a hand in the determination of what should be done—let the creditors help decide whether the business shall be liquidated, thrown into bankruptcy, or granted time for its revival.

Rule 58. *Agreements partially invalid may be enforcible as to the lawful part.* Sometimes, an agreement may contain some promises which are lawful and enforcible, while at the same time it may contain other promises which are not enforcible. The question may then arise: Shall we enforce the lawful part, or shall we take the view that the bad part of the agreement has contaminated and made invalid the good parts? A railroad company agreed with a manufacturer of locomotives to furnish power to transport these locomotives from the factory to other railroads, and it also agreed that it would not transport the machines of competing manufacturers of locomotives. The agreement contained three distinct promises. On one side there was the promise to pay freight for transportation; on the other side were the promises to haul their engines but not to haul the engines of competitors. The first and second of the promises were lawful, but the third was not because it is unlawful for a common carrier to refuse to carry goods as long as facilities are available. The last promise, however, did not materially affect the other two, so the courts would enforce the agreement to pay for the hauling and the agreement to haul the locomotives; but they would not give any remedy for breach of the agreement to refuse to haul locomotives for others. It is said of this rule: Where the unlawful and the lawful promises are severable, the lawful promises will be enforced.

If an agreement contains lawful and unlawful promises which are not severable, the whole agreement is held unenforcible. Lavery had an open account with Harris. Part of the account was for groceries and other supplies, and part of it was for the purchase of automobile tires in violation of rationing regulations. The account did not show how much of the amount due was for the lawful items nor how much for the unlawful items. Lavery gave a promissory note for the total amount of the account, but the note was unenforcible because there was no way in which the valid parts of the agreement could be separated from the invalid parts.

THE EFFECTS OF FRAUD, DURESS, AND MISTAKE

There are many written agreements to which the parties are competent and in which the specific objectives are lawful, but in which the background of the negotiations is such that no real agreements result. In such cases, there may be all of the appearances of agreements, but when the true facts are discovered, it becomes clear that the expressions of apparent assent have been based upon some kind of misapprehension. Some agreements of this sort are valid as contracts, and some are not. It is the purpose of the present discussion to indicate, in a general way, the rules by which the courts deal with such transactions.

Rule 59. *Fraud which conceals the nature of the transaction* *renders the transaction void.* Fraud is the term given to another concept which cannot be defined with complete accuracy, but, in the law of contracts, it may be regarded as any statement of fact known to be false by the maker of the statement, not known to be false by the person to whom it is made, intended to induce action, and resulting in the making of an agreement, provided the person deceived had a right to rely upon the statement. Such a statement may operate in either one of two ways. First, it may conceal the nature of the transaction which is involved. Thus, Selmer applied for admission into a certain organization. He was presented with a document which, he was told, was an application, but which was in fact a negotiable promissory note for fifty dollars. Selmer was not sufficiently educated to be able to detect the character of the paper, and in a suit on the note, it was held that this instrument was wholly void and that Selmer had incurred no obligation because of the fraud.[6]

Another illustration of this is found in a case in which a buyer of goods misrepresents his identity to the seller by mail. Blenkarn ordered goods from Lindsay, signed to the order the name Blenkiron & Co., and asked delivery at a place near to the place of business of the real Blenkiron Co. The goods were received by Blenkarn and sold by him to Cundy. In a suit against Cundy by Lindsay, it was held that the title of Blenkarn was void, and that therefore Cundy got no title at all. The decision was based upon the ground that the fraud had concealed the identity of the person who sent the order. This case must be compared carefully with a somewhat similar case discussed in connection with **Rule 60.**

Rule 60. *Fraud in the inducement renders an agreement voidable, but not void.* Probably the commonest effect of fraud

---

[6] If the paper were still in the hands of the person who induced Selmer to sign it, of course such person could not enforce it whether the instrument was void or merely voidable. In the particular case, the instrument was in the hands of a purchaser of the instrument, known as a "holder in due course." If the instrument were voidable only, the holder in due course could collect upon it, while if it were void, such holder could not collect upon it. This is one of the chief reasons for the importance of the difference between void and voidable agreements. The legal position of the holder in due course is discussed in Chapter VIII.

is that it results in inducing a party to do something which he would not have done in the absence of the fraud. For example, Bates was induced to agree to join a certain organization by fraudulent statements to the effect that the organization was in control of certain properties. As a part of the transaction, Bates signed a negotiable note for $300.00. This note was transferred to a holder in due course, who bought the note for its value before its maturity without knowledge of the fraud. If the note had been in the hands of the original payee, who knew of the fraud, or in the hands of any purchaser other than a holder in due course, the note would not have been enforcible because of the fraud. But, in the hands of the holder in due course, the note was enforcible. The fraud rendered the instrument not void as under **Rule 59,** but voidable only. Similarly, if Blenkarn, in the case discussed above, had presented himself at the place of Lindsay and taken away goods charged to Blenkiron & Co., his title would have been voidable only, as between himself and Lindsay; but if Cundy had then purchased the goods in ignorance of the fraud, the agreement (and the title) would not have been voidable against Cundy. The distinction between these two kinds of fraud is often very hard to make.

Rule 61. *Constructive fraud may operate as actual fraud.* There are some transactions in which, while there is no fraud in the sense of an actual statement of fact, yet the setting is such that there is an approach to fraud. One illustration of this is found in the discussion of **Rule 56,** and other aspects of the same thing are discussed in connection with **Rule 66.** The subject of constructive fraud should be regarded by the layman as a danger zone.

Rule 62. *Statements of honest opinion are not fraudulent.* When a seller of goods praises the quality of his goods to induce the purchaser to buy, it may be assumed, as a general rule, that he is honest in expressing his opinion of the goods. When such an assumption of honesty seems to the courts to be warranted, the fact that the maker of such statement is mistaken about quality will not affect the validity of any agreement induced by the statement. Also, there is a tendency to regard many puffing statements as to quality as expressions of opinion, even though such expressions may be made in very positive terms. Thus, such statements as *these are the best sheets you can buy anywhere, this is the fastest horse in the country, this is a good, strong horse,* and the like, are not regarded as statements of fact, but as statements of opinion. Of course, if the party who makes such statements can be shown to have known or suspected that these things were not true, then his statement is fraudulent because he has knowingly misrepresented the state of his opinion. In the latter case, his statement will be fraudulent, and agreements resulting therefrom will be invalid in accordance with **Rules 59** and **60**.

Rule 63. *Innocent misrepresentation will sometimes affect the validity of agreements.* There is considerable difference of opinion among authorities as to whether or not an agreement becomes invalid because of the fact that one party has without dishonesty misrepresented some fact, and that such misrepresentation has influenced the other party's decision to enter into the agreement. Probably most courts incline to the rule, in most cases, that such a misrepresentation should make an agreement voidable in so far as those agreements are concerned with sales of goods or land, but in connection with insurance contracts, most courts favor the view that such misrepresentations do not affect the validity of the agreement. In insurance contracts, such misrepresentations nearly always come from the insured, and they nearly always are related to the state of the health of the insured, or to the causes of death of his ancestors, or to other similar matters. In such matters, the insured is often limited to an expression of his opinion, so that what seem at first to be misrepresentations of facts may, in reality, be mere statements of opinion. The latter, as indicated in connection with **Rule 62,** do not affect the validity of agreements, so long as the opinions are honestly held.

Rule 64. *Duress renders an agreement voidable.* While the term duress is not strictly definable, its general meaning is coercion of a party to an agreement by a threat of an unlawful injury if such threat is made by the other party to the agreement. Such instances do not arise often in modern business practice, but they are sometimes encountered. Sherman began an action against

Galusha, alleging that he had been injured by eating impure
meat bought from Galusha. While the suit was pending, Sherman
and his attorney threatened Galusha with imprisonment, and by
this means induced Galusha to execute a note in settlement of
the claim. Galusha afterward brought a proceeding to set aside
the note and a mortgage securing it. In that proceeding, it was
held that the threats constituted duress, and that the agreement
was voidable and should be set aside. That the threat must be
one of an unlawful injury in order to constitute duress is shown
by the following case. Hart and Strong engaged in a dispute
about certain property which they had exchanged. They agreed
to a re-exchange, but a part of the re-exchange was a note executed
by Strong to Hart. Sometime later, Strong sought to avoid the
note on the ground that he had been induced to execute it by
a threat of Hart, by which the latter threatened to foreclose a
mortgage which was a part of the first exchange. There was no
doubt that the note was made under the influence of this threat,
but the threat to foreclose the mortgage was a lawful threat since
it was entirely lawful for Hart to foreclose the original mortgage
when the debt secured by it was unpaid. The threat in this case
was therefore not of the sort to constitute duress. Similarly, the
pressure of circumstances is not likely to be regarded as duress.
Horn received a telegram stating that his wife was very ill, and
he stated that he would enter into an agreement proposed by
Davis in order to cut negotiations short. There was no doubt
that Horn was induced to do this in part to enable him to return
at once to his wife, but when he sought to avoid the agreement
on the ground of duress, it was held that the agreement was
not made under duress, and that it was not voidable. The whole
subject of duress is considerably uncertain because of the difficulty of determining what is and what is not a lawful coercion.[7]

Rule 65. *Mistake of one party without fraud of the other
party does not affect the validity of an agreement.* Schotter sent
a telegram to Elsom, "Can deliver four hundred turpentine at

---

[7] The subject of undue influence and its effect upon agreements is even
more uncertain than that of duress. A brief treatment of commercial law can
do no more, effectively, than merely mention undue influence.

sixty-four." This was transmitted by the telegraph company as sixty instead of sixty-four. Elsom at once sent an acceptance of the four hundred "as per your wire." Schotter sent the goods and a draft based on the sixty-four rate and Elsom refused to pay this. Schotter accepted the payment of the account at the rate of sixty and sued the telegraph company. The latter sought to defend on the ground that the mistake prevented the making of a contract. The court held, however, that the contract was valid at sixty in spite of the mistake.[8] In another case, Kenny dictated a letter to Hale, offering for sale a certain lot for $4900. The stenographer wrote $4500, and Hale accepted the offer. Kenny sought to escape from the agreement on the ground of mistake, but it was held that the agreement was valid, in spite of the error. Again, many parties to agreements have been mistaken as to the value of property which they agreed to buy or to sell, but such mistakes do not affect the validity of the agreements.

Of course, if the mistake is such that a party should have been able to see the probability of a mistake, he could not reasonably rely upon the offer. This is another aspect of the discussion under **Rule 7**.

Rule 66. *Nondisclosure of all material facts is not necessarily fraudulent.* In general, there is no obligation upon a party to an agreement to inform the other party that he is laboring under the influence of a mistake. It is not generally regarded as fraudulent for one party to take advantage of the ignorance of the other. If Parsons knows that General Motors expects to buy certain land which is owned by Glenn, and if Parsons buys this land from Glenn, knowing that Glenn is ignorant of the intent of the corporation, Parson's knowledge of Glenn's ignorance is not fraudulent, and will not enable Glenn to avoid the agreement. There are a few exceptions to this rule. One who negotiates a negotiable instrument when the maker is known by him to be insolvent, one who pays a debt with a bad check, or one who delivers goods which appear superficially to conform to an agreement, but which, to his knowledge do not, is fraudulent; and any agreements based upon such action would be invalid because of the

---

[8] The telegraph company was held liable for the loss. See Ch. XII.

fraud. In applications for insurance, too, failure to disclose
material facts, even though information is not requested, may in
some cases constitute fraud. Thus, while failure to disclose information is usually not regarded as fraudulent, under some
circumstances disclosures may be regarded as equivalent to fraud.
Nondisclosure may thus become constructive fraud.

Rule 67. *Mutual mistake as to the subject matter will render
an agreement invalid.* In some instances, both parties to an
agreement may be mistaken either as to the existence of the thing
about which they agree, or as to precisely what the agreement
requires each one to do. In either of these kinds of cases, there
will be no contract. An example of the second kind of mistake
is found in an English case. The plaintiff agreed to sell and the
defendant agreed to buy certain cotton to arrive at Liverpool on
the ship Peerless from Bombay. Unknown to either party, there
were two ships named Peerless, both of which sailed from
Bombay with cotton for Liverpool. The defendant knew only
of the Peerless which left Bombay in October, while the plaintiff
knew only of the Peerless which left Bombay in December. There
was no contract, because it was impossible to tell which ship
was the subject matter of the agreement. In a similar case, Baker
owned two lots on Prospect Street in Boston. He had forgotten
about lot A since it was part of an inheritance and he had never
seen it. Green made an agreement with Baker for the purchase
of Baker's lot on Prospect Street, but Green knew only of lot A
and did not know that Baker owned lot B or any other lot on
that street. This agreement, too, was void since it was impossible
to determine which lot was the subject matter of the transaction.
Of course, in such cases, it is a necessary element that both parties
are honestly mistaken.

An agreement of the first kind above indicated is found in
a case in which Hill and Fuller entered into an agreement for
the purchase and sale of Fuller's horse to Hill. The horse was
in a stable when the parties had last seen him. After the price
had been paid, Hill went to get the horse and found that the
horse had been killed in a fire before the agreement had been
made. In such a case, Hill was entitled to the refund of his

money since the agreement was void because of the fact that the subject matter was not in existence at the time of the agreement, and this fact was unknown to the parties. If the horse had died after the making of the agreement and after title had passed, the buyer would not have been entitled to the return of his money,[9] and, of course, if the seller had known of the destruction of the horse when the agreement was made, the agreement would have been void because of the fraud upon the buyer by concealment of this fact.

Rule 68. *Mistake, as a general rule, does not affect the validity of an agreement.* From the previous discussion, it should be clear that the only mistakes likely to invalidate agreements are mistakes (a) as to the identity of the subject matter, (b) as to the existence of the subject matter, or, in some cases (c) by analogy to fraud, where the mistake conceals the nature of the transaction. In other cases, mistakes as to the qualities of goods, as to the meaning of language used in documents, as to the seller's title (except where title is warranted), and most other common kinds of mistakes do not affect the validity of agreements unless accompanied by fraud.

In the field of mistake, just as is true in other branches of the law, there are many technical and difficult questions, and it must be kept in mind that a textbook is only a chart of the general outline of the subject.

Rule 69. *Courts will sometimes reform agreements containing mistakes.* When a written agreement does not conform to the real intent of the parties upon some matter material to the agreement, courts will usually reform such agreements to conform to the true intent. For instance, if an agreement for the sale of land described the land, by mistake, as being in Will County when it was clearly in Kendall County, or if the court were convinced that the parties to a conveyance had intended that the purchaser should assume an existing mortgage but it was inadvertently omitted from the deed, and in a few other cases, the courts will reform the instrument so as to make it conform to what the

---

[9] Just when title passes in such a case is discussed in connection with the law of sales of goods in Ch. IV.

parties are trying to do. But it must be emphasized that this device cannot be used to change a contract; it is used only to arrive at an expression of the real intent of the parties, as of the time when they made the agreement. Mistaken reasons for making agreements are usually not recognized at all in this or other connections unless they fall into the classes discussed under **Rule 68**, or unless they are based upon fraud.

QUESTIONS AND PROBLEMS

1. Suppose that Mock promised to repair Dempster's garage floor in exchange for Dempster's promise to turn over to him some ration coupons from the ration book of Dempster's son, who had gone to the army. If the repair work were properly done, but Dempster refused to surrender the coupons, would Mock be legally entitled to recover anything for his work? If so, what? If not, why not? **Rule 48.**

2. In case you do not know whether or not there is a law in your state forbidding the making of contracts on Sunday, what should you do about protecting yourself against the possibility that an agreement made on Sunday might not be enforcible? Suppose you made an agreement on Sunday, but signed it on the following day. Do you believe, in the light of the last sentence of the paragraph on *Sunday Laws*, that this would make the agreement valid even if there were a Sunday law in the state?

3. A city ordinance provided that no driveways should be constructed from any street into any residential lot unless the curb were cut and relaid in accordance with the city's regulations. The Porter Cement Company laid a driveway, violating these regulations, to a lot which belonged to Jones. Jones refused to pay them for the work. Do you think that violation of the ordinance would deprive the company of the right to recover for its work? **Rule 50.**

4. Knox bought some fine steel tools from the Clipper Hardware Company. A clerk who sold the goods to Knox asked him what he intended to do with them. Knox replied that he intended to use them for entering a currency exchange in order to rob it. The clerk knew Knox well and charged the goods to his account. Do you think that, as the knowledge of the clerk is legally regarded as the knowledge of the employer, the right to recover the price of the goods would be lost? **Rule 51.**

5. In the absence of a specific provision for it in the statute, would the formation of an agreement such as that discussed under **Rule 53A** be punishable? **Rule 53B,** also.

6. Mennito sold his shoe-repair shop and business to Ponetti.

As a part of the sale agreement, Mennito promised that he would not open up a competing shop anywhere within two miles nor within a time interval of less than a year. Do you think such a promise would be enforcible by Ponetti? **Rule 54C.**

7. Read the discussion under **Rule 54E** carefully. Then write out a statement of your reasons why an attorney should be consulted in connection with the question of whether or not the good will of the business attaches to the driver or to the business or to both.

8. After reading **Rules 54** to **54G** inclusive, write down your reasons why no agreements should be entered into without consulting a competent lawyer, when such agreements are in the field of business competition. You may have to read these paragraphs several times to see your way into this, but it will be worth the effort in helping you to understand this part of the subject.

9. Page agreed to buy all of the products of a certain paper mill. This meant, of course, that the mill promised not to sell to any other buyer. Page did not pay for the paper, and when the mill sued him for the price, his defense was that this was a monopolistic agreement and therefore not enforcible. Do you think this defense was sound? Why? **Rule 58.**

10. Read the discussions under **Rules 59** and **60** very carefully. Do you understand the difference between these two kinds of fraud? Tell what it is, in your own words. Do you understand the effect of the two kinds of fraud upon the ability of the fraudulent party to pass some kind of rights to an innocent purchaser? Tell what it is, in your own words.

11. In the case stated under **Rule 60** in which Bates joined the organization, was he deceived as to what he was going to get or was he deceived as to what he was signing?

12. Alden wished to buy a lot on Vine Street. He asked Wilts, a real estate man, whether or not the street had been graded to its proper level in front of that lot or whether more grading would have to be done. Wilts said, "It is my belief that the grading has been done and paid for." In fact, it had not been done, and Wilts did not know anything about it. He really had no opinion at all. If Alden had bought the lot through Wilts and afterward learned of the facts, that the grading was not done and that Wilts knew nothing about it, could Alden rescind the agreement on the ground of fraud? If you think so, which kind of fraud do you think it was, and why? **Rules 59 and 60.**

13. In an application for a life policy, Grimes stated that there had been no cancer in his family. This was merely his opinion, but he wrote *no* after the appropriate question. After the policy had been

written, the insurance company learned that both the father and mother of Grimes had died of cancer. They notified him that the policy was cancelled on account of the misrepresentations. In your opinion was the answer of Grimes, when he wrote *no,* an opinion or a misrepresentation of fact, and why? Assume that Grimes was honest in his answer. **Rule 63.**

14. Mills ordered by telegraph 400 sacks of salt. The telegrapher erroneously sent the message to read 400 casks instead of 400 sacks. A sack was 14 pounds of fine salt; a cask was 400 pounds of coarse salt. The recipient of the telegram sent the 400 casks. Was Mills obligated to take and pay for them? **Rule 65.**

15. The closing sentence of the discussion under **Rule 66** is, "Nondisclosure may thus become constructive fraud." Give an illustration.

16. Lay and Blue were negotiating the sale of Blue's horse to Lay. Blue finally said, "I will take $160 in cash." Lay heard only the last part, and thought that the offer was sixty. Lay then said, "Did you say sixty?" Blue, supposing that Lay was merely abbreviating a hundred and sixty, said, "Yes, I said sixty." Lay then said, "All right; I'll take him." But, when Lay tendered only sixty dollars, Blue claimed that he was entitled to a hundred and sixty. Assuming that both men were entirely honest in this transaction, what is the solution of this case? **Rule 67.**

17. Laurence agreed to buy and Byrd to sell a certain house and lot in London, England. Some weeks later, they learned that enemy bombs had been dropped upon the lot a day before their agreement. The house was totally destroyed, and the lot was badly torn up. Byrd claimed that he was entitled to the price, but Laurence refused to pay. Assuming that the damage to the lot was such as to radically change its character, for whom should the decision be favorable? **Rule 67.**

18. Make a general statement as to the effect of mistake upon the validity of contractual agreements. **Rule 68.**

19. What is meant by the phrase *reformation of contracts?* Who does it and to what extent? **Rule 69.**

20. In general, what kind of threat of injury will usually be held to constitute duress? What is the legal effect of duress upon an agreement made under the influence of it?

Connecticut State Capitol, Hartford
Connecticut Development Commission

Delaware State Capitol, Dover
Underwood & Underwood

Florida State Capitol, Tallahassee
Underwood & Underwood

Georgia State Capitol, Atlanta
Underwood & Underwood

CHAPTER III

CONTRACTUAL OBLIGATIONS

Careful study of the law of the formation of contracts should make it possible for one to know how to make valid contracts and also to know when he has done so. It is, however, of equal importance that one should learn how to determine what his obligations are after he has made a contract. It might seem that this would be possible from a mere reading of the language of any agreement to which one is a party, but there is a great variety of instances in which parties to contracts are confronted with questions which are not answered by any of the language of their agreements. In connection with the solutions of such problems, there are a vast number of court decisions. From a study of these decisions, it is possible to deduce certain principles which the courts follow when they are called upon to determine the rights and obligations of parties to contracts, especially with regard to matters upon which the language used is silent or ambiguous. Another group of important questions is concerned with the law governing the termination of contractual obligations, while a third group relates to the processes and legal consequences of the assignment of contractual rights. These, also, are governed by principles deducible from the study of court decisions.

THE NATURE AND EXTENT OF OBLIGATIONS

In order to economize on space and reading time, the application of most of the rules in this field will be shown by reference to a single case. In this case, it is to be assumed, for the purposes of the discussion, that the parties are competent, that the objects of the contract are not contrary to public policy or law, and that all existing requirements of form have been met. In short, it is assumed that a contract has been formed, and the only questions, for the moment, are those relative to the character and scope of the obligations of the parties to the contract.

Betts was the owner of a vacant tract. Lynch was a small contractor. On June 27, 1940, these two men entered into a contract, the terms of which were, in effect, that Lynch should erect in a designated place on the land a small summer cottage with certain prescribed doors, windows, and hardware. He agreed to finish the work by August 15, 1940. Betts promised to pay $750 for the work and material on September 15, 1940, if the work were properly completed by August 15.

This agreement was a bilateral agreement when it was formed because at the time when the agreement was made, no work had been done and the price was still to be paid. There was an obligation on each side, each to be performed after the contract was made. But there was an important difference between the promise of Lynch and the promise of Betts.

Rule 70. *Promises in contracts may be conditional or un-conditional.* Notice that the contract states the promise of Betts to the effect that he will pay on September 15 if the work is properly done by August 15. That is, there is to be no obligation to pay until after the happening of the event designated in the agreement. To put it in another way, the proper doing of the work by August 15 is an event designated in the agreement, which must happen before there will be any obligation of the other party to pay. This event, the happening of which must precede the ripening of an obligation, is called a *condition* to the promise of Betts. And when the condition is expressed, as it is in this instance, the promise, as that of Betts, is said to be a *conditional* promise.[1] This definition must be clearly grasped because it has certain very important bearings upon contractual obligations.

The promise of Lynch, on the other hand, is not subject to any such expressed condition. Lynch promises to build the house by August 15. There are no ifs; there is no statement as to any event which is to take place before Lynch will be obligated to

---

[1] It will bear repetition that a conditional promise is one in which the condition is expressed in the contract.

build the house. Lynch's promise is called unconditional, and any other promise is called unconditional in the law of contracts if there are no expressed conditions to it.[2]

Sometimes the promises on both sides of a contract are conditional. Suppose, for example, that the facts of the above illustration were altered so that Betts agreed to furnish the lumber by August 1, 1940, and the remainder of the contract was as given above. Then Betts's promise to furnish the lumber would be unconditional, but Lynch's promise to build would be conditional because he promises to build if the material is furnished by August 15, and the promise of Betts to pay is conditional on the proper finishing of the work.

Rule 71. *Expressed conditions must be performed.* To return to the illustration as first stated, unless Lynch erects the building properly by August 15, there will be no obligation to pay the full price on September 15.[3] No matter what the reason is for Lynch's failure to perform the condition, the obligation to pay on September 15 will not become binding unless the condition takes place. This is a necessary consequence of the definition of condition: Some event which must take place before the promise will become binding. There can be no obligation to perform a conditional promise unless and until the conditions to it are performed.

Rule 72. *Expressed conditions may sometimes be substantially performed.* Suppose, in our illustration, that Lynch had completed the building on August 15 except for one of the doorknobs, which was missing. To be sure, he has not performed the whole of the condition, but the omission, as compared to the whole building, is not very important, and it would be absurd to say that Betts could escape all obligation to pay for the building merely because of the lack of this small item. In such a case,

---

[2] Do not make the serious error of supposing that unconditional means without any conditions. It means without expressed conditions, and, in a great number of instances, there are unexpressed or implied conditions to unconditional promises. The latter kinds of conditions do not make the promise conditional. The term absolute is used interchangeably with the term unconditional.

[3] Just what and when Betts must pay is not under discussion at this time. See Rules 72 and 79.

the courts would hold that the condition was substantially performed, and they would decide that Betts must pay the agreed price, minus what it would cost to supply the missing knob. This way of dealing with such questions is called the doctrine of substantial performance.

Rule 73. *Some conditions cannot be substantially performed.* There are some instances in which nothing short of complete performance will constitute performance of a condition. If our agreement between Betts and Lynch stated clearly that unless that building was completed by noon on August 15, Betts would not accept it nor pay for any of it, and if that were clearly understood when the contract was made, then a failure of ten seconds would not be substantial performance. Promises to pay rewards for lowering the record for the mile run, or for raising the record for the pole vault, and many others of similar character, simply cannot be substantially performed. The contestant either succeeds or he fails, and if he fails, the condition is not performed. To cases of the latter sort, of course, the doctrine of substantial performance cannot be applied.

Rule 74. *Expressed conditions are sometimes difficult to interpret.* Sometimes an expressed condition may be interpreted in a manner contrary to the superficial meaning of the expressions used. Nolan agreed to perform for Whitney certain mason work which was to be paid for upon the execution of a certificate of Morrill, an architect. The work was performed, except for some trivial defects in the plastering, amounting to about $200. The architect refused to give his certificate, and Nolan brought suit under the contract. The court held that the action of Morrill was unreasonable and that Nolan was entitled to recover the contract price minus the value of the trivial defects. This case has two important features. One feature is that the contract was enforcible without the performance of the act, which seems to be the condition, although the agreement states that the payment is to be conditioned upon the giving of the certificate and although the court recognized the rule that in a conditional promise the condition must be performed. The true meaning of this decision is that the real condition was not the certificate at all; the true condition was the doing of the work in a proper manner, and if the court can determine (as it could in this case) that the true condition was performed, then the promise is enforcible. The certificate was regarded by the court as one way (among other possible ways) of determining that the true condition had been performed. Conditions in contracts are rather often difficult to interpret. This difficulty should serve as a notice to the student that legal advice is desirable not only as an aid to the interpretation of such conditions, but also as an aid to the drafting of agreements which contain such conditions.

The other significant thing about this case lies in the fact that the promise to pay was enforcible even though the condition was not precisely performed. Thus, this case is an illustration of the application of the rule of substantial performance discussed in connection with **Rule 72,** and it shows how such instances are treated by the courts: they require the payment of the contract price minus the cost of performing the slight omissions.

Rule 75. *Conditions of satisfaction may sometimes be substantially performed, and sometimes they may not be.* Rather common are contracts in which the seller of goods or one who renders services performs under a *guarantee.* If the guarantee is looked at realistically, in those cases in which there is no obligation to pay until the work is finished or the goods delivered, the proper interpretation is that the customer promises, in effect, "I will pay the price if I am satisfied with the goods (or the work)." The Duplex Boiler Company repaired some boilers for Gardner under such an agreement for satisfaction. When the work was finished, Gardner claimed he was not satisfied. He made use of the boilers but refused to pay, insisting that he was not satisfied. He did not point out any specific defects in the work, but insisted upon his general dissatisfaction. Now, it was true that Gardner's promise was to pay if satisfied; but the court decided that if the work was done in such a way that a reasonable man should have been satisfied, then the condition was performed, and Gardner must pay for the work at the agreed price. The jury in the case found that a reasonable man should have been satisfied, and payment was ordered.

In another case, Bender ordered a painting of his hunting dog, promising to pay $500 if he were satisfied with the result. When the picture was finished, Bender refused to accept the picture or to pay for it, and the artist brought suit under the contract. In this case, it was held that if Bender were not satisfied, he need not take or pay for the picture.

The significance of these two cases is that, in the first case, the real condition was not satisfaction of the customer but the doing of the work in a reasonably satisfactory manner, while in the second case, the true condition was the actual satisfaction of the customer. In both cases, the terms of the agreements included promises to pay if satisfied. The line of distinction between these two types of cases involving satisfaction is drawn between the cases in which it is fair to judge performance by some current standard, as in the boiler case, and the other cases in which there is no current standard, as in the picture case. In the latter case, satisfaction is a purely personal thing, while in the former case, satisfaction is measurable in terms of usefulness. Another difference usually appears: namely, that in the boiler case the benefits of the work were put into the possession of the customer, while in the picture case he did not receive the picture at all.

It is of practical importance that the painter should insist upon some part payment upon the making of the agreement. Then, in case the customer is not satisfied, it will be necessary for him to sue to recover his payment. He will be entitled to it, no doubt, but he may be reluctant to sue for it.

Rule 76. *Unconditional promises in contracts may be subject to conditions implied in law.* Under **Rule 70**, it was stated that even unconditional promises may be subject to conditions. Such conditions are called implied because they are not expressed. They are included by court interpretations in five kinds of situations which are shown by the illustrations of the ensuing rules. Such conditions are never implied contrary to express stipulations, of course.

Rule 76A. *Continued existence of the subject matter of the contract is an implied condition.* In the illustration given under **Rule 70**, the promise of Lynch to erect the building by August

15 was unconditional. Suppose that the site for the building had been on the bank of a stream and that a change in the current had washed away the site. The land was the subject matter of the contract, but since it had been washed away, the obligation to erect the house was no longer enforcible. It would be absurd to require Lynch to pay damages for not building a house upon land which was no longer in existence. The continued existence of the land was an implied condition to the duty to build the house, and the failure of the condition to exist will operate as an excuse for the nonperformance of the promise.

Rule 76B. *Continued legality of performance is an implied condition.* In connection with the same case, suppose that before the work is finished, government orders forbid the use of lumber and the other materials for any private construction. Here, again, it would not be sensible to say to Lynch, "If you build this house, you will be punished for using the material; but if you do not build the house, you must pay damages for breach of your contract." For this reason, continued legality of performance is an implied condition to promises in contracts, and if performance becomes unlawful, the nonperformance is excused without penalty.

Rule 76C. *Noninterference with performance by the promisee is an implied condition.* Suppose that when Lynch came to the land to do the work, Betts refused to allow the work to be done; or, more practically, suppose that Betts had locked the gates and gone to South America, having forgotten about the contract. Once more, it would be foolish to say that Betts could recover damages for breach of the contract when the failure of Lynch was due to the act of Betts. On this ground, we find the third kind of condition implied in law.

Rule 76D. *Continued solvency of the promisee is an implied condition.* In the same case, if Betts should become insolvent before Lynch has finished the work, or even before he has begun the work, the insolvency of the promisee (Betts) will practically always operate as an excuse to the promisor. The same thing is true in connection with a promise to deliver goods on credit. Solvency of the promisee is nearly always an implied condition to any promise where the rule can be applied.

Rule 76E. *Continued physical capacity to perform a promise to render a personal service is an implied condition.* If the agreement were interpreted to mean that Lynch was to perform the work personally, and if he should become ill or be injured without any legal fault on his part, he would be excused for his nonperformance. This rule, it must be carefully remembered, applies only to promises to render personal services. It would not apply if Lynch had been a contractor who hired workmen to do the actual work.

For practical purposes, these five are the only conditions which are implied in law. Of course, not all of them apply in all cases since the nature of the agreement and the character of the subject matter will make a difference. Also, it should be kept in mind that these conditions are implied only when there is nothing in the agreement to the contrary. For example, suppose Lynch said, "I will build this building. If I cannot get the material, I will take that risk; if I become ill, I will hire someone in my place; and even if you become insolvent, I will build it." Under these facts, only two of the implied conditions could possibly be applied.

Rule 77. *Impossibility to perform a promise in a contract is usually not a legal excuse for nonperformance.* The essence of four of the five foregoing rules about implied conditions is sometimes stated in terms of impossibility of performance. Thus, it is said that impossibility of performance of a promise in a contract does not excuse nonperformance unless either the impossibility was specially provided for in the contract, or the impossibility is due to (a) destruction of the subject matter, (b) the ensuing illegality of performance, (c) some act of the promisee interfering with performance, or (d) physical incapacity to perform a personal service. Thus, impossibility to perform by Lynch because of bad weather, or because of strikes among his men, or because of business or economic or physical difficulties, will not excuse his obligation to erect the building unless such contingencies fall under some one or more of the implied conditions, or unless such contingencies fall within the stipulation in the contract. Here is another important reason persons who enter into contracts should seek the advice of experienced persons or of lawyers. In that way, it is possible to consider the desirability of including stipulations against strikes or other matters likely to interfere with performance.[4]

Rule 78. *Some contracts involve concurrent conditions.* Conditions are usually defined as events which must occur before obligations become complete. For that reason, most of them are called conditions precedent. In quite a number of cases, however, the phrasing of the agreements takes such form that it may be difficult to see that the promises are conditional on both sides of the transaction. For example, if two persons agree to the purchase and sale of a piano, the question sometimes arises: Is either party bound to take the first step in performance? Must the buyer offer the money first, or must the seller offer delivery first?[5] In such cases, it is said that the contract involves *conditions concurrent.* The meaning of this is that neither side can hold the other liable for nonperformance of the agreement without first offering performance himself. That is, the buyer must offer the price before he is entitled to expect delivery, and the seller must tender the goods before he can require payment for them. Thus, if neither one makes a valid tender of performance, neither can hold the other liable for nonperformance.[6]

Rule 79. *Sometimes promises are implied in contracts.* Consider once more the agreement between Betts and Lynch. If Betts should refuse to permit Lynch to do the work, Lynch could not recover the contract price in a law suit. The promise to pay the price was conditioned upon the doing of the work, and since the condition did not exist, there is no obligation to pay the price. However, this does not mean that there is no obligation at all on the part of Betts. If there were no obligation,

---

[4] It should be noticed that the doctrine of the substantial performance may be applicable to implied conditions as well as to expressed conditions; and it is to be remembered that some of the given implied conditions may be applicable even to conditional promises.

[5] This discussion refers to transactions in which the price is to be paid in cash simultaneous with delivery.

[6] Discussion of conditions subsequent is omitted since they are important chiefly to practicing attorneys. Such conditions are largely matters of pleading, i.e., proper presentment of a case before a court.

the contract would not afford any protection at all to Lynch. Therefore, it is said that there is an implied promise on the part of each party not to interfere with performance by the other. If Betts does not permit the doing of the work, he has broken this implied promise and can be held liable for breach of the contract.[7]

Rule 80. *Repudiation may be a breach of an implied promise.* If Betts announced, before time for performance, that he would not permit the work to be done, this would be called repudiation. Another name for the same thing is *anticipatory breach.* In case of a repudiation, the injured party may consider the whole agreement broken and bring suit at once for breach of contract; or, if he likes, he may wait until time for performance and then, if the performance does not take place, he may bring his suit as of the latter time, but he may not do anything meanwhile to increase the damages. For example, Mitchell agreed to deliver 1000 tons of sand to the Eagle Glass Works. Before time for delivery, the Eagle Works advised Mitchell that they could not accept the sand because their orders had fallen off. This was a repudiation because it was a violation of their implied promise to not interfere with performance of delivery. Mitchell was entitled to bring his suit at once and sell his sand elsewhere, or he might wait until time for delivery and offer it, hoping that the Works would change its position and would accept. But the assessed damages, if they would not accept the tender, would be measured as of the time of repudiation in most cases. In our case of Betts and Lynch, of course, if Lynch stated in advance of the time for performance that he would not perform, this would be a violation of his expressed, unconditional promise, and there would be no need to rely upon an implied promise.

Rule 81. *Failure to deliver an installment may be treated as a breach of contract.* This rule does not refer to promises to pay for goods by installment payments. It refers to those cases in which, for example, a seller agrees to deliver a large quantity of material, such as fuel or the like, in monthly installments of 500 tons each. A delivery of substantially less in any given month may be treated by the other party as a breach. This is somewhat

---

[7] **Rule 83**, relative to quasi contracts.

similar to repudiation in the manner in which the injured party may regard it.

Rule 82. *Joint obligations are both joint and several.* Under the old common law rule, if Howe and North signed an agreement together by which they bound themselves to pay for certain goods bought from Knowles, their obligation was a *joint* one. The legal meaning of a joint obligation under common law is such that if either of the joint parties could not be found or could not be served with process in a suit, then the other joint party could not be held liable. The creditor must sue both or neither if the one sued singly raised the objection that the obligation was a joint one. This was often used to the disadvantage of creditors. Two joint debtors would divide their property, and one of them would move out of the state. Each debtor lived, then, in a different state. The creditor was helpless. He could not sue the one remaining in the original state nor the one who had left the state. Either could object that the joint debt was owed by both together, and both could not be made subject in process in the same court in most cases. Modern statutes have changed this rule to that effect that now nearly all joint debts give rise to *joint* and *several* liability, so that the creditor of joint debtors can now sue either or both, whichever is convenient to the creditor.

Rule 83. *Some implied obligations are called quasi contracts.* There are numerous instances in which either there is no true contract at all or the obligations are uncertain, while, at the same time, some obligations are said by the courts to be implied by law. These obligations are called *quasi contracts.*[8] The obligations in such cases are implied in the interest of fairness and to prevent unjust enrichment. This branch of the law will always be flexible and somewhat uncertain because what is fair or reasonable or unjust enrichment will depend upon the peculiar circumstances of each case, and so long as that is true the law of quasi contracts cannot be standardized. The following illustrations are given as being indicative of this kind of case.

---

[8] The term *quasi* is a Latin word meaning as if. Quasi contract obligations are obligations which are not contractual, but which are treated as if they were contractual.

Take, as an example, the case of Mary Ellen whose uncle promised her some land.[9] The promise could not be enforced as a contract because the promise did not state either how much land or which parcel of land was to be conveyed to Mary Ellen. Under the rules of the law of quasi contracts, however, Mary Ellen was entitled to receive pay for her services at a rate which the court deemed reasonable for that kind of service. In another case, Wilson was employed as an editor, and his salary was paid three months in advance. At the end of the first month, Wilson was taken suddenly ill and was never able to work again. Under the law of quasi contracts, the employer, should he insist upon it, would be entitled to recover the unearned part of what had been paid. Strictly speaking, it would be unfair for Wilson to retain money paid him for work which he did not perform.[10] The flexible character of this branch of the law makes necessary the advice of an expert in connection with all such problems.

SUMMARY

The foregoing rules and illustrations should have made it clear that the correct determination of the obligations of any party to any contract depends upon several things:

First, it is necessary to know how to interpret that party's promises in the particular contract;

Second, it is necessary to know whether such promises are conditional or unconditional in the legal sense;

Third, in connection with conditional promises, it is necessary to know precisely and clearly the character and the meaning of each condition;

Fourth, one must answer the question: Have all of the conditions (to each promise) been complied with?

When all of these matters are properly understood and applied, then, if all applicable conditions have been complied with and if the promise in question has not been performed, the failure to perform such promise creates a liability for breach of contract. On the other hand, if any one or more of the conditions

---

[9] See **Rule 32.**
[10] Several other illustrations are discussed in *Law of Contracts and Sales,* referred to in the introduction of this book.

to a particular promise were not complied with, then there is no liability upon that particular promise.

The foregoing summary is applicable chiefly to promises which are conditional, although the last preceding paragraph applies to both conditional and unconditional promises. As to unconditional promises, it is necessary, first, to have the specific promise clearly in mind; second, one must determine which, if any, of the conditions implied in law are applicable in the particular case; third, if so, which ones, and whether or not they were complied with. Here, again, as to the unconditional promises, if the applicable implied conditions were executed, the maker of the promise will be liable only for nonperformance.

Finally, the transaction must be carefully considered for the purpose of determining whether or not any implied promises are involved in it, and, if there are any such promises, the matter of implied conditions, applicable to such implied promises, must be examined.

ILLUSTRATIVE CASES

The significance of this is that the determination of the obligation of any party to a contract may be a rather difficult and laborious task. This is especially true until one has had some experience with such problems. The analysis of several typical problems should make some aspects of the process a little easier than it first appears. The following problems are relatively easy.[11]

Lewis agreed to buy and Kuhel to sell the latter's car to the former for $400. Kuhel did not offer delivery, and Lewis did not offer to pay. May either hold the other liable for breach of contract? The promise of the seller is interpreted to be conditional, the condition being the tender of the price. The price not having been tendered, there is no liability of the seller for nondelivery of the car. Similarly, the promise of the buyer is interpreted as conditional upon delivery of the car, but, since delivery was not made, there is no liability of the buyer. Neither may hold the other liable until he himself offers performance.

Howard was employed to teach a certain school for nine

---

[11] They are taken from a list of problems found in *Law of Contracts and Sales,* referred to in the introduction.

months. The board agreed to pay him at the end of each month.
At the end of the seventh month, the school was closed by the
health officer. Was Howard entitled to pay for the eighth and
ninth months? In this case, we are concerned with the promise
of the board to pay a salary. This promise was clearly conditioned upon the doing of the work. The condition was not
complied with; therefore, Howard was not entitled to salary for
the months when he did not work.

Swift agreed to deliver 500 tons of coal within a certain
period. Before time for delivery, Swift's coal yard was carried
away by a flood, and all of his coal destroyed. He could not
get other coal in time for delivery. Is Swift liable for breach
of contract? Here the promise was unconditional. None of the
implied conditions apply to it, and therefore Swift is liable for
breach of contract. It might seem that the destruction of the
subject matter was a failure of one of the implied conditions,
but this is not true. No particular coal was to be delivered.
Any 500 tons of the proper quality would have been sufficient.
The subject matter of the contract was not destroyed, and therefore that condition does not apply. That condition applies only
when some specific thing is the subject matter of the contract.
This illustration also serves to show the importance of **Rule 77**:
that impossibility to perform is not usually an excuse for nonperformance.

Welch was employed as a cashier in the X Bank. He was
under a two year contract. While he was on a vacation, his
guide suffered a broken leg, and Welch stayed with him until
help could arrive. Welch was two weeks late in returning to his
job. Would the bank be entitled to dock Welch's pay for the
two weeks? The promise involved here is the promise to pay
salary. This promise is conditioned upon the doing of the work.
The work was not done, and therefore there was no obligation
to pay for those two weeks.

Suppose, under the facts of the case just discussed, that the
question arose: Would the bank be entitled to consider the contract broken by Welch's absence for the additional two weeks
without permission? Here, the promise to be considered is the

promise of Welch to devote his time to the employer's work. This was an unconditional promise. None of the implied conditions apply to it, and therefore Welch could be held liable for breach of contract. The bank could recover damages for its losses due to his absence if it chose, or it could consider the breach of the contract as a release from its obligation to continue to employ him. Therefore, it might employ some one to take Welch's place without incurring any penalty on its part.

These few instances have been given in part to show the manner of the application of some of the rules about conditions in contracts, and in part to impress on the student the need for advice in cases which involve questions of the nature and extent of contract obligations.

ASSIGNMENT OF CONTRACT RIGHTS

Assignment means transfer, but it does not refer to the transfer of those instruments which are called negotiable instruments. The law governing the transfer of negotiable instruments is discussed in a later chapter of this book. Assignment of contracts, as the phrase is used here, means the sale or gift of nonnegotiable contractual rights which are governed by the following rules.

Rule 84. *Contractual liabilities cannot be assigned.* One who is bound by contract to perform some act cannot assign this duty to some other person and thereby terminate the assignor's liability to perform the act. To be sure, it is common practice for a building contractor, for example, to sublet or farm out the actual doing of the work. A building contractor will hire a mason contractor, a carpenter contractor, a plumbing contractor, and the like to get the actual work done. This is sometimes called assignment, but it is not assignment in the legal sense. If the work is not properly done, the principal (or general) contractor is still legally responsible to the other party. Liabilities cannot be assigned.

Rule 84A. *Rights coupled with liabilities cannot be assigned.* If Smith is under contract to perform services as a teacher, he will have a contractual right to collect his pay for the services, if they are properly performed. Along with this right to collect, of course, there is the contractual right to be allowed to do the work and earn the money. Smith can assign the right to collect the money, if the work is done, as the discussion of a later rule will point out, but Smith cannot assign the right to do the work and earn the money, because this right is coupled with Smith's obligation to do the work. No rights can be assigned if they are coupled with liabilities in this way.

Rule 85. *Rights to require delivery of goods or to require services are not usually assignable.* If an author is under contract to write a book, his employer has a right to enforce this contract and to recover damages for breach of the contract. But if the employer decided that he did not want the book, he could not get rid of his obligation by selling this contract to someone else. If James wins a scholarship from a university, he has a contractual right to the services of the university within the terms of his contract, but he cannot assign this right to any other person. If Jones has a contract for the delivery of certain machines to him, he cannot assign the contract and require the seller to deliver the goods to the assignee. Of course, in any of these (or similar) cases, if the obligated party gives his consent, the change may be made, but the process will not be assignment. Also, in a few cases, the original contract may provide that such changes may be made, but, again, if they were made under such circumstances, they would not be assignments; they would be merely performance of the terms of the original agreements.

Rule 86. *One may assign a contractual right to collect money.* When a person renders services or delivers goods and thereby acquires a contractual right to collect the price, he is entitled by law to assign the right to collect this money, and he may assign the right to anyone.[12] Or when one has recovered a judgment in a suit for damages, he may assign the right to collect the money under the judgment.[13]

---

[12] This cannot be done if the original contract forbids it. For example, many employers forbid their employees to assign their wages. Where this is a part of the contract of employment, an attempted assignment of the wages is not valid.

[13] A right to collect damages for personal injury cannot be assigned until the claim has been reduced to a judgment. The right to sue is not transferable.

Rule 87. *One usually cannot assign more extensive rights than he owns.* This rule is extremely important because it is so little known and so seldom understood. Take a simple illustration. Suppose that Gates bought a car from the Auto Sales Company. He paid one hundred dollars in cash and signed an agreement to pay twenty-five dollars per month for eight months for the balance. This contract was a simple contract, not negotiable in form. On the side of the company, the contract was executed since it delivered the car. It then had a contractual right to recover two hundred dollars in eight payments from Gates. Now, if the Company wished to raise money in advance on this contract, it might sell the contract to the State Bank. The Bank then would have the same right to collect as the right which the Company had before the assignment. In many cases, no legal difficulty is encountered here, but in a large number of similar cases, very serious trouble might be met.

Suppose that the original contract contained a guaranty good for ninety days. This means that if the car does not meet the terms of the guaranty, Gates will not be obligated to pay the full price. He may even be able, in some cases, to rescind the whole contract. If this is the kind of contract which Gates made, then the Bank, to whom the assignment is made, will be under the same disability as the assignor. The Bank, even though it did not know of the guaranty, has no better rights than its assignor, and if there is any legal reason why the assignor could not have collected the money from Gates, then the assignee cannot collect it either. It is because of this rule—that an assignee can acquire no better rights than his assignor had—that installment sellers so often insist upon negotiable notes for installments, and banks will practically always refuse to buy nonnegotiable paper. They have learned that such paper is subject to this important rule, and they know better than to take the risks involved in assignments.

The same rule applies to assignments of wages. The employee will be entitled to collect the wages if he does the work, but if he does not do the work, he will not be entitled to collect the wages; and if the employee does not do the work, his assignee will not be able to collect anything under the assignment.

Rule 88. *The states do not agree as to the law in double assignments.* A right to collect money is called a *chose*[14] *in action.* Sometimes the owner of a chose in action assigns it first to one party and later to another without either assignee having knowledge of the fact that the claim has been assigned twice. This has no effect on the position of the debtor. He may pay the original creditor, after one or both of the assignments, and he will be discharged, if he pays without knowledge of the assignments. But when there are two assignees, the problem arises, which of them is entitled to collect from the debtor? In some states, the right of collection is given to the assignee to whom the assignment was made first; in other states, the right to collect is given to the assignee who first gives notice to the debtor that the assignment has been made. Since this is a matter of local law, any problems of this kind should be submitted to a local attorney.

Rule 89. *An assignment of a gift must usually be accompanied by some tangible evidence.* A savings account is a chose in action which is assignable unless the contract of deposit forbids it. When Emma Palmer said to her niece, "Minnie, I am giving you my savings account," but the deposit book was not delivered, the gift was not regarded as complete. In case Aunt Emma should die, the savings account would be distributed as a part of her estate and would not belong to the niece. Delivery of the bank book, or of an insurance policy, or of a note is usually sufficient to make a gift assignment valid.[15]

Rule 90. *Some contractual rights are not assignable at all.* Claims against the United States are not assignable until officially allowed and warrants have been issued for their payment. Salaries of public officials are usually not assignable. A claim for alimony cannot be assigned. Several kinds of common contract rights are not assignable because of the terms of the original agreements underlying them. Many employers forbid assignments

---

[14] Pronounced shows.
[15] If there is consideration for the assignment, no tangible evidence is necessary. It is safer, of course, to provide such evidence.

of wages by their employees. Most theater tickets are not assignable, and even many railway and steamship tickets are stamped *not transferable,* which means *not assignable.*

Rule 91. *At common law, no special forms are necessary for valid assignments.* Except for a few statutory rules, assignments may be quite informal, and they need not even be in writing except in the case of gifts. There are, however, a number of statutes in the various states which modify this rule. This is another reason why assignments should be supervised by legal counsel familiar with local laws.

It should be clear that, as a general rule, it is not good business practice to deal in assignments. Any obligations for the payment of money which are intended to be marketable, such as installment purchase conditional sales agreements, should be put into the form of negotiable instruments. If that is done, all of the uncertainties of the law of assignments will be avoided. The law of Negotiable Instruments is discussed in a later chapter of this book.

DISCHARGE OF CONTRACT OBLIGATIONS

The term, discharge of contracts, must be understood to mean: the termination of the obligation of a party to a contract, so that he can no longer be held legally liable for nonperformance of the contract in question. The most important kinds of events which will terminate contractual obligations are those discussed in the remainder of this chapter.[16]

Rule 92. *Contracts executory on both sides may be discharged by new agreements, as a rule.* As long as a simple contract has not been performed on either side, it may be discharged by a simple agreement of each party to release the other. For instance, after an agreement to paint a house and to pay for the work, but before anything has been done, the painter may ask to be released because he is too busy, or the owner may ask to be released because he has met with some financial reverses. When one party's request for release is met with a favorable response

---

[16] Some technical matters are omitted here since they are of little or no practical importance to the student of business law.

from the other, no more formality is necessary so far as the law is concerned. Of course, it may be wise in such cases to put the release into writing for the purpose of having good evidence, but the law does not require it. Even if the original contract were in writing, the mutual release need not be. This rule applies only to such agreements as have not been fully executed on one side or the other. If either side has been fully performed, then the release will be valid only if there is a consideration for it.[17] And the new agreement, in order to discharge the earlier one, must itself meet all of the requirements of the law of contracts.

Rule 93. *A contract may be discharged by novation.* Novation means a new agreement substituted for an old one. The release discussed under **Rule 92** might be thought of as a novation, but there are two other kinds of novation which should be noticed especially. Hill, by a written agreement, hired Watt as a chauffeur. Hill lost some of his property during a depression and could no longer afford to employ a chauffeur. He procured employment for Watt as a driver of a truck for another employer. The coachman promised to accept this and to release Hill from the former contract. Then the owner of the truck failed also, and Watt sought to recover from Hill on the original contract. The agreement between the truck-owner and Watt was regarded as a novation which discharged the original agreement between Watt and Hill.[18] In that case, the novation was between one of the former parties and a new party, but sometimes the novation is between the same parties. For example, Billings was erecting a house for Kane. While the work was progressing, Kane asked for additional specifications and for a change in the times of payments. This was agreed to by Billings. This would operate as a novation discharging the original agreement and substituting the new one for it.

Rule 94. *Contracts may be discharged by accord and satisfaction.* Fox owed Jennings a debt of $5000. There was no dispute as to the debt or as to the amount. Fox was unable to pay

---

[17] See the discussion under **Rule 35** *d*) and *e*).

[18] Note that this case shows, also, that an oral agreement might replace a written one.

the debt, and Jennings made the following agreement with Fox. Fox was to pay $3000 in cash, deliver $1000 worth of cement in bags, and assign certain patent rights to Jennings, in return for which Jennings agreed to discharge the original debt. The $3000 in cash was paid and the cement was delivered, but, when the delivery of the patent assignment was tendered, Jennings refused to accept it and subsequently brought suit for the remaining $1000. It is held in such cases that the agreement to accept something else in place of performance of an admitted obligation will not discharge the original obligation until the substitute has been completely performed. This is called discharge by accord and satisfaction. It is important to notice the emphasis on the word *and,* and it is important, also, to notice that satisfaction means, in this instance, performance.

Rule 95. *Contracts may be discharged by arbitration and award.* In modern business practice, there are numerous instances in which parties to contracts agree that they will submit any differences arising under contracts to arbitration. Sometimes this kind of agreement is made at the time when the original business contract is made; sometimes such an agreement (to arbitrate) is made after the original contract is made; and sometimes such an agreement (to arbitrate) is made after some dispute has actually arisen. In such cases, if the dispute is submitted to an arbitrator, if the arbitrator acts fairly, and if he makes a specific award, such an award is usually regarded as replacing the original contract. As to whether an agreement to arbitrate will be regarded by the courts as replacing the original agreement, the answer is usually in the negative. There is some uncertainty in this branch of the law, however, and it is safest to rely upon the probability that arbitration and award will operate as a discharge of a contract only when the arbitration has been honest, and the award has been made.

Rule 96. *A contract may be discharged by expiration of time.* If an agreement stipulates that it is to run for some designated length of time, it will, of course, end with the expiration of that time. Many employment contracts are of this kind, as are many partnership agreements. Even if no time is stipulated,

*STATUTES OF LIMITATION AS AFFECTING CONTRACT RIGHTS

(The numbers represent how many years must have elapsed)

State	Judgments	Contracts under Seal	Written Contracts	Open Acc'ts and Oral Contracts
Alabama	20	10	6	3
Arizona	5	6	6	3
Arkansas	10	5	5	3
California	5	4(c)	4	4
Colorado	20	6	6	6
Connecticut	No limit	17	6	6
Delaware	20	20	6	3
District Columbia..	12	12	3	3
Florida	20	20	5	3
Georgia	7	20	6	4
Idaho	6	5	5	4
Illinois	7 and 20(b)	10	10	5
Indiana	20	20	10	6
Iowa	20	10	10	5
Kansas	5(a)	5	5	5(d)
Kentucky	15	15	15	3
Louisiana	10	10	5	6
Maine	20	20	6	3
Maryland	12	12	3	6
Massachusetts	20	20	6	6
Michigan	10	10	6	6
Minnesota	10	6	6	6
Mississippi	7	6	6	3
Missouri	10	10	10	5
Montana	10	8	8	5
Nebraska	5(a)	5	5	4

* This table is reproduced from *The Law of Contracts and Sales,* by Christ, with the permission of Longmans, Green and Co.

STATUTES OF LIMITATION AS AFFECTING CONTRACT RIGHTS
(*Continued*)

(The numbers represent how many years must have elapsed)

State	Judgments	Contracts under Seal	Written Contracts	Open Acc'ts and Oral Contracts
Nevada	6	6	6	4
New Hampshire ...	20	20	6	6
New Jersey	20	16	6	6
New Mexico	7	6	6	4
New York	20	20	6	6
North Carolina	10	10	3	3
North Dakota	10	10	6	6
Ohio	5(*a*)	15	15	6
Oklahoma	5(*a*)	5	5	6
Oregon	10	10	6	3
Pennsylvania	20	20	6	6
Rhode Island	20	20	6	6
South Carolina ...	20	20	6	6
South Dakota	20	20	6	6
Tennessee	10	6	6	6
Texas	10	4	4	2
Utah	8	6	6	4
Vermont	8	8–15	8	6
Virginia	20	10	5	3
Washington	6	6	6	3
West Virginia	20	10	10	5
Wisconsin	20	20	6	6
Wyoming	5	10	10	8

(*a*) Kept alive by execution every five years.
(*b*) Complicated provisions.
(*c*) Two years if not executed within the state.
(*d*) Between merchant and consumer, two years.
Most of the states do not mention contracts under seal specifically. In such states, the same limitations apply as those which apply to written contracts.

a contract of partnership, for example, may be lawfully terminated by one partner without the consent of the others, after the expiration of a *reasonable time*. This is true of some kinds of employment contracts, too, but not most of them. Employment contracts should be made specifically terminable *at will* by either party without notice, or they should be for stipulated periods of time.

Rule 97. *Contracts may be discharged by breach.* This may at first seem rather strange, but what is meant is that if one party violates his side of the agreement, the other party may treat the agreement as discharged. In this way, breach is similar, in its legal effects, to repudiation discussed under **Rule 80.** The same thing is true of the effect of the fact that one party becomes clearly unable to perform. This also may be treated as a discharge by the other party.

Rule 98. *Contracts are discharged by performance.* This means that, if a party performs his part of a contract, he is discharged, not the other party. This, of course, is obvious, but it seemed desirable to mention it in order to get at the next rule.

Rule 99. *The effect of tender of performance is not discharge.* In contracts for the payment of money when the debt is due, checks, drafts, postal orders, and the like are not legal tender, unless the creditor agrees to accept them as such. Under the Act of May 12, 1933, all coins and all currency of the United States are legal tender for all debts, public and private. If Davis owes Rood $1000, and offers one hundred thousand pennies, this is legal tender; but, if Rood refuses to accept the pennies, the debt is not discharged. Davis still owes $1000. The legal tender does have a legal effect, but it does not discharge the debt unless it is accepted. The effect of legal tender—that is, of the tendering of full and proper performance—if it is refused, is this: If there is afterward a suit for the debt, the debtor will be relieved of the costs of the suit and he will be relieved of the obligation of paying interest from the date of the tender. This will be true only if the tender be kept good; it must be held available for the creditor at all times. One must remain willing and able to perform at any time after the tender, to keep the tender good.

Rule 100. *Contracts may be discharged by bankruptcy or by the Statute of Limitations.* If a debtor who is thrown into bankruptcy surrenders all of his assets to the court, and if he is discharged by the court as the result of the proceedings, then all of his contracts (so far as they were provable in bankruptcy)[19] are said to be discharged. This means that the debtor cannot thereafter be compelled, by legal process, to pay the debt so discharged. However, the bankruptcy statute also provides that if the debtor, after his discharge, promises in writing to pay the discharged debt, or if he does pay some part of it, as a part of the whole, then the discharge in bankruptcy is cancelled, and he again becomes liable for the original debt.

The same sort of attitude is taken toward discharge by the Statute of Limitations. After the statutory period, the debt is said to be outlawed, but a subsequent promise or a part payment will revive the original obligation.[20] Thus, discharge by bankruptcy or by the Statute of Limitations is really not a permanent discharge, but only a sort of suspension which the debtor can waive if he likes.

QUESTIONS AND PROBLEMS

1. What is the reason why it is important to be able to determine whether a given promise in a contract is conditional or unconditional? **Rule 70.**

2. How can one tell that the promise of Lynch, in the problem discussed under **Rule 70,** is unconditional? Write your answer.

3. Is a conditional promise one to which there are no conditions? **Rule 70** and footnotes thereto.

4. Write out an illustration of a conditional promise in which the condition cannot be substantially performed. See **Rule 73.**

5. When a party to a contract promises to pay if he is satisfied with the goods or services covered by the contract, how can one decide whether his promise to pay is conditioned upon actual satisfaction or upon whether or not he ought to be satisfied? **Rules 74** and **75.**

6. Write out the five conditions which are implied in connec-

---

[19] What is provable is highly technical. It cannot be discussed in this book.

[20] In some states, the Statutes of Limitations provide that the promise must be in writing to revive the debt. In others, it can be oral and have the same effect. As to the length of the period, see the table "Statute of Frauds," in the following chapter.

tion with promises in contracts unless the promises contain something which is contrary to such implications. **Rules 76** to **76E.**

7. What is the general rule with respect to the effect of impossibility of performance upon the obligations of parties to contracts? **Rule 77.**

8. Gray and Elson made a contract for the sale of Gray's horse and wagon to Elson for $50.00 in cash. Nothing was said in the agreement as to whether the money was to be paid before delivery or delivery was to be made before payment. If Gray did not tender delivery of the horse and wagon, could he be held liable for breach of the contract? Why? If Elson did not tender the money first, could he be held liable? Why? Which one is required to make the first tender? **Rule 78.**

9. In an agreement between Carlson and Witte, Witte was to paint Carlson's house, and Carlson was to pay $200 when the work was completed. If Carlson refused to allow Witte to do the work, could he be held liable for breach of contract? If so, what is the legal source of this liability if the contract did not contain any promise not to prevent the doing of the work? **Rule 79.**

10. What is the effect upon the rights of party A (to a contract) if party B repudiates the agreement before party A has performed? Be sure to state the rule fully. **Rule 80.**

11. What is the practical meaning of the joint debtors' laws, effective in most states, which provide that joint debtors are liable either jointly or severally? **Rule 82.**

12. List the questions which must be answered in order to determine the liability of a party who breaks a promise in a contract. You will find them under the summary on page 74. Copy them word for word if you cannot remember them.

13. Under the heading *Illustrative Cases* on page 75, note the second case, regarding Howard the school teacher. In this case, suppose that we change the facts to read, "The school was closed by the school board at the end of the seventh month because they thought that the students should go to work on neighboring farms." Under these facts, would Howard be entitled to pay for the eighth and ninth months? Why? Apply the reasoning given in connection with the Howard case as it stands in the book.

14. What is the practical meaning, to you, of the statement in **Rule 84** that contractual liabilities cannot be assigned?

15. If you are a prospective buyer of any good whatever, what is the practical importance to you of the discussion under **Rule 87**? Be sure to make your answer clear.

16. Grimes was the owner of a horse. He said to his son, Robert,

"I will give you the horse. You can go to my barn and get him any time you like." Robert did not get the horse immediately. Grimes died suddenly during the night. When Robert went to get the horse in a few days, the other members of the family (heirs to the estate of Grimes) objected on the ground that the gift was not valid. Was it valid or not, and why? **Rule 89.** What should have been done to escape the possibility of such a dispute as this?

17. Jones and Gilman made a contract in writing which was executory on both sides. (What does executory mean?) Before any work was done or payment made, Jones asked to be released, and Gilman stated that it was all right with him. Does this discharge the original contract, or does the law require that the release must be more formal than this? **Rule 92.**

18. Give an illustration other than the one in the book, which will show that you understand the rule of law about accord and satisfaction. **Rule 94.**

19. Jones did some work for Hayes and submitted a bill for $200.00, which Hayes thought too high. Hayes paid Jones $150.00 in legal tender. Jones refused to accept it and sued Hayes on the contract. The court decided that $150.00 was a sufficient amount since the price had not been originally agreed upon. Now, does the fact that Hayes tendered the proper amount (as determined by the court) discharge the whole debt? Explain your answer fully and clearly. **Rule 99.**

20. It is often said that a contractual debt is discharged by bankruptcy of the debtor or by the Statute of Limitations. In what sense is this statement true? In what sense is it untrue? What is the practical importance of your knowledge about this matter?

Idaho State Capitol, Boise
Johnson & Son, Photographers—Courtesy of Boise Chamber of Commerce, Boise, Idaho

Illinois State Capitol, Springfield
Courtesy, Herbert Georg Studio, Springfield, Ill.

Indiana State Capitol, Indianapolis
Underwood & Underwood

Iowa State Capitol, Des Moines
Underwood & Underwood

CHAPTER IV

CONTRACTS FOR THE SALE OF GOODS[1]

Rule 101. *The basic rules of contract law are applicable to contracts for the sale of goods.* All of the general rules for the formation of contracts are applicable to the transactions discussed in this chapter. Parties must be competent, the rules of offer and acceptance must be observed, there must be consideration, and the objects of such agreements must be lawful in order that they be enforcible.

Rule 102. *Some additional rules are necessary because of the existence of special problems.* In connection with contracts for the sale of goods, certain problems arise which do not arise in connection with any other types of contracts, and, therefore, special rules have been developed in order that the courts may deal with such problems in an orderly manner. These problems are concerned with four groups of questions. First, there is the group of questions in connection with the seventeenth section of the Statute of Frauds; second, there are difficult questions about the passing of title; third, there are questions as to how far the seller is held to have guaranteed the quality of the goods when there is no express warranty; and fourth, there are questions as to what remedies are available to either the buyer or the seller in case the contract is broken by either one or the other.

Rule 103. *Most of these rules are now embodied in the Uniform Sales Act.* These rules, concerning the groups of questions just enumerated, were mostly worked out by the courts,

---

[1] The author is greatly indebted to Longmans, Green & Co., New York, for their permission to adapt a considerable portion of this chapter from the author's book, *Law of Contracts and Sales*.

but since the courts in the various states did not always agree, it has seemed desirable to formulate a uniform statute in order to make the law uniform throughout the whole of the United States. This statute is called the *Uniform Sales Act*. It has been adopted in most of the commercial states,[2] and since most of the decisions of the courts, even in the other states, are in harmony with the rules as stated in the Sales Act, the present discussion is almost entirely confined to the law set forth in the act so far as the act is applicable.[3]

MAKING THE CONTRACT

Rule 104. *The Statute of Frauds must be complied with.* The Seventeenth Section of the Statute of Frauds has been incorporated in the Uniform Sales Act as Section 4 of that act, but it is still customarily referred to as the Statute of Frauds by nearly all authorities. The language of the Illinois statute is as follows:

A contract to sell or a sale of any goods or choses in action of the value of five hundred dollars or upwards shall not be enforcible by action unless the buyer shall accept part of the goods or choses in action so contracted to be sold or sold, and actually receive the same, or give something in earnest to bind the bargain, or in part payment, or unless some note or memorandum be signed by the party to be charged or his agent in that behalf.[4]

Every contract for the sale of goods, if the amount involved is equal to or greater than the amount set in the statute of the state whose law applies to the contract, must conform to the statute. If it does not, then neither party to the contract can enforce it in the courts of any state. There are a vast number

---

[2] The act has been adopted in Alabama, Arizona, Connecticut, Illinois, Idaho, Indiana, Iowa, Maine, Maryland, Massachusetts, Michigan, Minnesota, Nebraska, Nevada, New Hampshire, New Jersey, New York, North Dakota, Ohio, Oregon, Pennsylvania, Rhode Island, South Dakota, Tennessee, Utah, Vermont, Washington, Wisconsin, and Wyoming.

[3] These rules do not apply to contracts for the sale of land or the rendering of services.

[4] In all except five of the states, this statute is in effect in some form or other, even where the Sales Act is not in force. These states, as well as the differences in the values stipulated in the various states, are shown in the table on a following page.

of questions which have arisen in relation to the meaning of
this statute. Among the most important are those which concern
the matters discussed under Rules 104 to 107.

TABLE OF LEGAL AND PERMISSIBLE RATES[a] OF INTEREST AND AMOUNTS OF MONEY (SALES) IN THE STATUTES OF FRAUDS[b]

	Interest		Statute of Frauds (Amount Named or over)
	Legal Rate	Contract Rate	
Alabama	8	8	$500
Arizona	6	8	$500
Arkansas	6	10	$30
California	7	12	$200
Colorado	6	12[c]	$50
Connecticut	6	12	$100
Delaware	6	6	No law
District of Columbia	6	8	$50
Florida	8	10	No limit
Georgia	7	8	$50
Idaho	6	7	$500
Illinois	5	7[d]	$500
Indiana	6	8	$50
Iowa	5	7	No limit
Kansas	6	10	No limit
Kentucky	6	6	No law
Louisiana	5	8	No amount
Maine	6	12	$30
Maryland	6	6	$50
Massachusetts	6	Any	$500
Michigan	5	7	$100
Minnesota	6	8	$50
Mississippi	6	8	$50
Missouri	6	8	$30
Montana	6	10	$200
Nebraska	6	9	$500
Nevada	7	12	$50
New Hampshire	6	Any	$500
New Jersey	6	6	$500
New Mexico	6	12[e]	$50
New York	6	6[d]	$50

TABLE OF LEGAL AND PERMISSIBLE RATES[a] OF INTEREST AND AMOUNTS OF MONEY (SALES) IN THE STATUTES OF FRAUDS[b] (Cont.)

	Interest Legal Rate	Contract Rate	Statute of Frauds (Amount Named or over)
North Carolina	6	6	No law
North Dakota	4	7	$500
Ohio	6	8	$2500
Oklahoma	6	10	$50
Oregon	6	10	$50
Pennsylvania	6	6[d]	$500
Rhode Island	6	30[f]	$500
South Carolina	6	7	$50
South Dakota	6	8	$500
Tennessee	6	6	$500
Texas	6	10	$500
Utah	6	12	$500
Vermont	6	6	$40
Virginia	6	6	No law
Washington	6	12	Over $50
West Virginia	6	6	No law
Wisconsin	6	10	$50
Wyoming	7	10	$50

[a] In many states, these rates do not apply to small loans made by pawnbrokers or licensed loan companies. Also, in several states, the usury laws provide that corporations cannot avoid their interest contracts on the ground of usury.

[b] This table is taken from the author's *Law of Contracts and Sales,* by permission of the publisher, Longmans, Green & Co.

[c] Colorado; any agreed rate on debt of over $300.

[d] Illinois, New York, Pennsylvania; no restriction of loans over $5000 secured by certain collateral. This makes possible the call money market.

[e] New Mexico; 10 per cent on secured loans and 12 per cent on unsecured loans, by contract.

[f] Rhode Island; 30 per cent on loans over $50. On loans not over $50, five per cent per month for first six months; two and one-half per cent per month thereafter.

Rule 104A. *The Statute of Frauds does not require writing in all cases.* It is very commonly thought that the Statute of Frauds requires all contracts, within the amounts named, to be in writing. A careful reading of the statute will show that this

is not true. Writing is required only if there has been no acceptance and receipt and also no part payment.[5] This point is important and should be remembered.

Rule 105. *If a memorandum is required by the statute, it
need not be signed by both parties.* Notice that the memorandum,
when required, must be signed by the party to be charged or
his agent. This means that neither party can recover from the
other (if writing is required at all in the particular case), unless
the memorandum has been signed by the defendant. The party
to be charged does not mean the party who is to pay for the
goods; it means the party who is charged with violation of the
agreement.

Rule 106. *The Statute of Frauds does not apply to contracts
for services.* The courts in the past have been troubled a great
deal by the question: How can one distinguish a contract for
the sale of goods from a contract for work and labor? This
question arises in cases similar to the following one which arose
in the state of Massachusetts. Goddard was a builder of carriages.
Binney ordered a carriage built to rather unusual specifications.
The order was oral and no down payment was made. When
the work was done, the buyer inspected the carriage and expressed his approval, but he did not take the carriage. He promised
to take it next day, and to pay for it then. During the night,
a fire in Goddard's shop destroyed the carriage. Binney refused
to pay for a carriage which he did not receive, and when Goddard
brought suit for the price, Binney's defense was that this was a
contract for the sale of goods, and that it was not enforcible
because of the fact that there had been no payment, no acceptance
and receipt, and no written memorandum.

It was necessary first to decide whether this was a contract
for the sale of goods. If it was not, then the Statute of Frauds
would not apply. The court took the attitude that where a thing
is to be made under special order and would not be readily salable
in the general market of the maker, the most important thing about

---

[5] Earnest money to bind the bargain, is very uncommon. In this country
down payments are regarded as part of the price. Earnest money is not; it is
in addition to the price.

the contract is the service to be performed, rather than the goods. This contract, therefore, was said to be a contract for work, labor, and materials, and not a contract for the sale of goods. The Statute of Frauds did not apply, therefore, and the agreement was enforcible.[6] This rule is in effect in all of the states in this country except Missouri.[7]

Rule 107. *The memorandum is valid if made at any time before trial of a suit under the agreement.* If Binney had signed a statement of approval when he saw the finished carriage, and if this statement indicated an intention to take it and pay for it, that would have constituted a sufficient memorandum. The memorandum need not be formal; it may be on scratch paper, in the form of letters or telegrams or the like, and it may be made at any time before the suit upon the contract actually comes to trial. All that is necessary is that the memorandum show who the parties are and what they have agreed to do. Then, if it is signed by the party to be charged, the agreement is valid, so far as the Statute of Frauds is concerned.

THE PASSING OF TITLE

Rule 108. *Loss of property must be borne by the owner (at the time of the loss) unless some other person is legally chargeable with the loss.* This proposition is fundamental in our system of law. Unless some person has contracted to bear the loss, or unless someone's unlawful conduct is the cause of the loss, the owner of property must bear it. This rule makes it important that there should be some method by which it will be possible to determine who the owner of property is at the time when loss or damage occurs to the property. In the carriage case discussed above, for example, if the carriage belonged to Binney, he must pay for it; if it belonged to Goddard, then Binney need not pay for it. No matter which way we decide the question, one or the other must

---

[6] Binney was required to pay for the carriage because the title was held to have passed to him. This is discussed in a later part of this chapter.

[7] In Missouri, the so-called English rule is in effect. The substance of that rule is that if the contract contemplates that title to personal property shall change from one party to the other, it is a contract for the sale of goods. Under that rule, the Binney case would have been within the statute and not enforcible.

bear the loss unless it is insured or unless it can be recovered from the persons whose legal act was the cause of the loss. But even in either of the latter two cases, it would be necessary to know to whom the carriage belonged because only the owner could recover from the wrongdoer or from the insurance company.

Rule 109. *Title passes in accordance with the expressed intent of the parties to the contract, if possible and lawful.* If Goddard and Binney had agreed between themselves, by some mode of expression, that the title to the carriage would pass when it was finished, or when it was approved, or when it was delivered, or when it was paid for, or at any other stated time, the court would have followed this expression of intent, if possible and if the intent were not an unlawful one. But Goddard and Binney did not state when the title was to pass, and most parties to contracts for the sale of goods do not state their intentions to the passing of title. But when losses occur, someone must bear the loss; and for that reason, the courts must determine in some way who the owner was at the time of the loss. The rules for deciding whether or not title has passed from seller to buyer at the time of a loss (when no intent was expressed by the parties in that respect) have been incorporated into the Sales Act.[8]

Rule 110. *If the goods have been identified and are ready for delivery when the contract is made, title passes at that moment.* This rule is incorporated in the Sales Act, Section 19, Rule 1, which adds that in such cases, "it is immaterial whether the time of payment or the time of delivery, or both be postponed." Gale agreed to buy and Hill to sell a certain stack of hay in a field. It was to be held until paid for. Before the time of payment, the hay was burned up, but under this rule, the title had passed to Gale and he was obliged to pay for it. In a similar case, the hay was sold by the seller to a second buyer, Kinney, before Gale tendered payment. In the latter case, since the hay belonged to Gale, he was entitled to replevin the hay from Kinney. Thus, the rule protects the seller in case of loss, and it protects the buyer in case the seller attempts a second sale. A buyer in the position of Kinney,

---

[8] Keep in mind that the following rules do not apply unless the parties have failed to express their intent about the passing of title.

therefore, should make sure of the title of one who tries to sell to him, because if the seller (Hill) had no title, the second buyer (Kinney) would get no title.

Rule 111. *If the goods have been identified, but something remains to be done by the seller to make them deliverable, the title will not pass until that act has been done.* This rule is found in Section 19, Rule 2, of the Sales Act. Wilson agreed to buy a certain desk and chair from Neal, but it was agreed that the two articles were to be refinished by Neal. They were lost in a flood before the work was done, and Wilson was not obligated to pay for them since title had not passed. If the loss had occurred after the work had been done, Wilson would have held the title and would have been obligated to pay.

Rule 112. *If the contract requires the seller to deliver the goods to the buyer or to any particular place, title passes upon the completion of such delivery.* This is Section 19, Rule 5, of the Sales Act. This rule covers the ordinary cases involving sales by a store with a provision for delivery. If goods under such an agreement are lost before delivery has been completed, the buyer is not obligated to pay for the goods. The same rule applies to C.O.D. sales, goods shipped by parcel post, goods delivered by the delivery service of the seller, and, probably, goods sent by common carrier.[9] That is, the C.O.D. sale is regarded as a contract which requires delivery. Title does not pass in such a sale until delivery has been made. This rule (**Rule 112**) is applicable whether or not the subject of the contract has been identified at the time of the making of the contract.

Rule 113. *If the goods have not been identified, title passes upon the appropriation of proper goods to the contract by the seller with the buyer's approval.* This is Rule 4, Paragraph (1),

---

[9] There is some apparent conflict of authority on this last point. However, the conflict is mostly among text-writers since there is only one case in which a decision is recorded on the question. In that case, a purchaser of goods paid the price to a clerk in an express office. The clerk then went to look for the goods, and discovered that they had been stolen. The clerk refused to return the money and remitted it to the seller who also refused to return it, claiming that title had passed by appropriation of the goods (see **Rule 113** of this chapter). The court held that title had not passed and the buyer was entitled to the return of his money, which is in accord with **Rule 112**.

of Section 19 of the Sales Act. This rule is intended to cover the common cases in which the buyer orders goods from a catalog or by description. The goods are to be taken from stock by the seller and shipped to the buyer; or they may be manufactured, boxed, or bottled, by the seller; or they may be bought by the seller for the order. The greatest difficulty in applying this rule lies in determining what constitutes *appropriation* of the goods. In general, it may be said that when the goods have been clearly designated for the contract and put into the control of the buyer, the appropriation is regarded as complete. One instance of this is found in a case in which a machine consigned to the buyer was delivered by the seller to a railroad. This is regarded as complete appropriation.[10] Another illustration is furnished by a case in which the buyer ordered sixty cases of eggs. The eggs were packed in crates which were marked with the buyer's name and placed on a loading platform for him to pick up. They were destroyed before he got them, but it was held that the title had passed by the appropriation, and the buyer was required to pay for the eggs.

In this connection, consider the carriage case discussed under **Rule 106.** The title passed to the buyer in that case because the appropriation had been completed by the seller when the carriage was completed, and, in addition, the goods had been approved by the buyer.

The meaning of appropriation which has just been given is incorporated in Section 19, Rule 4, Paragraph 2, of the Sales Act.[11]

Rule 114. *If title is retained by the seller to secure the payment of the price, the risk of loss is upon the buyer.* This rule is found in Section 20 of the Sales Act. The rule is important because it modifies the rules which have just been discussed. Thus, when the seller takes a bill of lading for the goods for his own order,

---

[10] If the goods are consigned to the order of the seller, this being a common practice, the title does not pass until the bill of lading has been indorsed by the seller and the bill delivered to the buyer with the seller's consent. See **Rule 114,** however.

[11] It is again necessary to point out the conflict of ideas in this field because of the wording of Par. 2 of Rule 19, Sec. 4. No case has been found in which the risk of loss is put upon the buyer in a C.O.D. sale in spite of the wording of Par. 2 or Sec. 19, Rule 4. The rule is contradictory to Sec. 19, Rule 5, discussed in **Rule 112.**

he retains title, but, because of Section 20, the risk of loss is on the buyer.

Rule 115. *In a contract for the sale of an undivided share of a specific mass of fungible goods, title passes to the buyer at the time of the contract.* Fungible goods are goods of which the units are commercially equivalent to each other. Oil, wheat, cattle on the hoof, and coal are illustrations of fungible goods. Dickenson was the owner of a pile of wheat containing 6500 bushels. He sold to Shuttleworth 6000 bushels to be taken from this pile. Part payment was made, and a storage receipt was issued to Shuttleworth who then sold the storage receipt to Patchin. Before Patchin called for the wheat, Dickenson sold the entire mass to Kimberly who took the wheat away. In a suit between Patchin and Kimberly, it was held that since title had passed to Shuttleworth under the rule here discussed, Patchin was entitled to 6000 bushels from Kimberly. The latter must seek his remedy from Dickenson for the fraudulent second sale.[12]

Rule 116. *When goods are delivered on sale or return, title passes on delivery.* In such cases, the buyer, of course, may revest the title in the seller by returning the goods (or tendering them) within the time stated in the contract, or within a reasonable time if no time is stated in the contract.[13]

Rule 117. *When goods are delivered on approval or on trial, title does not pass until the expression of approval or the passing of time.* This rule is found in Section 19, Rule 3, Paragraph 2, of the Sales Act. The time referred to is either the time stipulated in the contract or a *reasonable time.* The only difficulty with the application of these two rules lies in determining which is a sale on approval and which is a contract for sale or return. This involves a question of fact which can never be clearly answered by any rule of law.[14]

Rule 118. *If the goods have perished before the making of the agreement, unknown to the parties, the agreement is void.*

---

[12] This rule is found in Sec. 6, of the Sales Act.
[13] Sec. 19, Rule 3, Par. 1 of the Sales Act.
[14] Bear in mind that the rule for the passing of title, as outlined above, operates only in the absence of expression of intent of the parties in the contract.

This is found in Section 7 of the Sales Act. It does not need illustration.[15]

Rule 119. *Generally, one cannot transfer a better title than he possesses.* Section 23 of the Sales Act reads as follows:

(1) Subject to the provisions of this act, where goods are sold by a person not the owner thereof and who does not sell them under the authority or with the consent of the owner, the buyer acquires no better title to the goods than the seller had, unless the owner of the goods is by his conduct precluded from denying the seller's authority to sell.[16]

(2) Nothing in this act, however, shall affect—(a) the provisions of the factors' acts, recording acts, or any enactment enabling the apparent owner of goods to dispose of them as if he were the true owner thereof.

(b) The validity of any contract to sell or sale under any special common law or statutory power of sale or under the order of a court of competent jurisdiction.

The factors' acts referred to in (2)(a) are in effect in Maine, Maryland, Massachusetts, New York, Ohio, Pennsylvania, Rhode Island, and Wisconsin. In general, those acts provide that when goods are shipped by carrier and the buyer has advanced money upon them, the shipper is regarded as the true owner (whether he is or not), to protect the buyer. In Massachusetts and Pennsylvania, this provision applies only if the shipper is in lawful possession of the goods.

Rule 120. *The holder of a voidable title can sometimes transfer a valid title.* This is an apparent exception to Rule No. 119, but in reality is a special case of Paragraph (1) of Section 23 of the Sales Act. One kind of voidable title is illustrated by the case which illustrated fraud in the inducement under **Rule 60** in Chapter II. Another illustration is afforded by a case in which an infant sold a machine and had it delivered, though he could have avoided the agreement. The purchaser's title was voidable, but if he had sold the machine to a buyer in good faith, such buyer would have a valid title, good even against the infant.

---

[15] See the effects of impossibility, **Rule 76A.**
[16] Preclusion of the right to deny the seller's authority to sell falls under the concept of *estoppel,* which is discussed in a subsequent chapter, dealing with the authority of agents. Par. (1) is a codification of common law.

Rule 121. *In most installment contracts, title does not pass until final payment because the contracts so provide.* Modern installment contracts for the sale of goods practically always provide specifically that title is reserved to the seller until the final payment is made, and also, in many cases, that any loss or destruction of the goods is to be borne by the buyer, even though such loss should occur before title passes. When the buyer realizes these facts, it should be clear to him that he should insure goods (under such contracts). Only in this way can be protect himself against the possibility that he might have to pay for goods which he cannot enjoy. These cases are discussed somewhat further under the rules concerning conditional sales.

Rule 122. *Sometimes the retention of goods by the seller may be regarded as fraudulent.* Section 26 of the Sales Act provides:

Where a person having sold goods continues in possession of the goods, or of negotiable documents of title to the goods, and such retention of possession is fraudulent in fact or is deemed fraudulent under any rule or law, a creditor or creditors of the seller may treat the sale as void.

This refers to cases in which the buyer leaves the goods in storage with the seller. Sometimes the seller sells the goods again to another purchaser in good faith, and sometimes the goods are attached by the seller's creditors. While title passes between the first buyer and the seller, the buyer who thus leaves the goods with the seller runs the risk that he may lose title to the goods because he (the buyer) may not be able to show that the sale to him was genuine. Many times, debtors, just before insolvency, make fictitious transfers of goods to their friends or relatives, issuing fake bills of sale and retaining the goods. Then, when the creditors of the seller try to seize the goods, the bill of sale is exhibited so as to deprive the creditors of their powers to take the goods for the satisfaction of their lawful claims. Then, when the creditors go away, the fictitious bill is either destroyed or held for another similar emergency. In some of the states, and in some kinds of cases, such retention is regarded as conclusive evidence of fraud; in other states and in other kinds of cases, retention merely raises the question of fraud, and the creditors are required to prove that the sale was actually fraudulent. In either case, the honest buyer may be put to a good deal of trouble to rebut the presumption of fraud by the seller. The only safe course for the buyer to take to avoid this particular risk is to take delivery of any goods he buys just as soon as possible after the contract is made.[17]

WARRANTIES MADE BY THE SELLER

The words *warrant* and *warranty* have the same meaning as the word *guarantee* or the word *guaranty* as the latter are commonly used. When one *guarantees* or *warrants* goods, he is doing two things. For one thing, he is representing something with reference to the quality of the goods, or their performance, or his title to them; and for another thing, he is promising that if the facts are not as represented, he will do something to make good the loss caused by the failure. Of course, a warranty may be made expressly, that is, there may be some kind of specific promise in the form of contract or part of a sales agreement to make good any loss if the representations concerning the goods are not true. When a seller of goods makes an express warranty, the following rules should be kept in mind.

Rule 123. *To protect a buyer, every express warranty should be specific.* The mere use of the word *guarantee* in a contract does not carry much meaning and is not worth much to the buyer as a protection in a considerable number of cases. *Satisfaction guaranteed or your money back,* for example, is a general warranty. It may prove to be of no practical value at all to the buyer because a guaranty of satisfaction, as has been pointed out in connection with contracts generally, may often be construed as the kind of expression which is subject to the doctrine of substantial performance. That is, the buyer of goods under such a warranty may find that, while he is not actually satisfied, he has no remedy against the seller because, in many cases, it will be held that if

---

[17] Of course, no attention need be paid to this risk when one is dealing with reliable sellers such as established department stores and other reputable dealers. Also, since the presumption of fraud is different in some states from the presumption in other states, local attorneys should be consulted in connection with any matters relative to such problems.

the goods come up to a commercially acceptable standard, he should have been satisfied; and when this interpretation is reached, the situation is treated as though the buyer actually had been satisfied, and the warranty, therefore, is not regarded as broken. The buyer should therefore insist that, if he is to have any express warranty at all, it should be made specific. In the case of a car, the tires should be guaranteed for a certain number of miles or months, the battery for a certain stipulated time, and the electrical equipment for a certain period of operation. In fact, a general guaranty is not worth very much, legally, because no one can be sure what it means.

Rule 124. *In small transactions, warranties are of little value legally.* In common purchases of goods at retail even specific warranties are not of much legal significance. The amounts involved are so small that the purchaser cannot afford to spend either the time or the money to insist upon his legal rights when such warranties are broken. If his tires are guaranteed for 25,000 miles, and if they wear out at 19,000, the buyer cannot afford a lawsuit to recover the few dollars lost. It is therefore much more important that the purchaser at retail should be sure of the integrity and business practice of the seller in standing behind his goods, than that the purchaser rely upon warranties. The same thing is true, whether warranties in a contract are express or whether they are implied, as is sometimes the case.

Rule 125. *In the absence of express warranties, the general rule is known as caveat emptor.* Caveat emptor is a Latin phrase which means: Let the buyer beware; that is, the buyer must take his chances as to the quality of the goods. This rule applies to all purchases of goods unless the transaction in a particular case falls within the limits of one or another of the exceptions which are stated in the ensuing paragraphs. Of course, when an article is sold *as is,* there is no implied warranty at all, and none of the exceptions will apply.

Rule 125A. *Under the Sales Act, there is a warranty of title unless there is an expression of intent to the contrary.* The general common law rule was that a seller of goods was held to warrant title to goods only if he had the goods in his possession at the time of the contract, but this has been changed by the Sales Act. Thus, every seller of goods can be held liable for the purchase price if the buyer loses the goods to the holder of a better title than the seller had. Remember that this rule does not apply if the seller indicates clearly in some way that he does not warrant the title.[18]

Rule 125B. *When goods are sold by sample and description, they must conform to the description.* In a case in which the buyer submitted samples of roots, stating that they were a certain kind, it was held that there was a breach of warranty when the seller delivered roots like the sample but not of the kind named. The goods must conform to the description whether they are like the sample or not. This rule is in Section 14 of the Sales Act.

Rule 125C. *If the buyer makes known the use to which the goods will be put and relies on the seller to furnish suitable goods, there is a warranty of reasonable fitness of the goods for the purpose.* Some large clay pots were ordered for use in a glass factory, and the seller was relied upon to furnish pots suitable for the work. The pots broke down under high temperature, and it was held that the seller was liable for breach of the warranty of fitness.[19] At common law, this warranty applies only if the seller is a grower or manufacturer of the goods; under the Sales Act, it applies to all kinds of sellers.

Rule 125D. *If goods are sold by description through a dealer, there is a warranty that the goods are merchantable under that description.* This warranty will usually cover foodstuffs which are sold by jobbers or wholesalers to retailers if the goods are not marketable when delivery is made, or, in some cases, when title passes. This warranty is usually, in fact, binding upon sellers other than dealers.

Rule 125E. *If a buyer has examined the goods, there is no warranty as to defects which inspection should have revealed.* This rule is found in Section 15, Paragraph 3 of the Act. Stated in this way, it is not an exception to the rule of *caveat emptor*. It is an

---

[18] This warranty does not apply to sales of goods by a sheriff or other person selling under legal authority (Sales Act, Sec. 13, Par. 4). This is also the common law rule.

[19] This rule, with the next four, is found in Sec. 15 of the Sales Act. The remedies for breach of warranty are discussed under **Rule 136.**

exception only by inferring that the rule means: There is a warranty as to defects which an inspection should reveal, only if the buyer does not inspect. At common law, there is no such warranty if the buyer had a chance to inspect, whether he did or not.

Rule 125F. *If an article is sold under a trade name, there is no warranty of its fitness for any particular purpose.* This rule applies to the sales of such things as patent medicines and the like. It needs no further discussion except that one should note that if the sale falls under **Rule 125C** or **Rule 125D**, the latter will of course apply even though the goods are sold under a trade name.

Rule 125G. *An implied warranty may result from a custom of trade.* It was once a custom among tobacco dealers to warrant that tobacco should remain sound and marketable for four months after the date of the sale. This was several times held to apply to the sale of tobacco in districts where this custom was in effect even though the particular seller did not know of the custom. This is in the Sales Act, Section 15, Paragraph 5.

Rule 125H. *In a sale of food for human use, there is an implied warranty of fitness for human consumption.* This rule is not incorporated in the Sales Act, but it is in effect in every state where the issue has come to the attention of the courts. The warranty is not very important because it applies to the retail buyer only, and the amount involved in any such case is apt to be rather small. In addition to that, the principle of this rule probably is covered by **Rule 125C.**

Rule 125I. *An express warranty does not exclude implied warranties unless inconsistent with them.* Thus, an express warranty of quality would not automatically exclude an implied warranty of title.

Rule 125J. *A buyer is generally entitled to inspect goods before paying the price.* This rule applies to such transactions as purchases C.O.D. from department stores, but, curiously enough, it has not been applied to C.O.D. sales in which the goods are shipped by common carrier. In the latter cases, there is generally no right to inspect. This difference probably is due to the fact that there is no right to inspect goods bought C.O.D. in any case, to begin with, because the contract C.O.D. means delivery will not be made until after the price has been paid; but department stores have for so long permitted their customers to inspect goods bought C.O.D., that this has become a governing custom which applies unless the seller makes it quite clear that there will be no right of inspection. Of course, common carriers sometimes do allow consignees to inspect C.O.D. shipments, but in the absence of specific provisions in the contracts, they are not legally obligated to do so.

Remember, again, that in the absence of express warranty or one of the above implied warranties, the buyer takes the risk as to the quality of goods purchased.

REMEDIES FOR BREACH OF SALES CONTRACTS

When one or the other of the parties to a sales contract has broken the agreement, the questions arise: What can the injured party legally do about it? What sorts of aids or remedies does the law provide for such violations? The answers will differ in different cases, and sometimes the differences will depend upon whether it is the buyer or the seller who is seeking a remedy. The remedies discussed here are incorporated in Sections 52 to 70 of the Sales Act, but specific references do not seem necessary.

THE SELLER'S REMEDIES

The seller may sometimes have a choice of as many as six remedies if the contract is broken by the buyer. These remedies are indicated in connection with the following rules.

Rule 126. *The seller may retain the goods without liability under some conditions.* The seller of goods, if he is in possession of the goods, is said to have a *lien* (a right to retain the goods), provided: (a) there is no agreement to sell on credit, (b) the stipulated credit period has expired, or (c) the buyer has become insolvent.

a) In a C.O.D. sale, of course, the seller may retain the goods until the price is paid, but the same thing is true in any sale unless the terms of the contract mean that there is to be delivery before payment.

b) Jones bought some wood from King who was to deliver

the wood within ten days; Jones was to pay for the wood within five days. Of course, King could not be compelled to deliver the wood within ten days if the price were not paid within five days. The application of illustrations *a)* and *b)* is not very frequent; such cases could be solved by the general principles of contract law.

c) Bain sold a large quantity of oak logs to Clay. The logs were to be delivered within thirty days, and Clay was to pay for them within three months. Before the delivery had been made, and before the time for delivery had expired, Clay became insolvent and Bain refused to deliver the logs. Clay's creditors tried to compel Bain to deliver the logs to Clay, but it was held that Bain had a seller's lien since he had the logs still in his possession, and that Clay's insolvency entitled Bain to retain the logs.

Rule 127. *The seller may sell the goods elsewhere under a valid seller's lien.* This is so closely related to the lien itself that quotation of Section 60 of the Sales Act is all that is necessary:

(1) Where the goods are of a perishable nature, or where the seller expressly reserves the right of resale in case the buyer should make default, or where the buyer has been in default in the payment of the price an unreasonable time, an unpaid seller having a right of lien or having stopped the goods *in transitu* may resell the goods. He shall not thereafter be liable to the original buyer upon the contract to sell or the sale, or for any profit made by such resale, but may recover from the buyer damages for any loss occasioned by the breach of the contract or the sale.

(2) Where a resale is made as authorized in this section, the buyer acquires a good title as against the original buyer.

(3) It is not essential to the validity of a resale that notice of an intention to resell the goods be given by the seller to the original buyer. But where the right to resell is not based on the perishable nature of the goods or upon an express provision of the contract or the sale, the giving or failure to give such notice shall be relevant in any issue involving the question whether the buyer had been in default an unreasonable time before the resale was made.

(4) It is not essential to the validity of a resale that notice of the time and place of such resale should be given by the seller to the original buyer.

(5) The seller is bound to exercise reasonable care and judgment in making a resale, and subject to this requirement may make a resale either by public or private sale.

Rule 128. *The seller's lien is lost by voluntary surrender of the goods or by waiver of the lien.* If the seller delivers the goods to a common carrier, having consigned them unconditionally to the buyer (by a so-called *straight* bill of lading), or if the buyer lawfully obtains possession of the goods, the seller's lien is lost. This should be clear from careful study of the conditions under which the lien exists, as stated under **Rule 126.** After delivery of the goods, the seller has no lien. Transfer of possession is regarded as a waiver of the lien. An agreement to sell on credit operates as a similar waiver.

Rule 129. *The seller may assert a right of stoppage in transit.* This right of the seller to stop goods in transit is similar to a lien. The Sales Act provides:

. . . . When the buyer of goods is or becomes insolvent, the unpaid seller . . . may resume possession of the goods at any time while they are in transit, and he will then become entitled to the same rights in regard to the goods as he would have had if he had never parted with possession.

The seller has this right when all of the following conditions exist: The seller is unpaid; title has passed to the buyer; goods are still in transit; the buyer is insolvent; and the buyer has not resold the goods. The exercise of this right does not revest title in the seller; it merely gives him a lien for the price, but unless the buyer tenders or pays the price, the seller may sell the goods elsewhere, just as he may do under his lien. If the buyer's creditors have seized the goods, this seizure does not interfere with the seller's right to stop the goods; they are regarded as still in transit. The right of stoppage is exercised by demand upon the carrier for return of the goods to the seller.

Rule 130. *The seller may rescind the contract under some circumstances.* Whether or not title to the goods has passed to the buyer, if the buyer defers payment for an unreasonable time, the seller may rescind the contract if he has a lien or if he exercises the right of stoppage. This, again, is closely related to the lien and the right of resale. The right of rescission cannot be exercised if the goods have been sold by the buyer to an innocent purchaser, or if a negotiable document of title (such as an order bill of lading) has been transferred to an innocent purchaser.

Rule 131. *The seller may recover the price of the goods if title has passed.* Unless the contract specifies that the price must be paid by a stated time, or unless the goods cannot be readily sold at a reasonable price, the right to recover the price depends upon the passing of title. If the buyer refuses to take delivery, the seller cannot sue for the price, as a rule, unless one of the above conditions is met.

Rule 132. *The seller may recover damages for breach of the contract.* If title has not passed, the seller's only remedy is a suit for breach of the contract unless the contract provides otherwise. In many installment agreements, the contracts provide that upon default, the whole price shall become due and payable at once, if the seller desires. In the absence of such provisions, the seller may sue for damages for breach just as he may do for breach of any other contract.

Rule 132A. *Damages for breach of sales contracts are measured by the difference between the contract price and the market value of the goods.* Of course, if the goods were made to special order and were not salable elsewhere, this difference would leave the whole of the price as the measure of damages.

THE BUYER'S REMEDIES

The remedies available to the buyer also depend upon the circumstances under which the contract is broken by the seller. Sometimes the buyer may *replevin* the goods; sometimes he may recover the value of the goods in an action of *trover;* sometimes he may rescind the contract; sometimes he may recover damages for breach of contract or for breach of a warranty; and in some rare cases he may have a decree for specific performance.

Rule 133. *If title has passed, the buyer may replevin the goods.* If title has passed and the seller refuses to deliver the goods when the buyer is lawfully entitled to delivery,[20] the buyer is entitled to a judgment ordering delivery of the goods. Of course, this kind of order is of no use if the seller no longer has the goods

---

[20] It must be kept in mind that the buyer is not always entitled to possession merely because title has passed. His right to possession depends upon the terms and interpretation of the contract and upon his performance of all of the necessary conditions.

in his possession, and for that reason the action of replevin is seldom used except in connection with a *writ of attachment,* which is a court order tying up the goods in the control of a court until the case is in some way settled.[21]

Rule 134. *If the buyer is entitled to possession, he may recover damages from the seller in an action of trover when the goods are unlawfully withheld.* The action of trover is used for the recovery of damages for the type of wrongful act known as *conversion* of goods. There are several kinds of acts which constitute conversion, but so far as the law of sales is concerned, one kind is of chief interest. If the seller unlawfully refuses to deliver goods to the buyer under a contract, such refusal constitutes conversion, and the buyer will be entitled to recover as damages the fair value of the goods. It is important to note, however, that this remedy can very seldom be used unless the buyer has paid the price; if he has not paid the price, he usually relies upon his remedy for breach of contract or an action of replevin. If the action of trover is used and it succeeds, the buyer is entitled to recover the fair value of the goods as of the time when the act of conversion took place.

Rule 135. *The buyer may recover damages for breach of the contract.* Since the sales transaction is primarily a contract, the remedy for breach may be an ordinary action for breach of contract. If the title has not passed (or even if it has passed), if the price has not been paid and if the seller unlawfully refuses to deliver the goods, the buyer is entitled to recover the difference between the contract price of the goods and the fair market value of the goods as of the time of the breach of the contract.

Rule 136. *The buyer may recover damages for breach of warranty.* Since a warranty and its obligation are contractual in nature, the action for breach is similar to any other action for breach of contract. The law regarding warranties and remedies for their breach is set out so clearly in the Sales Act that no more than quotation seems necessary. Section 69 provides:

---

[21] Whether the buyer can replevin the goods from a second buyer who purchased them from the seller is a very difficult question and should always be submitted to an attorney familiar with local law.

(1) Where there is a breach of warranty by the seller, the buyer may, at his election (a) accept or keep the goods and set up against the seller the breach of warranty by way of recoupment in diminution or extinction of the price; (b) accept or keep the goods and maintain an action against the seller for damages for the breach of warranty; (c) refuse to accept the goods, if the property therein has not passed, and maintain an action against the seller for damages for the breach of warranty; (d) rescind the contract to sell or the sale and refuse to receive the goods, or if the goods have already been received, return them or offer to return them to the seller and recover the price or any part thereof which has been paid.

(2) When the buyer has claimed and been granted a remedy in any one of these ways, no other remedy can thereafter be granted.

(3) Where the goods have been delivered to the buyer, he cannot rescind the sale if he knew of the breach of warranty when he accepted the goods, or if he fails to notify the seller within a reasonable time of the election to rescind, or if he fails to return or to offer to return the goods to the seller in substantially as good condition as they were in at the time the property was transferred to the buyer. But if deterioration or injury of the goods is due to the breach of warranty, such deterioration or injury shall not prevent the buyer from returning or offering to return the goods to the seller and rescinding the sale.

(4) Where the buyer is entitled to rescind the sale and elects to do so, the buyer shall cease to be liable for the price upon returning or offering to return the goods. If the price or any part thereof has already been paid, the seller shall be liable to repay so much thereof as has been paid, concurrently with the return of the goods, or immediately after an offer to return the goods in exchange for repayment of the price.

(5) Where the buyer is entitled to rescind the sale and elects to do so, if the seller refuses to accept an offer of the buyer to return the goods, the buyer shall thereafter be deemed to hold the goods as bailee for the seller, but subject to a lien to secure the repayment of any portion of the price which has been paid, and with the remedies for the enforcement of such lien allowed to an unpaid seller by Section 53.

(6) The measure of damages for breach of warranty is the loss directly and naturally resulting, in the ordinary course of events, from the breach of warranty.

(7) In the case of breach of warranty of quality, such loss, in the absence of special circumstances showing proximate damage of a greater amount, is the difference between the value of the goods at

the time of delivery to the buyer and the value they would have had if they had answered to the warranty.

In several states where the Sales Act is not in force, the buyer who has accepted goods cannot thereafter rescind the contract for breach of warranty. In the absence of fraud or special agreement, he must either sue for breach of warranty or wait until sued by the seller for the price and then show the breach of warranty as a reduction of his own liability for the price.

Rule 137. *The buyer may usually rescind the contract for breach.* If the seller breaks the contract, or if he states in advance that he will break the contract, the buyer usually is entitled to regard the contract as no longer in effect, and, if he has paid the price, he is entitled to recover it. The treatment of a contract as being no longer in effect is called rescission. In a few cases, courts have held that a buyer may not rescind if title to the goods has passed to him. In such cases, the buyer must rely upon some other remedy, but in most states (and under the Sales Act) the buyer's right to rescind does not depend upon the failure of title to pass. His right to rescind depends upon the seller's failure to perform.

Rule 138. *In rare cases, a buyer is entitled to specific performance.* As a general rule, courts will not order sellers of goods (or buyers, for that matter) to perform their contracts. The other remedies are usually regarded as adequate protection of the rights of the injured parties. But when contracts call for the delivery of certain rare or unique chattels, money damages are not regarded as adequate relief, and specific performance may be ordered. Some illustrations of these kinds of chattels are: patent rights, works of art, copyrights, trade-marks, valuable documents, and property of sentimental or unique value. Of course, if title has passed, the buyer may usually replevin the goods, as has been indicated earlier, but this is not regarded as specific performance although it does, by accident in some cases, have the same effect.

The student of commercial law must always bear in mind that the problems encountered in the law of sales offer extreme difficulties. Some of the difficulties arise from complications of law, but most of the trouble lies in the fact that differences in legal significance arise from minute factual differences. What is the meaning of language used in certain contracts; what is a fair market value; is a certain chattel unique; what was the intent of the parties as to title; were the goods appropriated to the contract; in what class does a given contract fall for the purpose of determining the passing of title; is a given contract within the Statute of Frauds; if so, was the Statute of Frauds complied with; did the buyer express approval of the goods? These kinds of questions render the law of sales very difficult, and it can be mastered only after a lifetime of study. This book does not attempt to state the whole of this branch of the law; it is enough to state some general rules, and to point out the nature of some of the difficulties. Expert advice should be consulted upon all but the very simplest problems.

CONDITIONAL SALES AND SALES IN BULK

A conditional sale is a contract for the sale of goods, under which possession is taken by the buyer and title is retained by the seller, usually until the payment of the last installment of the price. The commonest kind of conditional sale, of course, is the installment purchase contract.[22] In connection with conditional sales, some difficult problems arise from the general common law rule that a seller who reserves title to secure payment has no rights against an innocent purchaser of the goods from the first buyer. Purchasers usually are innocent in such cases since there is seldom any way in which they can learn that goods offered by sale to them have been bought under installment agreements, nor can such purchasers learn that the title is not in the person offering the goods for sale. The result of all this is that the reservation of title by an installment seller does not protect him as to the purchase price if the second sale is made to an innocent purchaser.[23]

To remedy this defect in the installment seller's position, conditional sales statutes have been passed in about a dozen states.

---

[22] Some installment sales contracts undertake to secure payment not by reservation of the title, but by the execution of a mortgage on possession of the buyer held by the seller.

[23] Note, too, that this rule is not in accord with the general common law rule that a seller cannot pass any better title than he himself has. **Rules 87 and 119.**

These acts vary in their details. In general, however, they provide that if the original installment contract is registered within a certain time from the date of the contract, all subsequent purchasers are put upon notice of the reservation of title. Thus, if the statute is complied with, there can be no innocent purchaser in the legal sense.[24] As a rule, the conditional sales statutes do not apply to goods sold for resale, and most of them do not apply to such goods as railway equipment, engine-room fixtures, bathroom equipment and other more or less permanent installations.

The term *sales in bulk* refers to the sale of a whole stock of goods by a business establishment. There is no reason why such sales should not be made, but certain precautions are necessary to safeguard the interests of all parties who may be affected by such sales. In the past, many business men, involved in financial difficulties, have sold their stocks of goods *in bulk* and eloped with the proceeds. Under the common law, an innocent purchaser of goods in bulk received a good title, and the creditors of the seller had no rights at all to the goods nor claims against the innocent purchaser under the *bulk* agreement. Thus, it was easy for insolvent men to defraud their creditors by simply selling out and taking the proceeds away with them, To remedy this, every state has adopted some kind of bulk sales act. These statutes provide that the sale of a stock of goods in bulk, without notice to that seller's creditors, will be invalid so far as such creditors are concerned. The creditors, in giving credit to a going concern, rely in a large part upon the stock of goods as a possible source of their payment; and under the bulk sales acts, they are protected in this reliance even though the stock is sold to an innocent purchaser. The stock can still be used to satisfy claims of the seller's creditors if those creditors have not been notified of the sale before it takes place. Thus, the purchaser of a stock of goods, from a retailer for example, runs the risk that he may have to pay for all of the seller's business debts unless the bulk sales law has been complied with. Such buyers should always consult competent legal counsel and should require a complete check of all of the creditors of the business.

---

[24] Under some statutes chattel mortgages are treated in a similar way.

QUESTIONS AND PROBLEMS

1. Look at the table on page 92. Write down on paper the amount named in the Statute of Frauds, the rate of interest collectible when a contract does not name any rate, and the highest contract rate which will be enforced, in your state.

2. Does Section 4 of the Statute of Frauds require that contracts for the sale of goods be in writing in order to be enforcible? **Rule 104A.**

3. Which of the parties must sign the memorandum when it is required by the Statute of Frauds? **Rule 105.**

4. Holt engaged a dentist to make a set of false teeth. The denture was completed, and a final fitting was satisfactory, but, as Holt's gums were somewhat sore, he left the denture with the dentist, intending to call for it the next day. During the night Holt died of a heart stroke, and his administrator refused to pay for the teeth. There was no memorandum, and no money had been paid although the price had been agreed upon. Was the dentist entitled to the contract price for the teeth under the rule of the carriage case? **Rule 106.**

5. As the Statute of Frauds is interpreted, does the law require that the memorandum (when required by law) must be made at the same time the agreement is made, or may the memorandum be made later? **Rule 107.**

6. When does the title pass to the buyer when goods are shipped C.O.D. by common carrier (express, for example)? **Rule 112.**

7. Who was the owner of the title to the carriage in the case discussed under **Rule 106**? Why?

8. What are fungible goods? Write down two illustrations. At what moment does title pass when there is a contract for the sale of a stated quantity to be taken from a designated mass of such goods if the parties to the contract do not state when they wish the title to pass? **Rule 115.**

9. Hill bought a piano on the installment plan. The title was reserved by the seller until the payment of the final installment. If the piano should be stolen or destroyed by fire, without the fault of Hill, would he be held liable for the price in spite of the fact that he does not own the instrument? **Rules 114** and **121.**

10. Explain why it is dangerous, in the legal sense, for a buyer of goods to leave the goods in possession of the seller. **Rule 122.**

11. Give two good reasons why a buyer should not rely too heavily upon a seller's guaranty of the quality of the goods. **Rule 123.**

12. What is the meaning of the expression *caveat emptor*? What is its practical importance to buyers and sellers of goods? **Rule 125.**

13. Jensen bought two plows and a harrow at a sheriff's sale of Brown's goods. After the sale, the goods were claimed by Henderson, who was able to prove that he had loaned them to Brown. The sheriff had no right to convey title to the goods since he was authorized to sell the goods of Brown only. Jensen therefore did not get good title and must surrender the goods to Henderson. How is it that the sheriff, as a seller of goods, is not required to give a warranty of title as indicated under **Rule 125A,** in the text?

14. Does a buyer of goods shipped C.O.D. by common carrier have a legal right to inspect the goods before paying the price and the charges if the contract does not specifically so state? **Rule 125J.**

15. Under **Rule 126,** which of the three illustrations is related to the matter of implied conditions in the law of contracts? We give no reference here because it is believed that the student can easily find the answer.

16. What is the seller's right of stoppage in transit? Under what types of transactions does it arise? What particular circumstances are necessary conditions to such a right? **Rule 129.**

17. Welsh had agreed to buy and Gates had agreed to sell to him six carloads of wheat (about 7500 bushels) at $1.10 per bushel. Welsh refused to take delivery of or to pay for the wheat, which was shipped on an order bill of lading to the order of the seller. The price of wheat at the time of the refusal to take delivery was $1.00 per bushel. What is Gates's remedy? Study **Rule 132** very carefully. You might turn to the discussion of the Measure of Damages, in Chapter XII. You will find some help there.

18. How does the general common law rule about one's ability to pass no better title than he has conflict with the first paragraph of the discussion of Conditional Sales on page 113.

19. How is the seller of goods under conditional sales contracts protected against the risks of resale by the customer before the price has been fully paid? Is this protection afforded sellers in all states? Page 114.

20. To what does the bulk sales law refer? To what kind of sales agreements? Explain why there is a need for such laws. Are laws relative to bulk sales statutory or common law rules? Page 114.

Kansas State Capitol, Topeka
Underwood-Stratton

Kentucky State Capitol, Frankfort
Underwood-Stratton

Louisiana State Capitol, Baton Rouge
Underwood & Underwood

California State Capitol, Sacramento
Sacramento Chamber of Commerce

CHAPTER V

THE LAW OF AGENT AND PRINCIPAL

The fundamental principle of the relationship called *agency* is that an employee is authorized, either expressly or by implication, to make contracts in the name of the employer. Such an employee is called an *agent,* and an employer who is bound by a contract made under such authorization is called a *principal.* It must be kept in mind that the agent in such cases is not a party to the contract, and also, that no agent can ever bind his principal unless the principal has performed some act which either authorizes the contract or can be used as a legal basis of implied authority. The first group of rules with which it is necessary to become familiar consists of rules of law concerning the creation of the agency relationship.

THE CREATION OF AGENCY

Rule 139. *The relationship must always be based upon some act of the principal.* Acts of a principal upon which his liability may be based may consist of direct authorization, subsequent ratification of an unauthorized transaction, or some act from which it is fair and reasonable to assume that authority has been granted to the agent, even though in fact no such authority was given; but always, before a principal can be held liable, it must be possible to trace the liability back to some voluntary act of the principal. Several illustrations covering different types of situations follow.

Rule 140. *Most agents are authorized by contracts of employment.* Contracts under which agents are employed are governed by the same rules which apply to other contracts. If such an agreement stipulates that the employment is to run for more than a year, it will be a contract only if the Statute of Frauds is complied with.[1] Clerks in stores, commission salesmen, and other types of commercial employees are authorized as agents under their contracts of employment.

Rule 141. *Many agents act gratuitously.* Many agents are authorized without any contract between agent and principal. If Smith asks his wife to take the family car to a mechanic for repairs, there is no contract between Smith and his wife; but the wife is authorized to enter into a contract with the mechanic, and that contract will obligate Smith to pay for the repairs just as though he had ordered the work personally. The wife is an agent, but she is a gratuitous agent. This does not depend upon the fact that she is the wife of the principal; the same rule would apply if you should ask your neighbor to buy a saw and charge it to your account at a hardware store. Gratuitous agencies are not very common in business, but they may be created.

Rule 142. *An agent may be authorized by estoppel.* Agency by estoppel is fairly common in business transactions. The authority in such cases is based upon an implication from the principal's conduct. In a well known case of this kind, Nixon employed Martin to buy a horse, giving Martin the purchase money. Martin bought a horse, paid the money for it, and took a bill of sale for the horse in his own name. When he bought the horse, he was acting as agent under contract, and the horse belonged to the principal, no matter what the bill of sale said. Martin took the horse and the bill of sale to Nixon and offered to deliver them. Nixon was not quite ready of take care of the horse, and he asked Martin to keep both the horse and the bill of sale for a few days. Martin agreed to do so, but he was no

---

[1] The liability of the principal under contracts authorized does not depend upon the enforcibility of the agreement between agent and principal. The person who deals with the principal through the agent is not affected by the validity or the invalidity of the agreement between agent and principal. Of course, the contract between the principal and third party must conform to all of the rules of the law of contracts, just as though such contract had been made by the principal in person.

longer an agent and he had no authority to sell the horse. For some reason, Martin at this point turned dishonest. He showed the bill of sale to one Brown, as an evidence of his ownership. Martin induced Brown to buy the horse for cash, and he then absconded with the money. When Nixon learned of this, he demanded his horse from Brown. Of course, the horse, as already stated, belonged to Nixon, and Martin had not been authorized by Nixon to sell the horse; but it was held, when Nixon sued Brown for the value of the horse, that Nixon was *estopped* to deny that he had authorized Martin to sell the horse. Nixon's conduct in allowing Martin to keep both horse and bill of sale had been the basis upon which Brown had been misled into supposing that Martin had authority to sell the horse. Since Nixon's conduct had misled Brown, it did not seem reasonable to permit Nixon, after Brown had acted upon the appearance thus created by Nixon, to deny that the implication raised by his own conduct was a true representation of the facts. This principle is involved in the legal doctrine of estoppel which applies not alone to agency, but to other legal situations as well. Whenever one person, by words or conduct, induces another to act in reliance upon a representation of fact, the first party will not be permitted in court to deny that the representation of fact was true: he is estopped to deny the truth of his first assertion if someone has acted in reliance upon it.

The principle of estoppel applies to another type of situation which is not uncommon. Suppose that the Littwell Publishing Company employed Clay as a subscription and delivery agent and furnished him with a written authorization card or letter. He collected subscriptions for a number of years and made proper accounting to the company. After several years, Clay left the employ of the Littwell Company, but he did not give up his authorization, and his former customers were not notified that his employment had been terminated. He called on several of the customers and took their renewal subscriptions, but he pocketed the money. When the subscribers complained that they did not receive their periodicals, the company, under these circumstances, was liable upon the subscriptions. It had not authorized the renewals, it is true, but its conduct in the past had carried over the representation of authority to the time after the termination of Clay's employment. Probably the only safe way in which an employer can escape the risk of such liability is to put a time limit on all letters of authorization of agents and to send a note to every subscriber served by a particular agent when that agent's authority comes to an end. Otherwise, there is always some possibility that there will be a liability by estoppel.

Rule 143. *An unauthorized act of an agent may bind the principal upon ratification.* When one person makes a contract in the name of another, the other may afterward ratify the contract so as to make it binding, just as though he had authorized it in the first place. The following illustration will indicate how and when ratification may become necessary or desirable.

Waite was a collector of paintings. He had been desirous for a long time of getting a certain painting which was held by Carey, another collector. Waite had not authorized anyone to buy the picture for him, but Gifford, a broker in such materials, knew of Waite's desire. Unknown to Waite, Carey offered this particular picture for sale at an auction. Gifford attended the auction, and, not having time to communicate with Waite, he bid upon the picture in Waite's name. The picture was "knocked down" to Waite who still knew nothing of it. The seller, of course, could not hold Waite liable for the price of the picture upon these facts. Waite had not made any contract; he had not authorized anyone to make a contract for him; and he had not indulged in any conduct which could be made the basis of an estoppel. However, as soon as the sale was concluded, Gifford notified Waite of what had been done, and Waite expressed his approval of it. This expression of approval constituted a *ratification* of the act of Gifford and made Waite a party to the contract. He could now be held liable to Carey for the price which Gifford had agreed to pay for the picture.

Rule 143A. *Unauthorized acts may be ratified only under certain conditions.* In the first place, one may ratify a previous unauthorized act of another only if the act is one which the principal could lawfully have performed himself at the time when it was performed. Suppose, for example, that when Gifford acted, Waite had been an infant and therefore incapable of acting as a principal. Under such circumstances his assent to the transaction, even if expressed after his majority, would not be binding. One cannot ratify an act which he was incapable of performing when it was performed.

In the second place, one may ratify only those acts which may lawfully be delegated to agents. This will be discussed further in another place; for the present it is sufficient to give an illustration: If the act performed by Gifford had been to vote at a political election in the name of Waite, such an act could not be ratified because it may not be performed by an agent.

In the third place, only those acts may be ratified which have been performed by the agent under pretense of acting for the principal. Thus, if Gifford had not pretended to be acting for Waite, the latter could not have ratified the purchase. Under such circumstances, Carey, upon learning that Gifford was not acting for Waite, could lawfully refuse to sell to Waite. This rule is one of the reasons one cannot ratify a forgery in most states. The forger does not pretend to be acting for the person whose name he uses. He pretends that such person has acted for himself.

In the fourth place, a ratification is binding upon the principal only if his ratifying act is performed with full knowledge of all the material facts. He need not know the legal effects of ratification, but he must know the material details of the transaction. For example, Gray was in possession of Fisk's horse. Gray sold the horse to Granger without Fisk's knowledge and accepted a check. Gray turned the check over to Fisk who thought that it came from Granger as a part payment of an old debt which the latter owed to Fisk. Fisk's cashing of the check was not a ratification of the sale of the horse for he did not have knowledge of the facts of the transaction.

In the fifth place, ratification of a part of a transaction with knowledge of the whole is usually held to be a ratification of the whole. The principal must take the burdens of the transaction along with the benefits. A book agent, without authority to do so, made an agreement with a justice of the peace to the effect that the agent's employer would accept for the purchase price of the book all of the fees of the justice during a certain week. The justice agreed. The price of the book was twenty dollars. The company upon receipt of the order sent the book. The fees for the week were only three dollars. The company sued for twenty dollars, but it was held that since they had ratified a part of the sale by sending the book, they had ratified the whole transaction and could recover only the amount of the fees. Knowledge of the facts is imputed to the principal by estoppel. See **Rules 142** and **160.**

In the sixth place, ratification need not be in any particular form unless the contract itself is one which requires authorization of the agent in some specified form. Thus, if the Statute of Frauds in a particular state requires that an agent to sell land must be authorized in writing, then, in that state, a ratification of an unauthorized contract must be made in writing. But many ratifications are made informally; in fact, many of them are made by implication. Johns was the owner of a horse. His son Fred traded the horse to a neighbor without Johns's consent. Johns saw the horse used by the neighbor, and he himself used the horse which had been received from the neighbor. When he at a later time sued for the return of the original horse, it was held that it was fair to imply from his conduct in keeping the horse for a while and not protesting within a reasonable time, that, if he did so with knowledge of the facts, he had ratified the trade. It was found that he had acted with full knowledge, and the trade was held to be binding upon him.

The legal effect of a ratification of an unauthorized contract is just the same as if the contract had been authorized in the first place. The agent is absolved from responsibility;

the principal becomes liable for compensation in accordance with general rules which are discussed later; and the contract is treated as though it had been made by the principal in person at the time when the unauthorized agent made it. Thus, a ratification, once made, becomes irrevocable just as any other contract. But if a principal whom an unauthorized person pretends to represent refuses to ratify what has been done, the agent may be held liable by the third person for breach of his warranty of authority. Every agent is held to impliedly warrant that he has authority from his principal to enter into contracts which the agent tries to make; if this is not true, whether he acts in good faith or not, he is liable. See **Rule 158.**

Rule 144. *Sometimes agency is said to exist by necessity.* At common law, if a husband fails to properly support his wife, the wife is legally authorized to pledge the husband's credit for necessaries for the use of the family. This is true at common law even though the husband has forbidden the wife to pledge his credit, and even though he has forbidden third persons to furnish necessaries to his wife upon his credit. This rule has been modified in many states by statutes which provide means by which the husband may escape this common law liability. This is not directly related to the law of agency, and it is a matter of local law which involves too many details for a general book. Another kind of agency by necessity is found in relation to the master of a ship. Under common law rules, the master of a ship is by implication authorized to pledge the credit of the ship's owner for necessary supplies and labor in certain emergencies. This is also sometimes called an agency by operation of law.

Rule 145. *Written authorization is not usually required.* As one might infer from the law of ratification and from the law of estoppel, written authority is not necessary, in most cases, to enable an agent to bind his principal to a contract. There are two important exceptions to this general rule.

Rule 146. *An agent's authority must be under seal if he is to execute an instrument under seal.* Of course, very few instruments are now required by law to be under seal, and a very small part of such instruments is executed by agents. The agent who sells property usually does no more than complete the negotiations; the signatures to important documents are nearly always affixed by the parties in person. Of course, when the contract or other transaction is made by a corporation, an agent must be employed; but his authority will usually be conferred by a vote which is recorded in the minutes of the corporation meetings, or it will be shown by a written instrument of some kind. There are few cases in which an agent's authority must be under seal, and when such cases arise, the instrument creating authority must, of necessity, be in writing.

Rule 147. *In some cases the Statute of Frauds requires written authority.* In many states the Statute of Frauds requires that when an agent is authorized to sell real estate, any contract which he makes for this purpose in the name of his principal will not bind the principal (or the third party) unless the agent's authority is in writing. This is not very important because, in the great majority of cases, the real estate agent is not an agent at all. He does not make a contract between buyer and seller. He merely conducts the negotiations, draws up the papers, and performs other similar services, and the documents are actually signed by the parties themselves, in most cases, or by their agents appointed for the purpose of signing. Thus, the agreement between a seller and a real estate agent need not be in writing unless the real estate agent is actually to make the contract in the seller's name. Aside from the exceptions indicated here, contracts of agency and authorization of agents may be conferred in any way, either formally or informally and either expressly or by implication.

Rule 148. *Every principal must be competent to act legally.* An infant cannot be a principal, and agreements made on behalf of any infants are wholly void in most states. This means that if an infant authorizes the making of an agreement in his name, he cannot ratify such an agreement even after he reaches his majority. This rule has been modified somewhat in a few states, but this is the only safe rule to follow: Do not deal with infants, either with them personally or through others appointed by them.

Similarly, a person who has been adjudged insane cannot make a valid agreement through an agent, and he cannot ratify such an agreement after he is adjudged legally sane.

Rule 149. *No one can be held liable as a principal without his assent expressly, impliedly, or by ratification.* Under this rule, a member of a club or an association (not incorporated) cannot be held liable for debts of the association unless it can be shown that such member has given his assent to the particular contract, or unless he has given his assent in advance by complying with the bylaws of the club. That is, the member cannot be held liable as principal for acts done by the association unless he has in some way, directly or indirectly, authorized the action. A member will be held liable, usually, for debts incurred for the purposes for which the club was founded, and practically always a member of an association can be held liable upon debts incurred as a result of a vote of the association if he voted on the side which authorized the debt. In many cases, even members who vote against such measures can be held liable on the ground that under the bylaws they are bound by majority rule; but members who do not favor such debts can escape liability, in most instances, by notifying the prospective creditor that such members do not agree to the debt. Of course, if this is a violation of the duties of the member, he may be expelled from the club, but he can in this way escape liability.

Rule 150. *An agent need not possess contractual capacity.* If the principal is satisfied with the ability of his agent, no more is necessary. A person may send his four-year-old son to the grocery store for food, and the person will be as liable as if he himself had gone. Many agents are under age: bank tellers, clerks in stores, collectors, and the like, are common illustrations.

Rule 151. *Some kinds of acts cannot be performed by agents.* No court will recognize an agency when one person is appointed by another to do something unlawful, immoral or contrary to public policy (in the legal sense). The power to make a will cannot be delegated to an agent; a duty to paint a picture, to appear upon a stage as an actor, or to perform a marriage ceremony cannot be delegated to an agent; nor can

one vote in a public election through an agent. Also, one who
has been authorized to act as an agent cannot delegate this
power to a third person (a subagent) unless such delegation
has been expressly sanctioned by the first principal, or unless
such delegation is customary in the business which the agent
has been selected to transact.

One common instance in which power to delegate authority
is implied is the fire insurance business. Insurance companies
customarily appoint district or local branch agents who, often
without consulting the company, select *subagents* in the persons
of banks or real estate firms; these subagents then, again without
consulting the insurance company, frequently instruct employees
of the banks or real estate firms to make contacts with customers.
These contacts are made in the name of and on behalf of the
insurance companies, and the resulting contracts are valid against
the insurance companies. This is for the reason that, while they
do not know the individual clerk in many cases, they do know
that this is the manner in which the business is carried on;
and since they have this knowledge, they are assumed to have
given their consent by implication. In paying insurance premiums,
however, it is wise to make checks payable to the insurance
company rather than to the agent. Cashing of the check by the
company will serve as evidence of ratification. Again, agents are
impliedly authorized to delegate authority to perform what are
known as *ministerial* duties. Ministerial duties are services which
are routine or mechanical, such as the service rendered by a
repairman in a garage. The contract is made by the owner of
the garage, but the work is done by the mechanic. The garage
is bound by the results, just as though the garage-owner had
done the work in person.

In this connection some kinds of *farming out* of work are
sometimes referred to as *delegation* while they really are not. If
Grimm hires a general contractor to erect a building, the contractor hires subcontractors to lay the bricks, install the plumbing
and lighting fixtures, and the like. This is sometimes called
delegation, just as it is sometimes called assignment; but it is not
delegation. The subcontractor does not have authority to bind

the owner of the house, and he is therefore not an agent at all.

Rule 152. *The burden of proving an agency is upon the party who asserts it.* Reeves authorized Jones to make a contract for the sale of Reeves's city lot. Jones made an agreement in Reeves's name to sell the lot to Kimball. Now, if Reeves refuses to sell to Kimball, and if Kimball should bring suit, Kimball must show that Jones was legally authorized to make the contract. In this particular case, the Statute of Frauds requires, in most states, that an agent be authorized in writing to make a binding contract regarding the sale of land. Similarly, if Kimball had cancelled the deal and Reeves had brought suit, then it would devolve upon Reeves to show that he had properly authorized Jones; or, if Jones had to sue for his commission, he would then have to show the proper grant of his authority before he could recover. In the latter case, Jones would not need to show compliance with the Statute, however, since he would be relying upon the promise to pay his commission, and that promise is not required to be in writing. In all cases, the task of convincing the court that the authority of an agent was properly granted rests upon the party who asserts and relies upon the agency.

Rule 153. *Certain duties are imposed upon agents by law, even when they are not mentioned in the contract or authorization.* Even a gratuitous agent, while he is under no contractual duty to act at all for the principal, is under certain duties which apply to all agents, if they act. These duties are usually classified under four heads.

Rule 153A. *An agent must exercise ordinary care on behalf of his principal.* Ordinary care means the degree of care which a man of ordinary prudence and skill would exercise under the circumstances. A bookkeeper was under a duty to check the books of his subordinates. Due to his failure to exercise due care, one of the men embezzled a sum of money, and the bookkeeper was held liable for the loss. In this connection, an agent is also obligated to use the degree of skill which he professed to have when he took the job. A collecting agent, for example, is under a duty to exercise due care and skill to prevent the escape of debtors from whom it is his duty to collect. The question, whether an agent has exercised the required degree of care and skill, is often very difficult, and one should be careful not to jump at conclusions in such matters.

Rule 153B. *An agent must obey instructions.* If an agent disobeys instructions, and if the principal is thereby caused to suffer loss, the agent may be held liable. Hill left a horse with Buck with authority to sell it, but with instruction not to take less than $300 for it. Buck sold the horse to Smith for $250. In a suit for the other fifty dollars it was held that the agent was liable. Of course, this rule does not require the agent to commit unlawful acts. There are some hard problems in this field, too, in which the advice of an attorney is necessary.

Rule 153C. *An agent must be loyal to his principal.* This means that, if it becomes necessary, an agent must place his principal's interest before that of his own. Certain things are distinctly forbidden by this obligation. An agent may not lawfully represent two principals on opposite sides of the same transaction unless he has the consent of both. If he does so, he will not only lose his right to a commission from either, but he may also be held liable for damages to either or both if loss results from his disloyalty. An agent may not make any personal profit for himself at the expense of his principal. A purchasing agent who accepted a bribe from a person selling goods to the principal not only had no remedy against his discharge by the principal, but also was held liable for damages in the amount of the bribe he received. In this connection, it is the agent's duty to inform his principal at once of any facts which the agent knows and which might affect the principal's interest, such as the probable insolvency of a debtor.

Rule 153D. *An agent must account accurately to his principal.* This duty is closely related to the duty of loyalty. The agent must account to the principal for all money or other assets which come into his control as a result of the agency. There are three things which this includes. An agent should keep his principal's money in a separate account—not with his own. If he is agent for more than one principal, he should keep a separate account for each one. If an agent deposits his principal's money in the agent's own account, and the bank fails, he will be liable to the principal for the loss; but if he puts the principal's money in a separate account, he will not be liable for its loss unless he has failed to exercise due care in choosing the bank of deposit. An agent must also keep accurate accounts of his principal's affairs and render frequent accounting. Finally, an agent must promptly pay all moneys due, and in some instances he may be held liable for interest upon such sums after they have become due and payable. This is especially likely to be true if the principal has demanded payment and it has been refused.

Rule 154. *The principal is obligated to remunerate his agent unless the agency is a gratuitous one.* When one employs an agent, even though there is no definite statement about the rate of pay, the agent is entitled by law to collect *reasonable* pay for his service. Of course, if the agency is clearly gratuitous, such as those discussed under **Rule 141,** there is no implied obligation to pay for the service. It should be noted, too, that the amount of pay to which the agent is entitled (in the absence of a specific agreement) depends entirely upon what is reasonable compensation. When such a case comes to suit, the courts will very seldom ask the principal's opinion as to what is reasonable. The agent makes his demand, and the court merely determines whether the demand is reasonable, and, if not, what is reasonable. It is sometimes a little hard to determine whether or not an agency is gratuitous, but a fairly safe guide is the following: If the agent performs the service as a business service, the agency is not gratuitous, and he is entitled to compensation.

Rule 155. *The principal must reimburse his agent for certain losses.* This rule does not mean that every agent is entitled to recover all of his expenses. Of course, a principal is not obligated to repay traveling expenses unless he has specifically agreed to do so, and he is not obligated to reimburse the agent for losses incurred through the agent's carelessness or unlawful conduct; but, when the agent is assured by the principal that certain goods belong to the principal, and when the agent is compelled to pay damages to the real owner (not the principal) because the agent unlawfully disposed of the goods without the real owner's consent, the principal is required to reimburse the agent for this loss. This subject is a rather technical one, and some aspects of it are difficult.

Rule 156. *An agent may be held liable for his own torts.* The word *tort* is a name given to certain unlawful acts such as negligence, assault, wrongful use of another's property, trespass, and the like. If a streetcar motorman negligently operates his car and in so doing injures a pedestrian, this is a tort. But the fact that the motorman is in the employ of the utility company does not relieve the motorman of his individual responsibility for his wrongful act. To be sure, injured persons do not usually sue the servant or agent of a corporation, but such agents or servants are nonetheless liable for their wrongful acts. They are not excused by the fact of employment.[2]

Rule 157. *An agent usually is not liable upon contracts made in the name of the principal.* When a contract is made by agent, it becomes one between the principal and the third person. The agent is not a party to it, and he has no liability under it. The resulting contract is precisely the same, in effect, as though the principal had made the agreement in person. But in order that this result be accomplished, the agent should make sure that the agreement is clearly in the name of the principal. The written memorandum should be signed in the principal's name with the agent's name below, thus: Jacob Marsh, principal, by Henry Adams, agent. Then there can be no mistake about it. If the agent signs the contract in his own name, the third person may hold the agent because of the signature, or, if he likes, he may hold the principal liable upon the contract because the latter authorized the agreement.

Rule 158. *An agent may become liable upon his warranty of authority.* Johnson understood that Williams had authorized him to buy a certain machine for Williams on credit. Johnson negotiated the purchase and signed Williams' name to the contract. Later, it became clear that Williams had not authorized the trans-

---

[2] The extent of liability of the employer is discussed in a later part of this chapter. (**Rule 159.**)

action, and since the seller could not hold Williams liable, he turned
to Johnson to make good the loss. In such a case, the agent is said
to warrant (guarantee) his authority. The fact that he was mistaken is not a good defense. One should make sure that he knows
his position before he attempts to act as an agent for any principal;
if he happens to be mistaken, he may find himself liable for breach
of his warranty of authority.

Rule 159. *The principal is liable for torts committed by the
agent within the scope of his employment.* Every employer of a
servant or agent assumes the risks of the misconduct of his employees in their relations to the public, so far as the misconduct
is directly related to the employment. This is the basic principle
which underlies the liability of a railroad, for example, for the
negligence of an engineer, the liability of an apartment house
owner for the negligence of his janitor in throwing snow from
the roof, and the liability of a bank for an assault upon a customer by an employee. But it must be kept clearly in mind that
this liability exists only when the servant's or agent's unlawful
act is done within his employment.

Rule 160. *The principal is liable upon all contracts made
in his name within the apparent scope of the agent's authority.*
This rule should be committed to memory. It is based upon
two principles: There must be an actual authority, or some act
of the principal which raises the appearance of authority; and,
in some cases, the actual authority may be either greater or less
than the *apparent* authority. Of course, the principal is liable
upon all contracts which he has actually authorized whether the
scope of the agent's authority is apparent or not to the third
person. In this field are the so-called *undisclosed principal* cases.
Suppose that Wade employed King, a broker, to buy five hundred
shares of a certain stock for him. Suppose that King, for his
own purposes and without instructions, bought the five hundred
shares from Gates upon credit in his own name. Now, of course,
there is nominally no contract at all between Wade, the buyer,
and Gates, the seller of the shares. Nevertheless, if King (the
broker) should not pay or if any other reason should give rise
to an occasion for it, Gates may, upon learning that the purchase

was authorized by Wade, hold Wade to the contract just as if
the agreement had been made in Wade's name to begin with.
That is, at the time of the transaction, King was in fact the
agent of Wade, but that fact was not disclosed to Gates. There
was an undisclosed principal, and in the undisclosed principal
cases, the third person may hold either the agent or the principal,
as a general rule.

The undisclosed principal cases are sometimes confused with
two other kinds of cases. For one thing, some persons seem to
have a tendency to confuse undisclosed principal cases with
ratification cases. They are easy enough to distinguish if one
just thinks about it. In the case of ratification, a person (agent)
pretends to have authority which he does not have; in a case
of undisclosed principal, the agent pretends not to have authority
which he does have. Another kind of case easily confused with
undisclosed principal is the case in which it is said that the
principal is undiscovered. In the latter kind of case, the agent
tells the third person that he is acting for a principal, but he
does not name the principal. In such a case, the third person
may not hold the agent upon the contract, but he may hold
the principal, and he is bound to the principal. In the undisclosed principal case, as we have seen, the third person may
hold either the agent or the principal. He may hold the agent
because the agent acted in his own name; or he may hold the
principal because the principal authorized the making of the
contract.

One of the most difficult questions in the law of agency is:
What is the meaning of *apparent scope of authority?* How is
one to know whether or not the act of the agent appeared to
be within the scope of his authority? There are two principles
to be kept in mind here. One is that the rule refers to what is
reasonably apparent to the third person; the other is that the
rule refers to what is apparent to the third person as a result
of what the principal does or says.

Suppose that Howard comes to your door and says, "I am
agent for the Curtis Publishing Company," and wants to sell
you a subscription to the Saturday Evening Post. It may be

that you have known Howard for a long time to be an honest man, and it is therefore reasonably apparent to you that he is authorized to make contracts of subscription to the Post. You pay him some money, but there is no contract between you and the publishing company unless (a) they have authorized Howard to act in this way or (b) they have done or said something which has led you to believe that Howard is their agent. In the case supposed, they had not appointed him and had said and done nothing about it. The authority of Howard was apparent in one sense of the word, but it was not apparent in the sense in which the word is used in the law of agency. Perhaps the meaning of the term apparent, as it is used here, will be clear if we refer again to the doctrine of estoppel. You will recall from **Rule 142** that when one person by his acts or words arouses in another a belief in the existence of certain facts, and when the second party acts in reliance upon the belief so created, the first party is *estopped* to deny that the facts were as he represented them to be. This is just what happens in agency when there is an *apparent* authority. The same idea is sometimes expressed by saying that the agent is invested with certain *ostensible* powers.

Here are some illustrations of apparent authority or ostensible powers of agents. In each case where apparent authority is found, it is reasonable to believe the agent had authority, and the belief was made reasonable by the principal's act. Defendant hired one Sides as an agent to conduct a retail store, but he requested Sides to conduct the business in the latter's own name. Sides bought goods on credit from Jaynes who knew that Sides was the defendant's agent to sell the goods. It was held that Jaynes could recover the price of the goods from defendant because the power to sell and to conduct the business imports a power to buy on credit. The power to buy or sell, generally, however, does not import a power to buy or sell on credit.

In another case, Roche was a merchant tailor. He went to Europe, leaving Lane in charge of the shop and instructed him not to buy any goods on credit. Lane induced the plaintiff to believe that he had authority to buy goods on Roche's credit and purchased some. Roche repudiated the deal as soon as he heard of it. It was held that on those facts alone, Roche was not liable. It was somewhat different from the Jaynes case. In the Roche case, the business was being conducted by Lane, a clerk, in the name of Roche. The mere presence of a clerk in charge of the business is hardly enough on which to base an assumption that the clerk has full charge of the business with authority to buy goods on credit, though it would justify an assumption that he had authority to buy anything for cash; but it would be so easy for Roche to leave some evidence of authority and so easy for the plaintiff to see it that it does not seem to be too much to ask that it be done. But in the Jaynes case the facts seemed to justify the assumption that the defendant did not care to appear to the world in general as the owner of the business; from his putting the agent in charge with authority to sell and to act in his name, it seemed reasonable to assume that the agent was also authorized to buy on credit.

In another case, the agent of a dock company had for some time, without actual authority, been in the habit of negotiating notes for the company. They had ratified a considerable number of such transactions. Then, without notice to the plaintiff of any change in the relationship, the agent negotiated a note to plaintiff, and the firm refused to ratify. It was held that the past course of conduct was enough to justify an assumption of authority. This was an act apparently within the scope of the agent's powers.

In another case, the bylaws of a corporation provided that the treasurer should have power to negotiate certain securities. The bylaws were known to plaintiff. The shareholders voted at a meeting to take away from the treasurer this broad power, but the plaintiff had no notice of the change. Thereafter, the treasurer negotiated some of the same old securities to the plaintiff. The company sought to repudiate the transaction, but it was held that the treasurer had acted within the apparent scope of his authority.

In many cases, the following or like facts appear. When Smith was on a vacation in Colorado, he called upon the owner of an auto livery concern to ask rates for a party of twenty-five. At the place of business a girl of about fourteen was in attendance. Without any hesitancy that he could see, she said that the rate was ten dollars per car for a day's trip in the mountains. (That was in 1919.) He arranged to take five cars. Smith's party took the five cars on the next day, and nothing was said about the rates. When they returned in the evening, the owner of the company demanded ten dollars per person per day. She did not deny that the girl may have said ten dollars per car. In fact, she said that the girl was always making mistakes of that kind. This girl was an agent; her authority appeared, from the fact that she was left in charge, to be such that she could make contracts. She did in fact make an agreement to furnish five cars, and it was reasonable for Smith to assume that she had been correct in her statement. She acted within the apparent scope of her authority, in the legal sense.

In another case Skipworth was owner of a line of coaches and engaged in the business of common carrier of passengers (not goods) for hire. He instructed his agents not to accept any goods (except personal baggage) for carriage, except at the owner's risk. The instructions were not known to the public. Lyle deposited goods with an agent of the carrier who did not advise him of the instructions. The goods were lost. It was held that the act of the agent was within the apparent scope of his authority and that the carrier was liable for the loss. But, when a bank permitted an agent to overdraw his principal's account, it was held that this was the equivalent of borrowing money, and that the fact that a manufacturer's agent keeps an account in a bank is not a sound basis upon which to assume that he is authorized to borrow money upon the principal's account. It was held, therefore, that the bank could not collect the overdraft from the principal. The overdraft was not within the apparent scope of the agent's authority.

The question often arises whether or not an agent for the sale of goods is impliedly authorized to warrant the goods. In general, it is the rule that an agent who is authorized to sell goods, unless there is a clear stipulation to the contrary which is known to the third person, has implied authority to warrant good workmanship, soundness of materials, general fitness of the goods, and the principal's title. Care must be exercised here to avoid confusion. It is not meant that the fact that the goods are sold by an agent raises such warranties; it is meant merely that the employment of an agent raises an assumption that if the agent makes such warranties, the warranties will be held binding upon the principal unless the latter in some way advises the third person to the contrary. This rule is of enormous importance in the business world because every day salesmen warrant the soundness and fitness of goods, but the rule does not make valid every warranty made by salesmen. For example, a salesman of pumps warranted that the boiler of the purchaser was big enough to operate the pump; a cloth salesman warranted that his cloth would wear like buckskin; a salesman warranted that rice would keep for a very long period of time. These warranties were quite unusual, and held not to be binding upon the principal. In case of doubt, the customer should, if the warranty is of real importance, require a written statement of warranty or a statement of the agent's authority to make a warranty; and he should see to it that the statement comes from some person in authority, particularly when he is dealing with the agents of corporations. The reason for this last statement is, of course, that a corporation cannot deal at all except through agents; therefore, whatever warranties are made must be made by agents. When one questions the authority of a corporation's agent, he can be assured only by another agent, and it is of the utmost importance to see that the assurance of authority comes from some agent who is himself authorized expressly or by implication to make such assurance in a manner which is binding upon the corporation.

There are a number of miscellaneous agency cases in which may arise the question of the agent's authority to bind the principal. Sometimes, a collection agent compromises a claim either by *taking off* a part of the whole debt or by accepting something other than money in payment. There is no implied authority on the part of an agent to do either one of these things in the absence of special circumstances. The agent who makes a contract of insurance usually has implied authority either to alter the terms of the policy or to waive the nonperformance of conditions. For example, a fire insurance policy provided that the policy should be void if gunpowder were kept upon the premises without the consent of the company. The agent who wrote the policy knew at the time that gunpowder was kept on the premises, and it was held that such knowledge was in effect a waiver of the condition by the company.

Sometimes, the question is asked whether stockbrokers are agents. It may be said in reply that stockbrokers commonly act in three capacities: they may be agents or creditors or pledgees. In the purchase of stock on margin, the broker is an agent if he buys in the customer's name or for the customer's account with the seller; if that is the case, when he buys the stock, he becomes a pledgee, and so far as he advances moneys he is a creditor. Very little of the legal rights of the parties depends upon whether or not the stockbroker is an agent; his liabilities upon his contracts and his rights, too, are generally clear enough.

The difficulties of problems of the scope of the agent's authority can scarcely be overemphasized. They arise from the difficulty of interpreting the meaning of the conduct of the principal. The essence of the problem is: What is it reasonable for the third person to believe as a result of the conduct or words of the principal? We can hold the principal, just as we can hold any party to a contract, only if we have some expression or conduct on his part which makes it reasonable for us to suppose that he will act as his conduct indicates. We cannot ever bind the principal upon the basis of what is said by the agent, whether it is true or not. We must find either that the principal has in fact authorized the agent and sent him out into the world as a representative, or that the principal has done or said something which justifies us in believing that he has so sent the agent out. If both of these things are lacking, there is no binding contractual relationship between the third person and one who he thought was a principal.

THE TERMINATION OF AGENCY

The creation of agency depends upon the express or implied authorization of the agent by the principal. The termination of the relationship is less simple. Once an agent has been authorized, either expressly or by implication, the principal may find it somewhat difficult to take away from the agent the power to bind the principal. The relationship may be terminated either by acts of the parties or by operation of law.

TERMINATION BY ACTS OF THE PARTIES

Rule 161. *Agency may be terminated by fulfillment of the agreement between the parties.* If the agent is employed for a certain stated time or for a special stipulated piece of work, of course, his authority ends when the time has elapsed or when the work has been done. If no stated time is indicated in the agreement, then the authority of the agent will end with the expiration of a *reasonable time*. For example, Martin authorized Schulte to sell Martin's land for $5500. About a year later the land was sold in Martin's name by Schulte. Martin repudiated the sale, and when suit was brought on the contract by the purchaser, the court held that the authority had terminated because the time between the authorization and the attempted sale was so long. In this connection it must always be kept in mind that, even though the authority has been terminated, the principal may be bound by the acts of the agent if the principal's conduct has led the third person to suppose that the authority still exists.

Rule 162. *Agency may be ended by renunciation by the agent.* In commercial agencies the agent is usually bound by contract to execute the authority given him. If he does not execute it and thereby violates his contract, he is said to have renounced his agency. He cannot revive the authority to act without the specific assent of the principal. These cases, of course, are merely illustrations of the law of contracts. The only reason for mentioning them here is to point out that when an agent has renounced his authority, he cannot revive it himself.

Rule 163. *An agency can be revoked by the principal.* In most cases a principal has the power to terminate the agent's authority, and he can exercise this power by merely notifying the agent that the relationship has come to an end. (Of course, it must be remembered that the principal must take proper steps to notify third persons who might know of the authorization. Unless such notification is given, the principal can be held under the principle of estoppel.) Again, in such cases it is necessary to remember that, if the agency rests upon a contract, the principal may be held liable for damages if he terminates the agency in violation of the contract. Violation of such a contract gives the agent a right of action; but whether or not the principal violates the contract in ending the agent's authority, the principal has the power to end the authority, and the agent has only his right of action. Even if the principal specifically promises the agent that he will not revoke the authority, it may still be done. The revocation of an agent's authority, in order to be effective, need not be in any particular form. The mere statement that the principal has done (or intends to do) the work himself, will usually be a sufficient revocation.

Rule 164. *An agent's authority is not revocable if it is coupled with an interest in the subject matter of the agency.* In some types of cases the agent is said to be vested with a property interest in the subject matter of the agency, and in such cases the principal has no power to revoke the agent's authority. It is not enough that the agent has an interest in his contract with the principal; he must have an interest in the property to be dealt with. The following should help make this point clear. Arnley was insolvent. He gave to Burns, one of his creditors, a power of attorney (power as an agent) to collect certain debts which were due Arnley and to apply the proceeds to Burns's claim against Arnley. Arnley tried to revoke this authority, but when Burns collected the debts anyway and withheld the amount due him, it was held that this collection was lawful under the authority originally granted him by Arnley. It was said that Burns had an interest in the subject matter—the debts to be collected. A common instance of this kind of interest is the interest of a pledgee to whom securities were entrusted as security for a debt. He was given an interest in the subject mat-

ter, and his authority to deal with the securities could not be revoked. The advice of an attorney should be sought in most cases
in this field.

TERMINATION BY OPERATION OF LAW

Rule 165. *The authority of an agent is terminated by death
of the principal.* If the agency is revocable, it is always terminated
by the death of the principal whether or not his death is known
to the agent or to the third party. Suppose that Smith was
appointed agent to sell Brown's farm machinery and that he
was authorized to give a bill of sale which would pass title to
the goods. On July 1st, unknown to Smith, Brown died. On
July 16 of the same year, Smith, still unaware of Brown's death,
sold the goods to Elson and issued a bill of sale. Under these
circumstances, any one of a number of things might happen to
raise the question whether or not the sale was valid to pass the
title to Elson. If Smith remitted the sale price to Brown's
address, the administrator might repudiate the sale and demand
the goods from Elson. The administrator would be entitled to
recover the goods, the money being returned to Elson and
Smith losing his commission. Or, on the other hand, Elson,
upon learning of the death of Brown, could repudiate the agreement without being guilty of breach of contract. If the agency
is one which the principal can revoke while he is alive, it automatically comes to an end upon his death.

Rule 166. *Death of the agent revokes his authority.* When
an agent dies, his authority does not pass to his estate nor to his
heirs. Of course, if the agent has a property interest in the subject
matter, that property interest will pass to his estate, and the agency-
authority will pass with it.[3]

Rule 167. *Bankruptcy of the principal terminates the
agency.* In this connection *bankruptcy* means formal bankruptcy,
not mere inability of the principal to pay his debts. In the strict

---

[3] Insanity of the principal occurring after the creation of the authority,
will terminate the agent's authority. The insanity of the agent will not terminate
it, although it gives the principal the right to revoke authority without being
guilty of breach of contract unless the authority was coupled with an interest in
the subject matter.

legal sense one is a bankrupt when his affairs have been put in charge of a court under the bankruptcy laws; when the proceedings come to an end, and if all goes properly, he is declared a bankrupt by the court and is given his *discharge in bankruptcy.* The mere beginnings of such proceedings are sufficient to terminate the authority of an agent of the bankrupt.[4]

Rule 168. *An agent's authority is terminated by destruction of the subject matter.* This principle is practically self-evident. If Hill has been authorized to sell Wilkson's horse, and if the horse dies before the sale is completed, any agreement made by Hill will not be valid. This is similar to the effect of destruction of the subject matter upon other kinds of contracts.

Rule 169. *The marriage of the principal will terminate an agency to sell the principal's real estate.* In all of our states a wife has some interest or other in the land of her husband. Therefore, if an unmarried man creates an agency for the sale of his land, his subsequent marriage will terminate the agent's authority. In many of the states (though not in all) a husband has some sort of dower interest in his wife's land. In the states where this is true, authority given by an unmarried woman to sell her land will terminate upon her marriage. In the states where a husband has no dower or similar rights to his wife's real estate, the marriage of a woman will not affect the powers of an agent who was authorized to sell her land. Again, the rules stated do not apply to any agency coupled with an interest in the subject matter. In such a case the agent's property interest precedes the dower right of the wife or husband, as the case may be, and the marriage does not affect the agent's powers.

QUESTIONS AND PROBLEMS

1. Are agents ever authorized gratuitously? If so, how do their obligations differ from those of agents under contracts? **Rules 140, 141,** and **153.** Is a gratuitous agent under legal obligation to act?

---

[4] The bankruptcy of a business agent terminates his authority too, but the same is not true of an agent with only routine or ministerial matters under his control. Even insolvency of either party justifies the other in terminating the relationship without penalty, in most circumstances.

2. Explain in your own words the reason for the liability of Waite to Carey in the case discussed under **Rule 143.**

3. If Jones, an infant 19 years of age, appointed Hemphill to act for him in selling certain property, the appointment would not be valid, and Jones would not be bound by acts of Hemphill. But suppose that after Jones reached majority, he ratified the appointment of Hemphill. Would he then be bound by those acts? **Rules 143A and 148.**

4. In which cases, as a general rule, does the law require that an agent's authority must be in writing to be valid and to enable him to bind his principal? **Rules 145 and 147.**

5. Does the law require that an agent himself, to be able to bind his principal, must possess contractual capacity? That is, may an infant act as agent so as to bind his principal? **Rule 150.**

6. In general, upon which party to a law suit will rest the burden of proving that an agency exists? **Rule 152.**

7. How much care does the law require of agents? Is it the same care in all circumstances? Is it the same for all agents? **Rules 153 and 153A.**

8. Wells was collection agent for Grimes. He deposited in his own account certain money which he had collected for Grimes. It was a reasonable thing to do because Grimes could not be reached until some time later to make payment to him. The bank was sound at the time of the deposit as far as anyone could tell. Wells immediately forwarded to Grimes a check covering the proper amount, but before the check reached Grimes, the bank failed. Who must stand the loss of the amount of the check, Wells or Grimes? **Rule 153D.**

9. State the general principle of **Rule 154.** How is it related to the general law of contracts? **Rules 143 and 356 to 360.**

10. Is an agent entitled to recover all the expenses of his activities in the absence of a specific promise by the principal to pay such expenses? **Rule 155.**

11. Kennedy was a driver of a grocery truck. While he was on his route delivering groceries, due to his own negligence, his truck collided with the car of Welch. What effect, if any, does Kennedy's employment have upon his personal liability? **Rule 156.**

12. Compare the discussions under **Rules 157, 158,** and **165.** Are there inconsistencies in these discussions or between the rules? Does **Rule 158** seem to contradict **Rule 157** or to be an exception to it? If an inconsistency does seem to exist, can you explain that there is none in reality?

13. Compare **Rule 158** with **Rule 153B.** Suppose that Golden instructed his agent, Knox, to accept no orders under $5,000. Now if

Knox accepted an order for $4,500 from Jenkins under such circumstances that there was no contract between Golden and Jenkins, could Jenkins hold Knox liable on his warranty of authority? **Rule 158.** On the other hand, suppose that the circumstances were such that there was a contract between Jenkins and Golden; would Knox be legally liable to Golden if losses should ensue from the making of the contract? What is the significance of these rules for the agent?

14. Commit to memory **Rule 160,** word for word. Do not try to put it into your own words. What is the most important (and perhaps the most difficult) thing about this rule of law? Explain as well as you can how this rule is related to estoppel.

15. What is a case of undisclosed principal? Give an illustration which is not in the book. Explain how such a situation differs from a case of ratification. **Rule 160.**

16. Why was there no *apparent authority* in the case on page 132 under **Rule 160,** in which Howard seemed to be a representative of the publishing company?

17. In the case on page 135 under **Rule 160,** which involved the hiring of the cars for mountain trips, the text indicates that the employer was bound by the promises of the girl. This would have been true even though the girl had directly disobeyed her instructions. Under what rule of law do the courts reach this result?

18. Hill bought an overcoat on open account at the X department store with the understanding that the price was forty dollars. When the statement of his account arrived, the coat was charged at sixty dollars. Hill immediately called on the credit manager, who promised that a correction would be made. Hill paid the forty dollars. Some time later, the store employed a new credit manager, who sought to collect the remaining twenty dollars from Hill. Hill held his receipt in full, but he had not been credited in full upon the books. Could he be held liable for the twenty dollars? What rule of law do you apply to this case? Upon its application, why do you get your result? This is a rather difficult problem.

19. Smith was employed to sell Henderson's farm with the agreement that he should receive a three per cent commission upon finding a buyer. Smith did find a buyer, but in the meantime Henderson died. His administrator refused to sell the farm to Jordan, the buyer. Does Smith have any legal right against the administrator? Give two reasons for your reply. There are two steps to be taken before you can get the correct result. **Rules 164, 165,** and **158.**

Maine State Capitol, Augusta
Underwood & Underwood

Massachusetts State Capitol, Boston
Underwood & Underwood

Michigan State Capitol, Lansing
Underwood & Underwood

Minnesota State Capitol, St. Paul
Underwood & Underwood

CHAPTER VI

LAW OF PARTNERSHIPS
AND CORPORATIONS

PARTNERSHIPS

Common law partnership is in the main merely an extension of the law of agency. If there is a partnership between Smith and Jones, consider Smith as the agent of Jones and Jones as the agent of Smith. Each is able to bind the other as principal within the *apparent scope* of the business. Also, the partnership relation may be set up by a simple agreement or even by estoppel, just as agency may be set up. About half of the states have adopted the Uniform Partnership Act. This act is largely a codification of the common law principles of partnership law. Though this branch of law is fairly uniform over the entire country, there are so many difficult questions in this field that it is extremely dangerous, legally, to set up or operate a partnership without competent legal advice.

Rule 170. *Every partnership should rest upon a carefully drawn written agreement.* A partnership is defined as *an association of two or more persons to carry on as co-owners of a business for profit.* The law does not require that such an association rest upon a written agreement, nor even that there must be a formal agreement of any kind. The mere act of doing business for profit by two or more persons as co-owners will constitute a partnership and involve all sorts of partnership liability. If there is a properly drawn written agreement, however, it will usually be fairly easy to determine the terms on which the firm is to operate, but in a surprising number of instances persons have set up partnerships without written agreements, and in many cases there is not even a clear understanding between the partners as to their mutual rights and duties. The danger of such procedure is shown by the wreckage of thousands of partnerships whose affairs have come into the courts. In many such cases losses which have been suffered can be clearly traced either to the fact that no clear agreement existed or to the fact that, if such an agreement did exist, there was no written record of it. A written agreement should exist in every case, not because the law requires it, but because common sense demands it. Such agreements should be submitted to a competent attorney for his approval before business operations are begun.

Rule 171. *The written agreement should be specific and comprehensive as to all terms of the contract.* A partnership agreement should indicate clearly the share which each partner is to have in the profits, the share of each in the management, the share which each is to bear if losses are incurred, the length of time during which the contract is to run, how remaining assets are to be divided upon dissolution, the limitations of the powers of each partner to bind the others to contracts with third persons, and other similar matters. If no such agreement is drawn up, or if any of the above questions are not covered by agreement, all of these questions will be answered in accordance with certain rules of law and without any regard to the actual intent of the parties.

Rule 172. *There is no single comprehensive test of the existence of a partnership in the absence of a written agreement.* A great many different tests have been devised by different courts and for different cases to enable them to decide whether or not there is a partnership in a certain case. No one of these tests can be successfully applied to all cases. The question is: When there is no evidence of an actual agreement, is it reasonable to treat the parties or their heirs as if a partnership had been intended?

Here are some problems which show the kinds of questions which may arise. Wiskler and Hagen, with no formal agreement, rented a mill and operated it, Hagen doing the actual operation. Wiskler brought some grain to the mill to be ground. Hagen paid the rent, and Wiskler paid for some repairs. Wiskler claimed a share in the profit of the mill, but Hagen refused, offering to pay for the repairs and to pay the balance due on account of the milling of the grain brought in by Wiskler. In all such cases the

courts take the attitude that the party asserting partnership in the
suit has the burden of proof. If Wiskler cannot convince the court
that there is a partnership, he will lose the suit.[1] In another case
Haug and his son were doing business under the name Haug
and Son. No agreement had ever been made. When the father
died, the question of partnership became important. If there were
no partnership, all of the father's property would go to another
son under a valid will drawn by the father. If there were a partnership, then a share of the firm still belonged to the son who had
worked with the father. The firm looked like a partnership, perhaps, but evidence showed that the father had done all buying
and that the son never made any contracts for the firm without
consulting his father. The son was unable to convince the court
that a partnership existed, and all the property went to his brother.
Whether this was right or wrong, no one can say. A written agreement would have prevented this uncertainty. In another case
Moulds loaned some money to Grey for use in Grey's business.
Moulds was to receive in return one third of the net profit of the
business until the loan was repaid. Before it was repaid, Grey
died, and Moulds claimed rights as a partner. All he could show
was the agreement about the profits. It was held that this, alone,
was not enough on which to base a partnership. The mere fact
of association, the mere fact of aid in management, the mere fact
of sharing in the profits, will not be enough to make certain a
proof of partnership in the absence of a specific agreement of partnership. There is no single, certain test of the existence of a partnership in the absence of a specific agreement.

Rule 173. *Whether associates are liable to third persons on
firm contracts in the absence of specific partnership agreements is
determined upon principles similar to those of estoppel and ratification in the law of agency.*[2] When a partnership exists, each
partner may be held liable upon contracts within the apparent
scope of the business,[3] just as an undisclosed principal under the

---

[1] Note the similarity to **Rule 152.**
[2] Compare with **Rule 142.**
[3] The extent of such liability is discussed under subsequent rules.

law of agency. But there have been a great many cases in which there was no real agreement, either express or implied, and where the question arose whether or not some person could be held liable as a partner. Beech leased a hotel from Miller, agreeing to pay daily, as rent, one third of the gross receipts of the business. Miller had nothing else to do, and he sat around the hotel a great deal and offered much advice and many suggestions. Some of the suggestions sounded like orders. Among other persons who dealt with Beech was Larson, a butcher, who sold meat to the hotel on credit. The meat was charged to the hotel on Larson's books. Beech was unable to pay, and Larson sued Miller as a partner. There was no allegation that there really was a partnership; the question was whether, from the appearances, Larson was entitled to assume that Miller was liable as a partner. In this case, the court thought that the mere giving of suggestions and advice was not sufficient basis for an assumption of partnership liability, but in many similar cases a very slight change in the kind and frequency of such suggestions has been held to warrant an assumption of liability. For example, Fletcher owned a farm which he leased to Pullen on shares for the operation of a seed and nursery business. Pullen advertised under the name Fletcher and Pullen. This advertising was circulated throughout the local community. Fletcher saw the advertising but did nothing to counteract or deny its implications. When Pullen failed in business, his creditors sought to hold Fletcher liable for the debts of the business. Of course, Fletcher was not actually a partner, and no one claimed he was, in the suit; the question was whether or not, as the result of his failure to counteract the impressions caused by the advertising, Fletcher was estopped to deny liability. It was held that, since Fletcher had knowledge of the advertising, and since he took no steps to counteract it, he was liable just as though he had been a partner in fact. If he had not known of it, or if he had taken reasonable steps to counteract the advertising, Fletcher would not have been liable. Even in such a case, assuming that Pullen honestly believed that the lease on shares constituted a partnership, a written memorandum would have made the matter so clear that Pullen could not have misunderstood it.

This may be summarized by saying that a partnership may exist as the result of an agreement, either formal or informal, between the parties. The agreement need not be written; it may be inferred from facts which justify the inference. However, it should be written. On the other hand, partnership liability may exist by estoppel even when there is no actual partnership.

Rule 174. *Partnerships may be conducted under almost any name.* A partnership's members may operate under any name which they care to adopt, so long as they do not infringe upon the rights of any other person. They may operate two branches in two different places under two different names. In fact, no firm name is necessary at all; the firm may operate under the name of the partners. But the liability of the members for firm obligations will not be affected at all by the character of the name.

Rule 175. *A partnership may conduct almost any sort of lawful business for profit.* In general, this rule needs no illustration; but it is necessary to remember that statutes prohibit the use of the partnership form in some kinds of business. For example, most of the states now prohibit the formation of banking institutions by partnerships. Such institutions are usually required to incorporate.

Rule 176. *The firm and each partner are bound by contracts of any partner within the apparent scope of the business.* Section 9 of the Uniform Partnership Act, codifying the common law, provides:

(1) Every partner is an agent of the partnership for the purpose of its business, and the act of every partner, including the execution in the partnership name of any instrument, for apparently carrying on in the usual way the business of the partnership of which he is a member binds the partnership, unless the partner so acting has in fact no authority to act for the partnership in the particular matter, and the person with whom he is dealing has knowledge of the fact that he has no such authority.

(2) An act of a partner which is not apparently for the carrying on of the business of the partnership in the usual way does not bind the partnership unless authorized by the other partners.

(3) Unless authorized by the other partners or unless they have abandoned the business, one or more but less than all of the partners have no authority to:

(a) Assign the partnership property in trust for creditors or on the assignees promise to pay the debts of the partnership.
(b) Dispose of the good will of the business.
(c) Do any other act which would make it impossible to carry on the ordinary business of a partnership.
(d) Confess a judgment.
(e) Submit a partnership claim to arbitration or reference.

(4) No act of a partner in contravention of a restriction on authority shall bind the partnership to persons having knowledge of the restriction.

This section is a codification of the common law. It is applicable no matter what the agreement of the partners is, as between themselves, unless the third person, dealing with the firm, knows of the agreement between the partners. A partnership was composed of Ames, Clay, and Bates under an agreement stipulating that Ames should not have authority to buy any goods for the firm without the expressed consent of Bates and Clay. Daly, who did not know of this clause, sold three barrels of oil to the firm under an agreement made by Ames who acted without the consent of the other two. The firm refused to take and pay for the oil, and when Daly brought suit it was held that the firm was liable upon the contract. In another case a partner executed a mortgage covering firm property to secure his private debt. This mortgage was held invalid in spite of the fact that the third person—the mortgagee—did not know it was firm property. The transaction, to secure the private debt of one partner, was not within the apparent scope of the business. If it had been a mortgage to secure a debt of the firm, the mortgage would have been valid.

Rule 177. *Notice to or by a partner is considered notice to or by the firm.* The principles applicable here are found in Sections 11 and 12 of the Uniform Act:

Sec. 11. An admission or representation made by any partner concerning partnership affairs within the scope of the authority as conferred by this act[4] is evidence against the partnership.

Sec. 12. Notice to any partner of any matter relating to partnership affairs, and the knowledge of the partner acting in the particular matter, acquired while a partner or then present to his mind, and the knowledge of any other partner who reasonably could and should

---

[4] Remember that this includes apparent authority.

have communicated it to the acting partner, operate as notice to or knowledge of the partnership, except in the case of a fraud on the partnership committed by or with the consent of that partner.

These two sections, again, are codifications of the law of agency: That notice to the agent is notice to the principal, and knowledge of the agent is knowledge of the principal. In one case, under Section 11, an employee of the firm signed the firm name to a note. Partner A had no authority to ratify the note, but he did admit, after the signature, that the employee had been authorized to sign it. It was held that this admission was good evidence. Even though partner A could not ratify, his admission of the validity of the signature is a different matter. Under Section 12, Harper contracted to deliver glass at a certain price to McIver. He then told McIver that he must charge a higher price. McIver did not agree to this. Harper then transferred the contract to a partnership of which he was a member. The firm, supposing that the second named price was the controlling one, filled the order, and when McIver refused to pay the higher price, the firm brought suit. It was held that the true price having been known to Harper, his knowledge was binding upon the firm.

Rule 178. *The firm and each partner are liable for torts within the scope of the business.* Another rule of the law of agency is applicable here. Section 13 of the Uniform Partnership Act provides:

Where, by any wrongful act or omission of any partner acting in the ordinary course of the business of the partnership or within the authority of his co-partners, loss or injury is caused to any person, not being a partner in the partnership, or any penalty is incurred, the partnership is liable therefor to the same extent as the partner so acting or omitting to act.

A member of a partnership in the drug business negligently prepared a prescription for the plaintiff who was made ill by taking the mixture. The firm was held liable for the negligence of the partner. This liability does not extend to crimes; unless the other partners have instigated or taken part in the crimes of a partner, they are not liable, nor is the firm liable in such cases.

Section 14 of the Act extends firm liability to somewhat cover such cases as the following: A firm of attorneys was acting for an estate. A part of the assets of the estate were bonds payable to bearer. These were used for his own profit by one of the attorneys without the knowledge of the others. It was held that the firm was liable for the ensuing loss.

Rule 179. *Partners are liable jointly and severally upon most of the partnership obligations.* This is the same principle as that discussed in connection with **Rule 82.** It is of great importance since it defines the extent of the liability of each partner upon the firm's obligations. It is one thing to know that if partner Ames makes a contract in the name of the firm and within the scope of the business, the firm is liable; it is quite a different matter to know whether partner Bates who did not know of the transaction or partner Clay who disapproved of it can be held personally liable for this contract of the firm. And the same situation might arise in connection with the commission of torts. Under the rule stated above (which is included in Section 15 of the Uniform Act), each member of a partnership may be held individually (severally) liable for the torts of the firm or of any member or employee of the firm, if committed within the scope of the employment; or they may be held liable (all or any part of them) together (jointly). Under modern law, this is true of both tort and contract liability in most states, as explained and illustrated under **Rule 82.** There are some difficult questions, however, with relation to how far this rule is applicable in some kinds of situations. Questions of joint liability should be submitted to competent local attorneys.

Rule 180. *A person admitted into an existing partnership is not individually liable for past obligations of the firm unless he specifically assumes such obligations.* This rule is included in Section 15 of the Act, which also points out that the share of such a partner cannot be distributed to him until all firm obligations have been met. Thus, while such a partner cannot be held liable individually for pre-existing debts of the firm, his share in the firm is subject to such debts.

In summarizing the above rules, it is most important to note that the nature of a partner's liability is such that his whole personal estate may be taken to satisfy the claims of creditors of the firm. Those claims may be the results of unlawful acts or of contracts which are unknown to and unauthorized by the partner held liable, if such acts or contracts are within the proper scope of the business. Every partner, therefore, runs the risk of losing not only what he invests in his firm but also his whole personal estate. He risks all this, too, not only upon the success of the business but also upon the competency, honesty, and good faith of his partners. These risks are in a large part responsible for the development of the business corporation, in which, as a rule, the investor's risk is limited by his investment. Again, a partner is bound to continue in the partnership so long as the agreement is in effect, and he cannot easily withdraw. This latter is so important that it seems worth while to devote more attention to it.[5]

Rule 181. *In many states partnership real estate cannot be held in the name of the firm.* The importance of this rule is that, if the firm real estate is in the name of a partner, he may dispose of it and give a good title to a person who does not know it is firm property, and even if the purpose of the transfer was not within the apparent scope of the business, the third party's title is secure. The rule works hardships upon partnerships since no one can be certain that a purchaser of property held in the name of a partner will know that it is firm property. The rule has been changed by the Uniform Act, but every partnership should consult competent legal counsel in matters in connection with the ownership of real estate. The rules in effect in the several states are so different, and the problems encountered are so complex that no further general statement can safely be made about this matter.

Rule 182. *Partners are bound to each other by contract.* The partnership relation is founded upon a contract, and the partners are all bound to each other by the terms of their contract whether expressed or implied. Any partner who violates the terms of the agreement will, of course, be liable under the ordinary rules of contract law. The other partners may either consider the contract broken and obtain a dissolution of the firm through court action, or they may recover damages for the breach. But there are

---

[5] See **Rule 187.**

other aspects of the relationship which are governed by other rules.

Rule 183. *Partners are entitled to equal rights in control.* In the absence of some provision to the contrary in the contract each partner has equal rights with all others to a voice in the control of the firm's affairs. Thus, if there are two partners, neither has more authority than the other; and if there are more than two, a majority is entitled to control the business even against the wishes of the minority so long as the terms of the agreement are not violated, that is, so long as they operate within the scope of the business. The majority may not change the nature of the business nor enlarge its scope without the consent of all partners unless the original agreement provides for such action. The majority may decide whether profits shall be distributed or used to enlarge the business, what policies shall be adopted for governing employees, and all similar questions.

Rule 184. *Each partner is entitled to an equal share of the profits.* Profits of a partnership are not divided in proportion to the amount invested by each unless the agreement so provides. All are entitled to equal shares of the profits, whenever any distribution is made. (See **Rule 191.**)

Rule 185. *Each partner is entitled to an equal share of property of the firm upon its dissolution.* This rule is parallel to **Rule 184**, and its application is not affected by any differences in the amounts of the investments of the several partners unless their agreement provides for such differences.

Rule 186. *All partners must bear an equal share of losses.* This is another rule parallel to **Rules 184** and **185**. Thus, if one partner should be sued and held liable by a creditor of the firm upon a firm debt, he must pay the creditor; but such a partner is entitled to recover equal shares of the amount paid from all of the other partners. The same principle holds if there is a deficit upon distribution of assets at the time of dissolution. These principles will be illustrated in the discussion of dissolution.

Rule 187. *A partner cannot transfer his share in a partnership.* In connection with **Rules 84** and **84A**, it was pointed out that one cannot assign his liabilities nor his rights which are coupled with liabilities. A partnership share includes both rights (in management, in profits, and in assets) and liabilities (for contracts, for torts, and for performance of his obligations to his partners). A partner, therefore, cannot transfer his share because it consists of a combination of rights and liabilities. A partner may assign his right to a share of the profits in his firm, but the assignee cannot collect anything until all of the obligations of the firm have been met. By such an assignment a partner cannot escape his liability for previous debts of the firm; he may still be held liable. Also, if a partner should try to withdraw without the consent of his copartners, he may find that he has violated his contract with them. Even if a partner obtains the consent of the other partners to his withdrawal, he still cannot escape liability for pre-existing debts; and he cannot escape liability for future debts of the firm unless he takes proper legal steps to notify creditors and prospective creditors of his withdrawal. If a partner obtains the consent of his partners and a release from existing creditors and gives proper notice to prospective creditors, he may withdraw; but this will end the old partnership, and if the remaining associates wish to continue, they need a new contract. If they wish to take in a new partner, it may be someone designated by the retiring partner or someone else; but in no case can the retiring partner sell his share and compel the other partners to accept his assignee as a new partner. Legal problems concerning the attempted transfer of partnership shares should always be entrusted to competent authorities.[6]

Rule 188. *Partnerships may be dissolved for several reasons.* At common law a partnership is dissolved by (a) the expiration of the time agreed upon originally, (b) the withdrawal of a partner either in violation of his agreement or with the consent of his partners, (c) an attempt of a partner to sell his share, (d) the death of a partner, and (e) war between the countries of which the partners are subjects or citizens. Insolvency of a partner does not usually effect a dissolution, but under the Uniform Partnership Act bankruptcy of either the firm or any of its members will oper-

---

[6] The rules of law are about the same in their relation to either trading or nontrading partnerships. In the latter, as a rule, the apparent scope of the business is usually held to be very much limited. Illustrations of nontrading partnerships are firms of lawyers, doctors or other firms which render services, as distinguished from firms which operate stores or otherwise engage in trade.

ate as a dissolution. If a partner becomes insane or violates the partnership agreement, courts of equity will usually order a dissolution upon petition of the other partners.

Rule 189. *Dissolution of a partnership does not terminate its affairs.* The dissolution of a partnership means that its privilege to operate as a firm has come to an end, but it does not mean that the obligations of the firm or those of the members have been terminated. Also, the dissolution of a partnership does not terminate the powers of the partners to do whatever is necessary for the settlement of the partnership affairs. For example, the firm of Hawes & Madden was dissolved by the withdrawal of Hawes. After his withdrawal, Hawes collected certain debts from persons who owed money to the firm. This, Hawes was entitled by law to do, even from those debtors whom he told of the dissolution. He then absconded with the money without even reporting the collections to the other partners. Madden sought to collect from these same debtors and brought suit against them, claiming that they should not have paid the claims to Hawes when they knew that the firm had been dissolved. The court held that these collections were binding upon the firm and operated as full discharges of the debtors because any member of a firm, after dissolution, has power to perform any acts which are for the apparent purpose of winding up the affairs of the firm. It is difficult for one in the position of Madden, in this case, to protect himself against this kind of loss. The mere publication in newspapers of the facts of dissolution probably would not be a sufficient protection in most cases. It is probably necessary to address some kind of notice to each individual from whom such collection might be sought. Mailing of such notices, properly addressed, would probably be sufficient. This rule is merely an application of **Rule 176**.

Rule 190. *Dissolution of a partnership does not terminate liability of partners.* It should be clear without illustration that the dissolution of a partnership has no effect at all upon the liability of any members of the firm to third persons. In fact, it is precisely upon dissolution that such persons may find it desirable to turn to the partners to make good the debts of the firm. But, beyond that, dissolution does not eliminate the risk of additional liability upon contracts which may be made after dissolution within the apparent scope of the business. Dillon had sold goods on credit to the firm of West, Holt, and Baker. West withdrew from the firm and afterward contracted with Dillon for the delivery of a bill of goods to the firm without disclosing the fact that he had withdrawn. The goods were accepted by West, and, when the firm refused to pay, Dillon sued Holt and Baker. Just as in the agency case discussed under **Rules 142** and **149**, the court held that the firm was bound to pay under the principle of estoppel.

Rule 191. *A withdrawing partner may be held for debts contracted after dissolution.* This rule is merely the reverse of **Rule 190**. If West, the retiring partner in the preceding illustration, did not take proper steps by publication or the like to give adequate legal notice of his withdrawal, he could be held as a principal upon debts contracted after he had left the firm. Old creditors of the firm are entitled to actual notice of dissolution; new creditors may not rely upon the former character of the firm if proper notice of the dissolution has been adequately published.[7]

Rule 192. *Upon dissolution firm assets must be distributed as required by law.* In the simpler types of cases, the assets of a partnership are distributed as follows when the firm has been dissolved:

1. Payment of all debts to creditors who are not partners.

2. Payment of debts other than capital owed by the firm to partners.

3. Repayment of capital investments to partners.

4. Division of remainder equally among all partners unless their agreement specifies otherwise.

An illustration or two will show how this works. Suppose we find a given firm with assets of $30,000. Debts to general creditors amounted to $12,000, A's capital paid in was $5,000, and B's was $4,000. B had, in addition, loaned the firm $3,000. Upon dissolution they must first of all pay the $12,000 to the outside creditors,

---

[7] Note the similarity of this rule, too, to the matter of estoppel. What is adequate publication is generally governed by local statutes. When dissolution is the result of the death of one of the partners, such notice is not necessary, and the estate of the deceased partner is not liable. The death is regarded as a matter of public knowledge.

which will leave $18,000. They must then pay $3,000 to B for his loan, leaving $15,000. They then pay to A and B their invested capital which takes an additional $9,000 and leaves $6,000. This is divided equally between A and B, so that each receives the same amount of profits. Suppose, with the same obligations, the amount of assets was $20,000. Now, after paying the outside creditors and repaying the loan of B, there remains but $5,000. In view of the fact that the business began with $9,000, there has been a loss of $4,000, which must be divided equally between A and B. Therefore, of the $5,000 remaining we must pay $3,000 to A and $2,000 to B. In every case, unless the agreement stipulates otherwise, profits or losses are divided equally between the partners, and the greatest care must be observed in determining what the amount of the loss is.

In general, when a firm becomes insolvent, the firm creditors are entitled to the firm property until it is exhausted, and the creditors of each individual partner are entitled to the property of their several debtors. When the firm is insolvent and all of the individual members are also insolvent, the property of the firm and of all the members is placed together. Then all the creditors of the firm and of the members must add their claims together, and an equally proportionate share is paid to each. That is, if the assets of the firm and all of the members will pay only fifty per cent of all the claims against both the firm and all the members, then each creditor, whether a creditor of the firm or of one of the members, will receive fifty cents on the dollar on his claim.

When one or more of the partners, or the firm, is bankrupt, the rules for distribution are too complicated for discussion here. They can be properly applied only under the supervision of attorneys thoroughly familiar with the laws of bankruptcy. This branch of law is applied in the federal courts.

SUMMARY

Some of the more important rules of the law of partnership may be summarized as follows:

· 1. A partnership may be formed without formality by an ordinary simple contract.

2. The terms of the contract are binding upon the partners, just as other contracts are binding.

3. Each partner is the principal of the others, and each is the agent of the others unless the agreement contains stipulations to the contrary.

4. In the absence of agreement to the contrary, losses and profits are to be borne equally by all the partners.

5. Creditors of the firm may hold any one or more of the partners liable for the firm's debts.

6. Partners' shares in the business are not transferable.

7. In a partnership of more than two, the majority may control the management of the business unless there is some agreement to the contrary.

8. Partnerships are dissolved by death of a partner, by withdrawal of a partner, by the expiration of the stipulated time, by mutual agreement, and by illegality.

9. No partner is entitled to remove any of the partnership property without the sanction of the others or until the assent of creditors has been obtained.

10. Should any partner break his part of the agreement, he may be held liable in damages, just as any party to any other kind of contract.

CORPORATIONS

The risk of loss to a partner is so great that it is practically impossible to use the partnership form of organization for any business in which small investors are to take part.[8] Since every partner can be held liable for a share of the loss, which does not depend upon the amount of his investment, a man who invests a hundred dollars in a partnership risks the same amount of loss as a man who invests a hundred times as much. When it is remembered that any partner may be held liable for all of the firm's debts, it is clear that the small investor should not assume such large risks with a small investment. On the other hand, a man who invests

---

[8] Limited partnerships are impractical, too, for large organizations. This is in a large part due to the fact that the partners with limited liability have little or no voice in management.

a hundred thousand dollars in a business is not willing, in most cases, to share authority equally with another investor who invests only a thousand dollars. In order to raise enough capital for modern industries, it is necessary to tap the vast resources of capital which small investors can contribute. The partnership is not suitable, in part because of the reasons already given, and in part because a partnership meeting of many hundreds (or even thousands) of investors, where each had an equal voice, would be extremely clumsy. To the questions thus raised, modern business men have worked out most of the answers by developing the corporation. The technical legal name of the corporations so used is *private corporations for profit,* which distinguishes them from *corporations not for profit,* such as churches, clubs, and the like, and public utilities.

Rule 193. *Corporations may be formed only by express legislative permission.* A corporation is not a common law form of organization. No parties can form a corporation by mere contract. The investors in corporations are relieved of most of the risks which have been found burdensome to partners, but, in order to avoid those risks, such investors must have the consent of a state or of the national government. Such consent is in the form of corporation statutes.

In earlier times, each corporation was created by a special act of legislation, which applied to one corporation only; but it has now become the universal practice in this country that each state legislature enacts general incorporation laws under which any persons who comply with such laws may organize corporations without consulting the legislature of the state for organization.[9]

Rule 194. *The requirements for incorporation are similar, but not identical, in most states.* The general incorporation laws of the several states are similar in outline although their details

---

[9] Some corporations are organized under national legislation. National banks have been so organized since 1863. It should be remembered that the general incorporation laws of the several states nearly always are confined to general business. Banking, railroading, dealing in real estate, insurance, and some other businesses may be carried on by corporations, in most states, only if the corporations are organized in compliance with special statutes concerning such businesses. The kinds of business so supervised and the details of the legislation differ in the several states.

vary. They provide that a stated number (usually three) of citizens of the states and of the United States may incorporate by following certain rather simple formalities. It is extremely important, however, that these requirements, simple as they are, be complied with under the advice of a competent attorney. The reason is that, if the parties who seek to incorporate should in any substantial way fail to comply with all of the legal requirements, they can be held liable as partners, and partnership, of course, is the very thing they usually wish to avoid. For example, when a statute required that a certain portion of stock subscriptions should be paid in cash, a certificate of incorporation stated that payment had been so made. Later, it turned out that payment had been made by a check which had not been paid when the certificate was filed. The check was not honored when presented, and it was held by a court that no corporation had been formed. Therefore, the stockholders were held liable as partners for the debts of the organization.

Rule 195. *The same organization may be a corporation for some purposes and not for other purposes.* Sometimes, even though certain substantial requirements of corporation laws have not been complied with, the courts will hold that the association has some corporate powers. For example, in 1874, the city of Cleveland conveyed to Perun certain real estate, subject to a mortgage which was not recorded until 1879. Before the recording of the mortgage, Perun organized a corporation under the state corporation laws, but some rather unimportant requirements of the law were not complied with. Perun then conveyed the same real estate to the corporation, and the corporation sold parcels of the land to certain individuals. All of the members of the corporation and all of the buyers of land supposed that the laws had been complied with. In 1879, the state of Ohio brought a suit to dissolve the corporation on the ground that the statute had not been strictly complied with. The petition of the state was granted, and the society was dissolved. The rule was laid down that no corporation has a legal right to exist unless it has complied strictly with the laws of the state. If it has complied strictly with the laws, it is called a corporation *de jure* (pronounced dee jury), which means a corporation by legal right, and the state cannot dissolve it. But, if the law has not been strictly complied with, there is neither a corporation *de jure* nor a legal right to act as a corporation.

Following this case in which the corporation was dissolved, came a suit on behalf of the city of Cleveland. The city claimed that since the corporation had not been properly organized, it had no power to take the title to the real estate; that since the corporation had no title, it could not give a title to the purchasers; and that the city was therefore entitled to recover the land. The court, however, applied the following rule: If the incorporators have made a good faith attempt to comply with the law and if the association has transacted business in the honest belief that the law has been complied with, there is a corporation *de facto*. This means that there is a corporation in fact, even if not *de jure*. In the case of a *de facto* corporation, persons who have dealt with the association as a corporation cannot rescind their dealings with it, even though the state is able to dissolve the association. Thus, while the state of Ohio could dissolve the society of Perun, the city of Cleveland could not use this dissolution as a means of recovering the land which the society had sold in good faith.

Rule 196. *A subscription to stock is controlled by the law of contracts.* Subscriptions to the stock of a corporation may be either contracts to purchase shares, contracts of purchase, or mere offers to buy stock. In addition to this, many subscriptions are transactions between the subscriber and a promoter or some other person and not transactions with the corporation at all.

Rule 196A. *There can be no contract with a corporation before its incorporation.* Hahn was a promoter for a corporation. Before incorporation, he induced Walker to sign a blank which contained the words, "I hereby subscribe for the number of shares placed opposite my name." The number was 100. About six months later, still before incorporation, Walker advised Hahn that he was withdrawing his subscription. The corporation was organized soon after this, and when Walker refused to take 100 shares, the corporation sued him for breach of his contract of subscription. It was clear that Walker had made no contract with the corporation when he signed the blank because there was no corporation at that time. So far as the corporation was concerned, this blank was merely an offer. An offer may be revoked at any time before acceptance. The corporation could not accept before it came into existence. Walker's withdrawal, therefore, cancelled his offer before it was (or could be) accepted, and there was no contract. The following rule will always be applied, no matter what the language or the form of the instrument is: There can be no contract with a corporation until after it has been incorporated.

Rule 196B. *A subscription may be a contract with other subscribers even though not with the corporation.* Mallory was a promoter who induced Hansen to sign the following: "In consideration of the signatures of the preceding subscribers, and in consideration of the promise of H. Mallory that he will allot to the undersigned the numbers of shares noted opposite their several names, I hereby agree to purchase the said numbers of shares at their par value." This was signed by Hansen before the incorporation of the company. Here, as in the previous case, there was no contract with the corporation, and, so far as the corporation was concerned, this was merely an offer which could be withdrawn at any time before acceptance; but the signing of this instrument did constitute a contract between Hansen, on the one hand, and Mallory and the other subscribers on the other. This was a contract to buy shares.

Rule 196C. *A subscription may be a contract with the corporation, but still merely a contract to purchase shares.* The Penny Pen Company, after incorporation, permitted Smith to sign an instrument which read: "The undersigned agrees, within thirty days of notification to him of the opening of the subscription books of the Penny Pen Co., to purchase sixty shares of the common stock of the said company at $100.00 each." This did not constitute a contract since there was no promise of the company that they would notify him nor that they would sell shares to him; but if they did send the notice of the opening of the books, this would be an acceptance, and there would then be a contract to buy the sixty shares.

Rule 196D. *A subscription may be a contract of purchase.* If the subscription is made after incorporation, if the price is paid at the time of the subscription, and if the subscriber becomes the owner of shares at the time of his subscription, then the contract is one of purchase. Such subscriptions are somewhat rare since most subscriptions in one way or another provide that ownership of the shares shall pass at some time after the actual making of the contract.

The foregoing rules and illustrations should make it clear that subscriptions for stock may have different legal effects, and expert advice should generally be sought by the subscriber before he signs.

Rule 197. *Shareholders, as such, are not liable for the corporation's debts.* A corporate shareholder can be held liable to pay the corporation for his shares as per his contract, but this liability, in general, can be enforced only by the corporation, and it is limited by the amount he promised in his contract;[10] but he is not liable to the corporation's creditors.[11]

Rule 198. *All shareholders are prima facie entitled to vote.* In the absence of contrary stipulations in contracts of subscription, each share of stock in a corporation entitles the owner to one vote in corporate meetings. This is true of all kinds of stock whether common or preferred, registered or unregistered.[12] Thus, preferred shareholders do not lose their votes merely because they hold preferred shares unless their contracts so provide (as they usually do).

Rule 199. *Shareholders are entitled to vote by proxy.* Again, unless their contracts provide otherwise, shareholders may delegate to others their voting rights, but the proxies must also be qualified voters in the corporations in which the voting rights are delegated.

Rule 200. *Only registered shareholders are entitled to vote.* Under modern procedure, bylaws of corporations practically always provide that voting rights are restricted to shareholders of record (registered) at some stated time (usually ten or fifteen days) before the date of any given meeting. This is done in order that

---

[10] In some cases holders of shares which have been issued at less than par value can be held liable for the difference between what they paid and par value; this liability is for the benefit of creditors of the corporation. The liability is based upon technical rules, and problems of this sort should be entrusted to an expert.

[11] The double liabilities of bank shares are statutory exceptions to **Rule 197.**

[12] Stipulations may be found in statutes, in charters, in bylaws, or in the contracts themselves.

corporate officers may have an accurate record of qualified voters.

Rule 201. *No shareholder is entitled to a dividend unless the corporation books show a profit and a dividend is declared by the board of directors.* This is true of the holders of both common and preferred shares. If a *dividend* should be paid out of capital when there is no proper surplus, creditors of the corporation may compel the shareholders to refund money paid to them under such circumstances.

Rule 202. *All shareholders are entitled to dividends at the same rate, prima facie.* Preferred shares are entitled to dividends before common shares only if the contracts so provide. To be sure, the reason for preference very often is precisely a preference as to dividends, but unless the contracts of subscription of both the common and preferred shares contain provisions to the contrary, all shares are treated the same in the distribution of dividends, just as in relation to their voting rights.[13]

Rule 203. *Preferred dividends are cumulative unless the contract provides otherwise.* In a given corporation, 200 shares were preferred as to dividends, and 1000 shares were common. In 1927, there was a surplus of $3,000, but no dividend was declared on either kind of stock. In 1928, there was a surplus of $5,000. The directors proposed to pay a five per cent dividend on the preferred stock, which would take $1,000, and a two per cent dividend on the common, which would take $2,000, leaving $2,000 for working capital. The preferred shareholders objected to this, claiming that they were entitled to dividends at five per cent for both 1927 and 1928, before the common shareholders were entitled to any dividend. In this, the preferred holders were correct. That is what is meant by the rule stated above. Of course, preferred dividends may be made noncumulative by the terms of the subscription contract.

Rule 204. *Owners of preferred shares are entitled to participate equally in all dividends above the preferred rate.* A corporation had a surplus of $50,000. There were 200 shares of five per cent preferred and 1000 shares of common, each share with

---

[13] The same is true as to the distribution of assets upon dissolution of the corporation. See **Rule 213.**

par value of $100.00. The directors decided to pay five per cent to the holders of preferred for the current year and fifteen per cent to the holders of common, distributing $16,000 and leaving $34,000 in the surplus fund. But this could not lawfully be done unless the agreement of subscription so provided. After the common stock receives an amount per share proportionate to the amount paid each share of preferred, any other dividend must be paid to both kinds of shares, share and share alike, unless there is a valid agreement to the contrary. Thus, if the directors wished to use only $16,000 for dividends, they must distribute it as follows: five per cent to the preferred—$1,000; five per cent to the common—$5,000; and the remaining $10,000 equally to each of the 1,200 shares—an additional dividend of eight and one third per cent to all shares. Thus, preferred shares would participate in dividends unless there were a valid previous agreement to the contrary.

Rule 205. *Dividends become debts as soon as declared.* Once a dividend has been declared, it becomes a corporation debt which cannot lawfully be rescinded. Shareholders entitled to such dividends may recover them in an action of contract, even though the directors subsequently vote to cancel the dividend.[14]

Rule 206. *A shareholder may transfer his shares without the consent of other shareholders.* In many states, the courts hold that even a bylaw is void if it provides that no shareholder of a corporation can transfer his shares without the consent of other shareholders. Of course, reasonable restrictions upon transfer are held valid. For example, a bylaw may provide that transfers of stock are not effective until registered on the corporation's books.

Rule 207. *The majority of voting shareholders can control the corporation.* This majority rule is well known, of course, but it is not widely realized that it is subject to two important qualifications. One is that the bylaw may lawfully provide for more than majority votes to control on stipulated matters; and the other is that the majority cannot change the terms of the contracts entered into between the corporation and the minority shareholders.

---

[14] Of course, it must be kept in mind that the declaration of a dividend has this effect only if it is lawful to begin with.

Illustrations of the second are as follows: A majority of the voting shareholders cannot lawfully dissolve a going concern nor change the nature of the business; a majority cannot deprive the minority of their rights in control; a majority cannot create lawful preferred shares without the consent of the minority.[15]

Rule 208. *Corporations are bound by the acts of duly authorized agents, only.* Every agent of a corporation, to be able to bind the corporation as a party to a contract, must be appointed and authorized in accordance with the general rules of the law of agency. A stockholder is not an agent merely because he is a stockholder; a director is not an agent of the corporation to deal with the public merely because he is a director; even an officer is not necessarily an agent. Just as in all other cases of agency, the question, whether the principal (the corporation) is bound by the acts of some person, is a question, the answer to which depends upon (a) whether the person was, in fact, authorized to act for the corporation, (b) whether the principal created an apparent authority, and (c) whether the principal ratified the act after it was performed. Thus, one does not necessarily have a contract with a corporation merely because one has dealt with the president of the corporation. To be sure, certain officers are customarily entrusted with similar duties in so many different corporations that one may assume, for example, that a cashier of a bank has the authority to accept deposits and make contracts concerning them; but this kind of authority comes under the heading (b). In dealing with a corporation officer on important matters, one should make sure that there is a basis for the official's authority or apparent authority.

Rule 209. *The board of directors has power to direct the general policies of the corporation.* No act of the directors is recognized as legal and valid unless the board acts as a board in some kind of formal meeting. In such a meeting the board may appoint agents (one of their number, if they like), they

---

[15] Sometimes, if the minority is extremely small, and if upon petition to a court it seems that the minority is unreasonable, courts will order the minority to either give consent to the changes or accept a fair price for their shares. These cases are quite rare, however, and they usually are so decided as to prevent control of the majority by the minority.

may declare dividends (if there is a surplus), and they may decide other matters of policy. A majority of the board may control at such meetings unless the bylaws make some other provision; and so long as the directors act in good faith, within reason, and within the scope of the charter, the stockholders have no legal right to complain. The stockholders may, of course, elect new directors when the proper time comes.

Rule 210. *Acts performed by a corporation beyond its charter powers may be valid or invalid.* Such acts are known as *ultra vires* acts.[16] There are three ways in which the validity of an *ultra vires* agreement may come before the courts.

a) The Whitney Company was incorporated to make and sell firearms. It made an agreement to manufacture 20,000 padlocks. The locks were delivered, but the buyer refused to pay on the ground that the agreement was *ultra vires* and therefore void. It was *ultra vires,* true enough, but since the act had not been an unlawful or criminal act, and since performance by the corporation was complete, the court held that the corporation was entitled to collect the price of the locks. This agreement had been executed by the corporation.

b) Long conveyed some land to the Georgia Railway. The price was paid and the conveyance made. The railway had no power under its charter to buy this land. Long offered to return the price and demanded the land. It was held that he was not entitled to it since this agreement had been executed on both sides.

c) The Central Railway agreed to lease a certain strip of its right of way to Kennedy so that he could extend his field of grain. Before any work had been done or any money had been paid, the company learned that this lease was ultra vires and cancelled the lease. Kennedy brought suit for breach of contract, but the court held that an executory ultra vires agreement is not enforcible either by or against a corporation which is a party to such an agreement. This agreement was executory on both sides.

Rule 211. *A corporation may be dissolved only by consent of the state of its incorporation.* The corporation is a creation of

---

[16] The second word is pronounced vī'rēz.

the state, and its existence cannot be terminated without the state's expressed consent. The corporation's existence may be terminated by legislative action, only if the charter so provides; a charter may be forfeited with the assent of certain state officials (the secretary of state, as a rule); upon petition of the members to a court of competent jurisdiction the court may dissolve the corporation. Mere failure to do business, sale of all assets, or even bankruptcy, does not terminate a corporation's life although any of the latter may be deemed sufficient reason for dissolution by a court. However, dissolution is not automatic.

Even when a charter expires, while the corporation may not lawfully continue doing business, it is not extinct. A receiver should be appointed to wind up its affairs. Dissolution upon the petition of the stockholders will usually be denied unless all stockholders join in the petition, or unless it appears that dissolution is the best course for the interests of all those who are concerned.

Rule 212. *Upon dissolution, creditors' claims must be satisfied in full before shareholders are entitled to any part of the corporate assets.* This is clear except for one matter. If the same person is both a creditor and a stockholder of a corporation, upon dissolution, this person is entitled to collect his debt in full without regard to the fact that he is also a stockholder. He has two separate contracts: one as a stockholder and one as a bondholder or other kind of creditor. In one relation, he shares equally with other creditors of his class; in the other, he takes his share under his other contract as a stockholder.

Rule 213. *All shareholders share, at the same rate, the remaining assets upon dissolution.* This is similar to **Rule 202.** Here, again, the rule is followed only if there are no contrary provisions in the shareholders' contracts. But a preference as to dividends does not imply a preference as to assets upon dissolution. Each preference must rest only upon its own specific provision. Also, under this same rule, if preferred shareholders are entitled to unpaid, accumulated dividends for past years, they are entitled to these before common stockholders are entitled to any of the assets upon dissolution.

QUESTIONS AND PROBLEMS

1. Give two reasons why every partnership agreement should be written and signed by all partners in the organization. **Rule 170.**

2. Name two different things which may be taken into consideration in determining whether or not a partnership exists in a particular case, as between the partners. **Rule 172.**

3. Name two types of circumstances which may be taken into consideration in determining whether or not a certain person may be held liable as a partner for the debts of a firm, even though there is no partnership between the persons associated in the business. **Rule 173.** Indicate how this is related to agency by estoppel.

4. In the last paragraph under **Rule 176,** why is it that there was liability for the oil in spite of the fact that the purchase was contrary to the agreement between the partners? Why would there be no liability if one of the partners had mortgaged some of the firm's property to secure his own debt, as indicated in the same paragraph?

5. What is the practical meaning of the rule that partners may be held liable jointly and severally for any or all of the firm debts in most states? **Rule 179.**

6. Jones joined the partnership of Ames and Smith. He did not agree to assume the firm's debts which then existed. He could not be held liable on those debts, as indicated under **Rule 180.** But suppose that six months after Jones joined the firm, they distributed a dividend to all partners. On what ground, if any, might this be objected to by persons who were creditors before Jones became a member?

7. Is a partner's liability for the firm's debts limited to the amount of his investment? If not, is it limited by anything at all so far as the law is concerned? **Rule 180.**

8. Two remedies are suggested for the partner who is injured by a breach of the partnership contract by other partners. What are those remedies? **Rule 182.**

9. In the absence of any special provisions in the contract of partnership, what is the basis of control of the affairs of a firm, within the scope of the agreement? Is it investment? Is it the proportionate share in the profits? Is it majority control? **Rule 183.**

10. Memorize **Rules 184, 185,** and **186** until you can write all three of them without looking at any reference.

11. Suppose a partner wishes to sell his share in the firm. To what extent can he do this with the consent of the other partners? To what extent can he do it without the consent of the other partners? **Rule 187.**

12. Name four reasons for which the courts will declare that a partnership has been dissolved. **Rule 188.**

13. Jones was a partner in the milling firm of Jones and Glass. Jones withdrew from the partnership with the consent of Glass, and Glass formed a new partnership with Kent. Glass and Kent failed to meet their obligations. Johnson, a creditor of the firm with claims which were dated before the withdrawal of Jones, being unable to collect from Glass or Kent, brought suit against Jones. Could Jones be held liable on such a debt if he did not have the specific release from Johnson when he retired from the firm? **Rule 190.** Suppose that Johnson also tried to hold Jones liable for the firm's debts which were contracted after the withdrawal of Jones. Under what circumstances, if any, could Johnson do this? **Rule 191.**

14. If a firm and all of the partners are insolvent, how do the courts divide the firm property and the personal assets of the partners among the two kinds of creditors, those of the firm and those of the individual partners? **Rule 192.**

15. Write out in full the summary of rules of the law of partnership on page 157 following **Rule 192.**

16. Is there any way in which persons who wish to form a corporation, and thus escape the liabilities of partners, can do so by common contracts as they could form a partnership? **Rule 193.**

17. What is a *de facto* corporation? Can the members of such an organization be held liable as partners? **Rule 195.**

18. Read **Rule 196A** carefully and compare it with the discussion of agency. What rule of agency law is applicable to situations like those suggested in connection with **Rule 196A**?

19. If any of the signers of the document mentioned in connection with **Rule 196B** should refuse to accept shares offered them by the corporation after incorporation, would the corporation have any legal right to damages for breach of contract? Read **Rule 196B** very carefully before you answer this question.

20. Compare **Rule 197** with **Rule 186.**

21. Are all shareholders entitled to vote in shareholders' meetings unless their contracts of subscription specifically deny them this right? May a shareholder vote by proxy unless his contract provides otherwise? **Rules 198** and **199.**

22. What are the necessary conditions for a shareholder to collect a dividend on his stock, provided his stock is a kind which is entitled to a dividend if these conditions are fulfilled? **Rules 201, 205.**

23. Are preferred shares always entitled to preference in the payment of dividends? Are such shares always entitled to preference in the distribution of assets upon dissolution of their corporation? **Rules 202** and **213.**

24. What are cumulative dividends on preferred stock? Are

holders of preferred stock entitled to cumulative dividends unless their contracts specifically provide for such dividends? **Rule 203.**

25. A certain corporation had a profit of $3,000,000 available for distribution. There were 10,000 shares of five per cent preferred stock and 20,000 shares of common stock. The directors proposed to pay $50,000 to the preferred shareholders, $200,000 to the common shareholders, and to use the remaining $2,750,000 in the business. Assuming for the present that they may lawfully use the remainder of the profits for the business, is it lawful for the directors to divide the $250,000 as they proposed to do? If so, why? If not, what should they do with it, assuming that only $250,000 is to be used for dividends at that time? **Rule 204.**

26. Suppose that four-fifths of the voting shareholders of a certain corporation engaged in the hardware business voted to have the charter amended to permit the manufacture and sale of wooden furniture because of the scarcity of metals for the hardware trade. Can the four-fifths control the one-fifth to this extent? (Assume that all shareholders were present and voting.) **Rule 207.**

27. A partner is an agent of his firm, whether the firm likes it or not, and he may bind it to contracts with third persons unless the other partners give proper notice to such third persons. How far does a stockholder in a corporation have a similar power? Does it make any difference, so far as you can tell, whether he is a holder of common or preferred stock? **Rule 208.**

28. Read again question 25. In that question it was assumed that the directors could use eleven-twelfths of the profit in the business and that the shareholders would have to be satisfied with one-twelfth of the profits, if the directors so decided. Now consider this question: Does the board of directors have legal power to dispose of the profits? If so, is their power unlimited? If it is not unlimited, do you think that the directors in question 25 exceeded the limit of the power? Why? **Rule 209.**

29. A partnership dissolves automatically upon the happening of certain events indicated under **Rule 188.** Is the same thing true of a corporation? **Rule 211.**

30. Suppose that there are three classes of stock in a certain corporation: Preferred A, Common A, and Common B. Upon the dissolution of the corporation, in what order will these several classes of shareholders receive repayment of their investments? That is, what rules are followed to determine the order of payment to them? Do they all share alike, or are some paid in full and others in part? **Rule 213.**

Mississippi State Capitol, Jackson
Underwood & Underwood

Missouri State Capitol, Jefferson City
Underwood & Underwood

Montana State Capitol, Helena
Underwood-Stratton

Nevada State Capitol, Carson City
Underwood-Stratton

CHAPTER VII

LAW OF PERSONAL PROPERTY

BAILMENTS AND CARRIERS

This branch of the law is concerned with the rights and duties of storage-keepers, repairmen, carriers, innkeepers, and other depositaries of goods, whether they act gratuitously or for hire. The transactions which are involved in such relationships are known as bailments.

Rule 214. *A bailment is a transfer of possession of goods without a passing of title.* There are almost as many definitions of the term bailment as there are writers on the subject, but the most important thing is to understand in a general way what the term refers to and what the legal relationships are which arise from such transactions. The chief characteristic of bailment is that every bailment consists of a transfer of possession of goods without a passing of title. The person who makes the delivery is known as a bailor, and the person who receives possession is known as the bailee. It is not even necessary that the bailor be the owner of the goods.[1] Deliveries of goods to warehouses or to carriers, deliveries under conditional sales contracts, deposits of goods for safe keeping, the lending of books or other articles (for hire or free), the leasing of personal property such as linotype machines or rent-a-car automobiles, and many others, are bailments.

Rule 215. *Bailments are usually said to be of three classes.* The classification of bailments is usually made upon the basis of the benefit to be derived from the transaction. One class of bailments is that in which a bailor delivers possession of chattels to a bailee

---

[1] Bailment refers to personal property (chattels) only. It never refers to dealings with real property.

for the sole benefit of the bailee. The loan of a book, an umbrella, an automobile jack, or even a lead pencil, when no charge is made for the use of the thing loaned, is an illustration of this class of gratuitous bailment. A second class, also gratuitous, consists of instances in which goods are delivered to a bailee for the sole benefit of the bailor. For example, a delivery-truck driver is unable to leave a package at the home of the addressee and leaves his package next door. The bailee derives no benefit and makes no charge. The benefits will accrue to the driver since he will avoid an extra trip, and to the buyer since he will not be compelled to wait another day for his goods. The third class is most important commercially. The storage of grain in elevators, the delivery of goods to carriers for transportation, the hiring of drive-yourself automobiles, the checking of parcels for fees at railway stations, leaving a pair of shoes or a watch for repairs, and many other similar bailments are intended to produce benefits for both bailor and bailee.

Rule 216. *In every bailment there must be actual or constructive transfer of possession of chattels.* A common example of constructive transfer is the delivery of a bill of lading with a draft upon the buyer of goods. One bailee of the goods is the holder of the bill of lading, but he does not have the goods —he has only constructive possession. Again, if goods are delivered to a servant for his master, this is regarded as constructive delivery to the master himself, and the master becomes a bailee. In every bailment there must be actual or constructive delivery of goods to a bailee.

Rule 217. *No one can become a bailee without his own consent.* Walsh was carrying a sack of wheat along a road when Johnson drove by with a wagon loaded with other sacks of wheat. Without Johnson's knowledge, Walsh placed his sack of wheat in the wagon, intending to get it back again when he should reach a mill which was the destination of both. At a ford in a stream, the water was rather high, and Johnson, to make sure that the horses could pull him through, tossed out three of his own sacks of wheat and Walsh's sack. Walsh's sack was torn on a jagged stone and the wheat lost from it. Walsh claimed that

Johnson was a bailee and bound to act as such. It was held otherwise because a man cannot be made a bailee without his own consent. If Johnson had discovered Walsh's sack and left it in the wagon, he would have been a bailee; consent would have been implied from his keeping of it. But if he had tossed it out as soon as he saw it, he would not have been a bailee at all.

Rule 218. *A bailor need not be the owner of the goods.* A finder of lost property does not become the owner of it, but he has a sufficient interest in it to enable him to make a bailment of it. A boy was set to digging in a lot at the instance of the owner of the lot. The boy found a tin can full of gold pieces, which he deposited with a storekeeper for safe keeping. The storekeeper-bailee refused to surrender the coins to the boy on demand, claiming that since the coins did not belong to the boy, he could not make a bailment. But, in an action at law, it was held that a finder of lost goods has a right to possess them until the true owner has been found, and that this right enables the finder to make a bailment. As bailor, the boy had a right superior to that of his bailee, and the storekeeper was ordered to return the coins to the boy.[2]

Rule 219. *A bailee has a property interest in the bailed goods.* This property interest of the bailee is sufficient to entitle the bailee to legal protection against any person (even the bailor) who may seek to take the goods away from the bailee unlawfully. Jackson leased a boat to Kelly, creating a bailment. Before the end of the lease-period, Jackson's creditors took the boat away from Kelly, and Kelly was entitled to recover damages from the creditors of Jackson. Jackson had no right to the boat himself until the period of the lease-bailment was ended, and Jackson's creditors, in general, could not acquire any better right to his goods than he himself had. Kelly had a real property interest, as bailee, even though he was not the owner of the boat.

Rule 220. *A bailee may not deny his bailor's title.* Cleaves borrowed a gun from Fletcher. When Fletcher asked for the

---

[2] The legal position of finders is discussed in the latter part of this chapter.

gun, Cleaves refused to return it, claiming that it was his own gun to begin with. In Fletcher's action, it was held that the bailee could not, after taking possession of the goods under a bailment, afterward escape the duties of a bailee by denying the validity of the bailment under which he got possession. Of course, if title is transferred to the bailee after the bailment, he can set up his title as a defense to a demand for return of the goods. This happens often under contracts for sale on approval. The buyer is a bailee until he expresses his approval. If he does express approval, and the seller afterward demands the goods, the passing of the title under the contract is a good defense.

In another kind of case, **Rule 220** does not apply although it might at first seem applicable. Walker brought to the Golden Ore Company twenty bags of ore for assaying and sampling. Before Walker came to get it, it was demanded from the ore company by the Apex Mining Company under the claim that Walker or some other person had stolen the ore from the mining company. In that case the rule applied was this: When a third person asserts to the bailee a better right than the bailor had (when such third person demands the goods as his own), it then becomes the duty of the bailee to determine without error whose the goods are. If he makes a mistake and delivers the goods to the wrong person, no matter how careful the bailee may be, the latter may be held liable in an action of trover for conversion of the goods. This rule sometimes acts very hard upon the bailee when conflicting claims are presented for the same goods. He chooses a person to whom to deliver at his own peril.

Because of this hardship, a device has been provided by courts of equity by which the bailee can escape from his inconvenient position. This remedy is called a bill of interpleader. When the conflicting claims arise, the bailee may at once apply for relief to a court of equity. His bill of interpleader informs the court of the facts of the case, states that he is holding the property until the court advises him what he should do with it, and asks the court to call in the rival parties and decide to whom the goods should be delivered. When the proceeding is ended, the court names the person who is by law entitled to the goods, the goods are delivered to him either by the bailee or by the court, if they have been in the meantime delivered into court, and the costs are usually taxed against the losing claimant. This remedy is often used in behalf of elevators, warehouses, carriers, and other depositaries of goods for commercial purposes.

Rule 221. *The bailor should warn the bailee of hidden dangers.* Of course, this duty of the bailor operates only when he knows (or when, by the exercise of ordinary care, he should know) of hidden characteristics of the goods which might be dangerous to the bailee. Suppose that Smith loaned his car to Johnson. Johnson drove out of the garage into the street. The car's brakes were defective, and Johnson was unable to stop before crashing into a truck. Smith was a bailor. If he knew, or if he could have known (by the exercise of ordinary care) that the brakes were defective, he could be held liable both to the owner of the truck and to Johnson if the latter had been injured in the collision. The bailor's responsibility in such cases rests solely upon his failure to exercise the duty just discussed. His liability does not rest upon ownership.[3] In general, an owner of property is not responsible for damage done by the use of his property by his bailees unless he has neglected his duty as bailor.

Rule 222. *The bailee must return the goods at the end of the bailment.* If no claim has been made in conflict with the bailor's claim,[4] it is the bailee's duty to return the goods to his bailor upon termination of the bailment. If he does so in good faith, he is relieved of all responsibility for the goods. This is sometimes extremely important. For example, a man named Laton brought certain sugar to a warehouse for deposit. During the absence of the owner of the warehouse, a clerk permitted Laton to store the sugar there. When the owner returned and learned of the transaction, he at once ordered Laton to take the sugar away, and the latter did. Then the true owner of the sugar, from whom Laton had acquired it by fraud, came to the

---

[3] In two or three states, there are special statutes contrary to this general rule and applicable to owners of automobiles, but such statutes are by no means common.

[4] See Rule 220.

warehouse and demanded the sugar. When it was not delivered, he brought an action against the warehouseman for dealing with his goods without his consent. It was held that the warehouseman was a bailee of Laton and that he had performed his duty by returning the sugar to the bailor, provided he acted before he had notice of the plaintiff's claim, and provided he acted in good faith, as he had done in this case. Of course, sometimes the bailment agreement provides that, upon the termination of the bailment, the goods are not to be returned to the bailor but passed on to someone else. When that is true, of course, it is the duty of the bailee to make the delivery agreed upon. This happens daily in the case of railways and express companies. They are bailees with instructions to deliver the goods not to the bailor, in many cases, but to some consignee named by the bailor. If the delivery is made properly, the carrier is not liable even though the shipper was not the true owner nor acting for the owner.

Rule 223. *The bailee must exercise ordinary care with the goods.* It is said that in a bailment for the sole benefit of the bailee, the bailee is under a duty to exercise great care to prevent loss or injury to the subject matter; that in a bailment for the sole benefit of the bailor, the bailee is under a duty to exercise only slight care of the subject matter; and that in a bailment for the benefit of both parties, the bailee must exercise only ordinary care. What is the practical meaning of all this? First, take the case of a bailment for the benefit of both parties. Brown deposited a quantity of palm leaf with Racine. The latter was to make the palm leaf into hats if he should care to do so, and whatever was left he was to return to Brown, who was to pay for what he used at a stated rate. This transaction was a bailment. Possession of the leaf was transferred to Racine, but he did not become the owner of it until he used some of it for hats. It was a bailment for the benefit of both parties; Racine's benefit was that he was to have the leaf at hand ready to use, should he want it; Brown's benefit was that there was a possibility of a sale and that the leaf was cared for in the meantime by the bailee. Racine did not use any of the leaf for hats and did not buy any. When he came to deliver the leaf back to Brown, however, a considerable part of it was spoiled and useless. Brown demanded damages for the loss of his palm leaf, but Racine declined to pay anything. In a suit for the value of what was spoiled, the court said that the question to be decided was whether Racine had properly cared for the leaf while he had it. The rule was laid down that a bailee under a bailment for mutual benefit is under a legal duty to exercise that degree of care which a man of ordinary prudence would have exercised with his own goods under the same circumstances.

It is important to note that it was not enough for Racine to treat the goods as he in fact treated his own; he must exercise the same amount of care as would have been exercised by a man of ordinary prudence in the same circumstances—with the same kind of goods, in the same climate, at the same time of year, and so on. This is the rule generally applied in bailments for mutual benefit. Of course, no general rule can be stated which will enable us to determine what a man of ordinary prudence would have done; this is a question which must be solved separately for each particular case. It is often a very difficult one, but the bailee can protect himself by exercising just a little more care than seems to him would be exercised by a man of ordinary prudence. If he does this much, he probably will be safe.

The degree of care required in the other kinds of bailments can be measured in terms of the rule stated above. If the bailee is to get all of the benefits of the bailment, as he does when he borrows some article for his own accommodation and is not expected to pay for the use of it, it is reasonable to expect him to be more than ordinarily careful. This is the practical meaning of *great* care. On the other hand, the bailor may leave property in the hands of the bailee for the keeping of it for the accommodation of the bailor. If one steps into the corner store and asks permission to leave his suitcase for a few moments, this kind of bailment is created. Under such circumstances, it is said that one cannot reasonably expect the bailee to exercise as much care over the suitcase as it would be reasonable to expect if he were to be paid for the service. Thus, in such an instance, it is said that he may exercise somewhat less than ordinary care. This is the meaning of *slight* care.[5]

Rule 224. *Parties to bailments may determine their own rights, but in the absence of stipulations the law fixes rights and duties.* Perhaps it ought to go without saying that the parties to a bailment may, by the terms of their contract, agree to any group of rights and liabilities which they think desirable, and, so long as their stipulations are not unlawful, they may do so. But, just as is true in connection with the law of sales, the parties to bailments commonly do not make any stipulations at all, or, at most, merely the most elementary ones, as to what are to be their respective rights and liabilities. It is in the absence of any stipulation by the parties, or when their stipulations (as happens rarely) are unlawful, that the courts have worked out rules which describe the rights and liabilities of the parties.

Rule 225. *Bailee's right to use is limited.* A bailee may not lawfully use the subject matter for any purpose other than that which was stipulated or which may fairly be assumed to have been intended. For example, Greer hired a horse to drive from town A to town B and return. He drove to town B but made the return trip by way of town C. He did not drive the horse improperly, but the distance was about twenty miles greater than it would have been had he gone directly back to town A. It was held that the driving home by the different route was a violation of the rights of the bailee under the bailment, and he was held liable in an action of trover for conversion of the horse. It is likely, however, that the same result would not be reached if the bailment were one of an automobile and if the excess distance were not more than it was in the horse case, unless it were very clear that the distance was strictly limited by the contract. But even in the case which involves an automobile rather than a horse, it is the duty of the bailee to use

[5] In two very common kinds of mutual bailments, the general rule about exercising care has no application. These two kinds are (1) the acceptance of goods for transportation by a common carrier, and (2) the taking of custody of a guest's goods by an innkeeper. The obligations of these two kinds of bailees are discussed in connection with subsequent rules.

the car only for the purpose of the bailment. The difference
between the two cases, so far as there is any difference, arises
out of the fact that while it may be clear that it is unreasonable
to drive a horse by a return route which is twenty miles longer
than the going route, it is not by any means certain that twenty
miles extra driving would be a violation of a bailment of an
automobile. In such cases, however, everything depends upon
what it is reasonable to suppose was a legitimate use of the
article bailed, and any other use is unlawful and will render
the bailee liable.

Rule 226. *The bailee is not obligated to keep the subject
matter in good repair.* The bailee of goods is not responsible
either for ordinary wear and tear nor for any other loss or injury
which occurs unless he assumed such responsibility when the
bailment was made, or unless the loss or injury is due to his
failure to exercise the requisite degree of care, or unless the
loss or injury is due to the bailee's willful act. Hayes was the
bailee of a horse which belonged to French. The horse became
sick through no fault of Hayes, and it was held that the owner
must pay for the care and cure of the horse. But, when Riley
rented a machine from Lowden, agreeing to keep it in perfect
repair, and when the machine was damaged by an accident
through no fault of Riley, it was held that he was liable to pay
for the repair of it because he had assumed that risk. Sometimes, a business custom or usage puts the risk upon the bailee.
When the Wabash Railway rented certain cars from another
railway company, the cars which were delivered were defective
and had to be repaired before they could be used. It was held
that since there was a custom among railroads to the effect that
the borrower of cars must repair them, the Wabash must pay
for the repairs; but, in the absence of some such custom or an
assumption of the risk in the contract or some legal fault, the
bailee is not responsible.

Rule 227. *A bailee for repairs must exercise the degree of
skill he professes to have and obey instructions.* For example, if
my neighbor asks me to help him grind the valves in his Ford,
and if I do not profess to have any special skill in the matter

but agree to help him, the degree of skill which he can expect of me is much lower than that which he is entitled to expect if he takes the car to a professional automobile mechanic. In one case, however, a car was taken to a garage by the owner, who, in the absence of a mechanic, agreed to permit a helper to work on the car. Some damage was done due to the helper's inexperience; but since the owner of the car knew that he was dealing with a helper, neither the garage keeper nor the helper could be held responsible if the helper were not negligent.

But, if my neighbor had specifically directed me to take special care to mark each stud and nut as removed, and if I had neglected to do so, I could be held responsible to him for loss or damage due directly to my failure to carry out his instructions. This latter duty is not related to my skill nor to the fact that I am acting gratuitously.

Rule 228. *A bailee for hire is entitled to a lien for his charges if there is no agreement to the contrary.* The bailee's lien is his right to retain goods until his charges have been paid. It is very important, and, though it has been modified somewhat in many states by statutes, an understanding of the bailee's common law lien is likely to prove useful.

In the first place, the bailee who performs work upon or in connection with the subject of the bailment has a lien upon only those goods in connection with which or upon which he does work. Wright was a printer. Lyon deposited certain book plates with Wright from which Wright was to print books. Wright had no lien upon the plates for his charges because he did not do any work upon or in connection with the plates. He did, however, have a lien upon the printed pages unless it was agreed that the work was to be paid for at some time subsequent to delivery. In another case, Cole had borrowed a horse and, during the period of the bailment, he had loaned a sum of money to the owner of the horse. The money was not paid when due, and Cole kept the horse as security; but it was held that he had no lien upon the horse for the debt because the two transactions were separate. It is otherwise, however, when a garageman does work upon a car, when a smith shoes a horse, or when anyone does work on material for another. In the absence of a previous agreement, the bailee has a lien upon the property until the price of the work is paid.

In the second place, the lien is specific not only as to the subject matter upon which the work is done, but it is specific also in the sense that the lien exists for the charges due upon the particular job only. If a person takes his car to a garage for repairs, the garage operator has a lien for the price of the work done at that time, but he has no lien for charges for work done in the past, nor for work done upon some other car. For instance, Carson owned two cars, and he took one to the Amco Garage for repair work. When the work was done, it was charged to him upon the books. Before he paid for the first work, he took the car in again. The garage keeper would not permit him to take the car until he had paid both bills. Carson paid the second bill and demanded the car, and when delivery was still refused him, he brought an action and recovered damages for conversion of the car. The meaning of this is that the lien of the bailee was good for the charges in the present transaction only. The same would have been true had Carson taken the second car in for repairs. The garage would have had a lien for the charges in that transaction only; it could not have lawfully held the second car to secure the payment of the charges for work upon the first.

In the third place, the bailee's lien may be lost by failure to exercise it at the proper time. A mill owner had a common law lien upon certain lumber which he had sawed. A statute gave him a lien and a right of attachment. He brought suit under the attachment statute, and it was held that he had thereby forfeited his common law lien. When the suit under the statute failed because he had not filed certain notices required by the statute, his common law lien was gone, and he could not fall back upon it. He was compelled to rely upon an ordinary action of contract for his remedy.

In the fourth place, the common law lien is lost when the bailee voluntarily parts with possession of the property. Taylor made certain repairs upon a wagon for Tucker. He had a lien on the wagon for his charges, but he allowed Tucker to take the wagon away and thereby lost his lien. It is not every act which looks like surrender of possession, however, which will forfeit a lien. Wells had repaired an engine for the owner, and, when the work was done, he delivered the engine to an express company for shipment to the owner. Before it reached its destination, the owner became insolvent, and Wells ordered the express company to retain possession of the engine. It was held that his delivery of the engine to the express company did not constitute a surrender of the goods so as to forfeit the lien since the express company was the shipper's agent. This, of course, is closely related to the rule of stoppage in transit, which permits the shipper of goods to assume the right of disposal of goods when they are en route to his consignee, provided the consignee becomes insolvent before he has either received the goods or disposed of the bill of lading to a purchaser in good faith. The right of stoppage in transit was discussed earlier in connection with the law of sales of goods. Again, if one has a lien upon property, and if the property is surrendered to the assignee of the claim for which the property is held, the lien is not lost. In the absence of an agreement to the contrary, a common law lien is assignable and enforcible by the assignee of the claim if he has possession of the property which is subject to the lien.

In the fifth place, a common law lien is lost if the debtor tenders the correct amount of the debt and the creditor refuses to accept it, claiming more. Page was the owner of a harness which had been left with Wilson for cleaning and repair. When the work was done, Wilson demanded $50 for it. Page tendered twenty dollars, and, when it was refused, he paid the money into court and sued in trover for the value of the harness. Upon the trial, the court found that twenty dollars was a reasonable price for the work, and it was held that the tender of a reasonable amount upon a disputed claim discharges the creditor's lien. The debtor, Page, was entitled to his harness because of his tender, which he had kept good by paying the money into court. The retention of the harness after the good tender was a wrongful act and a conversion. The lien was discharged by tender.

In the sixth place, the bailee's lien does not give him the right to sell the property in order to collect his claim. The X railway company had a lien upon a shipment of flour for freight charges. The charges were not paid, and the company's agent sold the flour in order to collect its charges. It was held to be a conversion of the flour. The same thing would have been true at common law even though the flour had been about to spoil; the common law lien does not give the bailee the right to sell the goods. It gives him a right to merely hold the goods until the claim is paid or a reasonable amount is tendered in payment for the debt which is subject to the lien. Carriers' liens have been modified by statute in practically all of our states. If goods are not called for or if charges are not paid within certain periods of time (usually six months or a year), and if proper notice of sale is published as prescribed in the statutes, the carrier may sell goods at a public sale. The same is true in many states of repairmen of different kinds. This is the meaning of the signs one often sees in repair shops *Not responsible for goods not called for in thirty days*. But it must be remembered that this right of the bailee to sell the goods is not a common law right. It exists only where there is a statute to that effect. These statutes are matters of local law, which cannot be cited in detail here.

The common law lien is important not only to the bailor and the bailee; it is often of considerable importance to the bailor's creditors. For, if the bailee has a lien, the property subject to the lien cannot be taken by the bailor's creditors until the charges due have been paid to the bailee. The reason for this is that the creditors of the bailor have and can acquire no better rights to the property than the bailor himself has, so the bailee's rights are often of importance to the bailor's creditors.

In closing the discussion of liens, two points will bear repetition. One is that almost any kind of stipulations may be made about liens. The other point to remember is that the matter of liens has been so extensively dealt with by legislation that the law in practically every state has been very considerably modified, as far as it concerns liens.

Rule 229. *Bailments may be terminated by consent or acts* *of the parties.* Since bailments arise from transactions which involve the consent of the parties,[6] they may be terminated by consent of the parties. In this regard, bailments, especially commercial bailments, are contractual in character, and they may be terminated in much the same ways as may be used to terminate contracts in general. If a bailment has been formed for the duration of a stated time, as is the case when an automobile has been rented or when any personal property has been leased for a given time, it becomes the duty of the bailee to return the property when the time expires, and it becomes the right of the bailor to demand the return of the goods.

In some cases, the property has been bailed, not for a stated period of time, but for the accomplishment of a stated purpose. When this is the manner of the making of the bailment, the accomplishment of the purpose or even the passage of a reasonable length of time without accomplishment of it, in some cases, will give the bailor the right to terminate the relation. For example, when a typewriter is leased for the doing of a certain amount of work, the bailor is entitled to demand the machine as soon as the work is completed, or, if it is not completed within a reasonable time, he may demand it anyway. In either case, refusal to deliver it would be a wrongful act upon the part of the bailee and render him liable in an action of trover for conversion of the goods.

It is usually held, too, that when the bailee uses the property in a manner not contemplated by the agreement, the bailor may then terminate the relation; and it ought to go almost without saying that the parties may terminate a bailment by mutual agreement whenever they give their mutual consent to do so. In a gratuitous bailment, whether the benefit accrues to the bailor or to the bailee, it is usually held that the bailor may lawfully demand a return of his property at any time except when the bailment is for a specified time or purpose. In the latter case, the consent of the bailee is necessary up to the time the purpose is accomplished or the agreed time expires.

In discussing the termination of bailments by acts of the

---

[6] See the discussion of the finder-bailee in a following rule.

parties, it is said that certain acts terminate the bailment. The true meaning of this statement is perhaps a little different from what one might expect unless he considered the matter very carefully. Suppose, for example, that goods were turned over to a truckman for delivery at a certain destination. Suppose that when the truckman arrives at the appointed place, there is no one to receive the goods. In a sense, the object of the bailment is accomplished—the goods have been delivered; but the bailment is not terminated because the goods are still in the possession of the truckman, and his duty to exercise care and the like is not ended. An even clearer case is that in which a watch is left with a jeweler for repair. When the work is done, the object of the bailment is completed, but the bailment is not ended. The real significance of the statement about termination of bailments by acts of the parties is this: Certain acts of the bailee give the bailor the right to demand the property and make it the duty of the bailee to return the goods.

Rule 230. *Bailments are sometimes terminated by operation of law.* In some instances, the termination of bailment by operation of law results in an actual termination and not in a mere change in the rights of the parties. For example, if the subject matter of a bailment should be destroyed through no fault of the bailee, the relationship is wholly ended. There is no more possession, no more duty, and no more rights, with respect to the subject matter. In the case of a deposit of lumber by Spencer with a cabinet maker for the manufacture of furniture, there was a bailment; and when the wood was burned, through no fault of the cabinet maker, the bailment was ended. There may have remained some contractual rights and duties, but the bailment was wholly terminated. In other cases, termination by operation of law amounts to about the same thing as termination by acts of the parties; it gives rise to rights on behalf of the parties, rather than actually putting an end to the relationship.

Rule 231. *Certain events make possible the termination of bailments.* The events most commonly said to bring about termination of bailments by operation of law are death of bailor or bailee and change in the legal status of the parties. But these events do not always terminate bailments. In bailments for the sole benefit of the bailor, death of the bailor is said to end the bailment. His representative (administrator or executor) succeeds to his rights, however, and may demand the goods. This effect does not take place if the bailment is for a specified purpose or time. In the same kind of bailment, the death of the bailee does not usually terminate the bailment unless the bailment involved a relationship of trust or confidence reposed in the bailee. In the latter case, the bailee's death does end the relationship. Much the same attitude is taken generally when the bailee or bailor becomes insane or bankrupt. It is perhaps best to say here what the student may have already suspected: The subject of termination of bailments is in considerable confusion. There are two fairly safe guides for the business man. One is the fact that bailments are consensual (almost contractual) in character, and that they may be terminated as contracts may be terminated. The other is that the duties and rights of the parties do not automatically come to an end upon the occurrence of any of the events which we have discussed except the destruction of the subject matter. When these two guides do not lead to a conclusion which seems to be sound or in line with common practice, the best thing to do is to consult an attorney or some other person experienced in these matters.

In bailments for the sole benefit of the bailee, the death of the bailor vests in his representative the same rights as the bailor himself had: the bailment can be terminated at once unless it was one for a specified time or purpose. But the death of the bailee probably terminates the bailment, giving the bailor the right to reclaim the property in every case of this kind.

When the bailment is of the mutual sort, common in commercial transactions, death or bankruptcy does not change the relationship of the parties any more than death discharges a contract. This is of particular importance in that type of bailment known as a pledge, in which possession of chattels is transferred to secure the performance of some kind of obligation. The pledge, however, is of much more importance as a collateral security device than it is as a bailment.

COMMON CARRIERS AS BAILEES

It has already been suggested that those bailments which consist of the delivery of goods to a common carrier for shipment are among the most common commercial bailments, and that certain peculiarities in the law of carriers made it desirable that we discuss them and their duties in a separate place. A common carrier is anyone who offers his services as carrier to the public generally for hire.[7] Express companies, railway companies, ferryboat companies, local transporters of baggage and freight, and taxicab companies (so far as they are carriers of baggage) are usually all common carriers. The Pullman Company, turnpike companies, irrigation companies, tugboat and towboat companies, postmasters and letter carriers, and the post office, among others, are not common carriers. (The Pullman Company is designated a common carrier for certain purposes of the Interstate Commerce Acts, but it does not come within the limits of the rules which are discussed here.)

First of all, the common carrier is under a legal obligation to carry for all and to furnish equal facilities for all, so far as he is able to do so. If a common carrier, having facilities, refuses to furnish them to any member of the public applying for service, it may be held liable for the damage caused by such refusal. The difficulty, of course, is in establishing the fact that facilities were really available. Of course, the carrier may properly refuse to accept for transportation goods which are improperly packed, goods which are in themselves of a highly dangerous character, or goods which it is unlawful to transport, and it may lawfully demand its payment in advance. Aside from these limitations, when goods are offered to common carriers for shipment, they must accept the goods if facilities are available.

Rule 232. *Common carriers are liable as insurers of goods.* It is the duty of the bailee for hire (in a mutual bailment) to exercise ordinary care over the goods and ordinary skill of the kind which he professes to have, in order to accomplish the purposes

---

[7] There are two states which do not require that a common carrier must be one who offers his services to the public. These states are Pennsylvania and Tennessee, and peculiar rules apply in those two states.

of the bailment. The common carrier, however, is under a much more onerous duty. He is an insurer of the goods and must assume all the risk of loss or delay to the shipment unless the loss or delay should be the consequence of one of the five causes discussed in the following paragraphs. And even if the loss is due to one of those five causes, he still must show that he has exercised ordinary care to avoid such perils or to minimize the loss after the goods have been actually exposed to the danger. And if the carrier deviates from the usual or agreed route without a reasonable excuse, he becomes absolutely liable for loss caused by the delay ensuing. The five conditions which excuse the carrier from his absolute liability for loss or delay, but not from the exercise of ordinary care, are as follows:

a) *Acts of God.* No one can say just what the meaning of this phrase is. It has no place in the law at all except in the law of common carriers, and the different meanings attached to it make its significance a matter of local law. It probably includes such events as strokes of lightning, earthquakes, and volcanic disturbances, but what else it means must be locally determined. It is always less extensive than the term inevitable accident, however.

b) *Acts of the public enemy.* This means, practically, that if goods are taken from a carrier or destroyed by an organized, invading, hostile force, the carrier is not liable. Its chief significance is historical rather than practical.

c) *Acts of the shipper or the shipper's agent.* Such acts may consist of improper packing or stowing of goods by the shipper or by his servants, or of such an act as occurred in the following case. James shipped a carload of household goods, with a man in charge of the car, on the X railway. The man in charge was furnished with a lantern which he in some way upset, thereby setting fire to the goods, which were destroyed. It was held that whether the act of the man was negligent or not, the loss was due to the act of the shipper's servant, and the company was not liable.

d) *Acts of public authority.* This refers to such events as the confiscation of goods by government officials, the seizure of diseased

or injurious goods, or the attachment of the goods by some authorized officer. In such events, the carrier is excused from the duty
to deliver the goods, provided the act was performed by a recognized public official only, acting within the scope of the police
power of the state. These cases are not very common.

  e) The inherent nature of the goods. Sometimes, the goods
are destroyed due to some inherent quality of the goods themselves.
Liquid material may evaporate, or, as in one case, barrels of
molasses may ferment and explode. In such cases, the carrier is
excused from his duty to deliver. This exception becomes particularly important in the carriage of livestock. On the one hand,
the animate character of this class of freight necessitates the furnishing of special facilities for handling it; on the other hand,
many losses are due to the fact that the animals, as living or-
ganisms, are susceptible to perils which do not affect inanimate
freight and the occurrence of which may relieve the carrier of
liability.

  What has been outlined here is the common law duty of
carriers, both as to their duty to accept goods for shipment and as
to their duty to deliver the goods promptly and to the right consignee. These regulations have been revised by the state legislatures and by Congress under its power to regulate interstate
commerce. They cannot even be sketched in a treatment as brief
as this must be. The business man engaged in such activities as
make desirable some knowledge of these questions should employ
competent counsel to work out rules for his guidance in the jurisdiction in which his work is carried on.

  Sometimes, carriers have sought to *contract out* of this onerous
common law liability. However, it has been held that provisions
upon bills of lading or other shipping documents, so far as such
provisions seek to limit the carriers' liability to the exercise of
ordinary care or less, are not operative unless the shipper actually
expresses his assent to the limitation. If he refuses to consent, the
carrier must accept the goods, if properly packed, under its common law liability. Mere publication of notice by the carrier is not
enough; it must be shown that the shipper actually knew of the
limitation and that he expressed his approval. But it is agreed

everywhere that if the shipper actually does give his consent, the carrier may become liable as an ordinary bailee only. It is also a well settled law that the carrier may effectively limit his liability *as to amount* by the publication of notice to the effect that he will not assume liability beyond a stated amount upon any single shipment, unless the shipper shall notify him of the value of a particular shipment in excess of that amount; and he may make this added amount of his liability the basis of a differential rate charge. This matter, too, is complicated by the existence of more or less minutely detailed regulations in the different states and by the many provisions of the several acts of Congress which affect interstate commerce. Limitations as to the time and manner of presentation of claims for damages to shipments are held to be valid as a general rule, provided such limitations are reasonable, and provided they are brought adequately to the attention of the shipper.

Rule 233. *A carrier may sometimes be liable as a warehouseman only.* Two other matters in connection with the liabilities of common carriers may be discussed under one head. They arise from the fact that the question, whether or not a common carrier was in a given case acting as a common carrier or as an ordinary bailee, often must be answered. For example, goods were deposited with the Y railway company for shipment, but, before they were loaded into cars, the shipper advised the freight agent that he might not ship them after all and asked that they be held pending his orders. While they were in the custody of the railway company, they were destroyed by fire through no fault of the company. It was held that the company had not accepted the goods for shipment, and so was not acting as a carrier but as a warehouseman, whose duty, in general, is that of an ordinary bailee. The same kind of situation not infrequently arises when goods have reached the freight station at the point of delivery and are being held pending the consignee's calling for them. In such cases, if proper delivery is tendered and refused, the carrier becomes a warehouseman with duties as such. Likewise, should the consignee ask the carrier to hold the goods temporarily, it usually acts as a mere warehouseman. Aside from either of these events, the carrier continues to be responsible as a carrier until the goods are finally delivered in good order to the proper person.[8]

Rule 234. *A pledge (or pawn) is a kind of bailment.* Any deposit of a chattel as security for the payment of a debt or for the performance of any other obligation is a pledge. It is also a bailment because possession is transferred without a transfer of title. All of the rules of the law of bailments apply to pledges. Since the pledgee is a bailee, he must exercise due care with the property; he must return it upon the termination of the bailment; and he may not use the pledged article for his own purposes unless the agreement specifically permits such use.

Rule 235. *If the obligation is not performed by the pledgor, the pledgee may either keep the pledge or sell it to realize the amount of his claim.* This rule does not need illustration, but it must be kept in mind that these powers of the pledgee may be modified by statute or by the agreements of the parties. Also, in most states, a pledgee is required by law to notify the pledgor either in person or by publication before he may lawfully sell the pledge, unless the contract provides otherwise. State statutes have modified the legal position of pawnbrokers, in many states.

Rule 236. *Documents of title are often pledged instead of the actual goods.* It frequently happens that the property to be pledged is unwieldy and inconvenient to handle,[9] or that the pledgor wishes to retain the property and use it to produce income with which to pay the debt covered by the pledge. Under such circumstances, the actual deposit of the goods is impractical, and business men have worked out some modifications of the pledge. Suppose Gilman is the owner of 50,000 bushels of wheat which is worth $1.09 per bushel, and that he wishes to borrow $10,000 upon the security afforded by some of this wheat. It might be physically possible to deposit the actual wheat with the bank, but

---

[8] Under the common law, an innkeeper is liable as insurer of the baggage of his guests. This obligation has been modified considerably by statutes in the various states. The details of these statutes differ, of course, but as a rule they provide that if the innkeeper furnishes a place for the deposit of his guests' valuables, he cannot be held liable as insurer. Local authorities should be conulted on this matter.

[9] For property such as livestock, carloads of grain, and machinery in warehouses, documents of title are often pledged.

it certainly would be inconvenient for the bank if some 10,000 or more bushels of wheat were dumped into its lobby; and if the bank had very many borrowers of this kind, the difficulties would be insuperable, even though wheat is regarded as adequate security for certain types of loans. To overcome such inconveniences, it has become customary for owners of quantities of fruit, vegetables, grain, coal, cattle, and other bulky goods, to draw up or cause to be drawn up certain documents which can be used as security in place of the goods. These documents are drawn up in such ways that only the holders of the instruments are entitled to the goods represented. When this is done, lenders of money are willing to accept such instruments in pledge in lieu of the actual goods. If the goods are in storage, as in an elevator or warehouse, the depositor is a bailor and the warehouseman is a bailee. The latter issues a storage receipt or warehouse receipt. If the goods are in the hands of a carrier, the latter, as bailee, issues a bill of lading. If the goods are in a dock warehouse, a dock receipt may be issued. The use of such instruments as collateral security is illustrated in the following pages by discussing the uses of bills of lading.

Rule 237. *A straight bill of lading cannot be used as collateral.* Bills of lading are of two kinds, called either straight bills or order bills. The straight bill is illustrated in Fig. 1. A careful reading of the instrument will disclose that it is a receipt showing that the carrier has received certain goods and has engaged to deliver those goods to John Smith at Elmyra, New York. Delivery to any other person may not lawfully be made unless such person is the agent of Smith, and delivery may be made to Smith at Elmyra whether or not he presents any bill of lading. Since this is true, the straight bill of lading cannot be used as security for a loan. There is no way of assuring the lender that the goods have not been or will not be delivered to Smith, nor is there any practicable way of making sure that the goods will be delivered to the lender if the loan is not paid. Therefore, straight bills of lading are not used as collateral.

Rule 238. *An order bill of lading may be used as collateral.* In the order bill of lading, Fig. 2, notice that the goods are to be delivered to the order of the shipper. This form is sometimes used

Fig. 1. Uniform Straight Bill of Lading

(Uniform Domestic Order Bill of Lading, adopted by Carriers in Official, Southern, Western and Illinois Classification territories, March 15, 1922, as amended August 1, 1930, and June 15, 1941.)   F. D. 2636
400M 10-27-41
8½x11

UNIFORM ORDER BILL OF LADING—ORIGINAL
THE PENNSYLVANIA RAILROAD COMPANY

1

RECEIVED, subject to the classifications and tariffs in effect on the date of the issue of this Bill of Lading, the property described below, in apparent good order, except as noted (contents and condition of contents of packages unknown), marked, consigned, and destined as indicated below, which said company (the word company being understood throughout this contract as meaning any person or corporation in possession of the property under the contract) agrees to carry to its usual place of delivery at said destination, if on its own road or its own water line, otherwise to deliver to another carrier on the route to said destination. It is mutually agreed, as to each carrier of all or any of said property over all or any portion of said route to destination, and as to each party at any time interested in all or any of said property, that every service to be performed hereunder shall be subject to all the conditions not prohibited by law, whether printed or written, herein contained, including the conditions on back hereof, which are hereby agreed to by the shipper and accepted for himself and his assigns.

CAR INITIALS AND NUMBER **M.D.T.** **64821**

The surrender of this Original ORDER Bill of Lading properly indorsed shall be required before the delivery of the property. Inspection of property covered by this bill of lading will not be permitted unless provided by law or unless permission is indorsed on this original bill of lading or given in writing by the shipper.

AT *Chicago, Illinois*
No. *(108)*
FROM *Proviso Produce Company*

DATE	SHIPPER'S NUMBER
March 10, 19	

CONSIGNED TO
ORDER OF *Proviso Produce Company*
DESTINATION *St. Louis*   STATE OF *Mo.*   COUNTY OF

Received $ *none*
to apply in prepayment of the charges on the property described hereon.

_____ Agent or Cashier

NOTIFY *J. B. Wilkes 231 8th St.*
AT *St. Louis* STATE OF *Mo.* COUNTY OF

Per _____
(The signature here acknowledges only the amount prepaid.)

ROUTE   DELIVERING CARRIER

Charges Advanced $ *none*

Subject to Section 7 of Conditions, if this shipment is to be delivered to the consignee without recourse on the consignor, the consignor shall sign the following statement: The carrier shall not make delivery of this shipment without payment of freight and all other lawful charges.

_____
SIGNATURE OF CONSIGNOR

←—— If charges are to be prepaid, write or stamp here, "To Be Prepaid."

WEIGHED AT _____

Note—Where the rate is dependent on value, shippers are required to state specifically in writing the agreed or declared value of the property. The agreed or declared value of the property is hereby specifically stated by the shipper to be not exceeding _____ PER _____

★ If the shipment moves between two ports by a carrier by water, the law requires that the bill of lading shall state whether it is "carrier's or shipper's weight."

	GROSS	TARE	ALLOWANCE	NET

SHIPPER *Proviso Produce Co.*
PER *A. M. C.*
Permanent Postoffice Address of Shipper *1247 E. 12th St., Chicago, Ill.*

AGENT *J. B. Smith*
Per _____

NO. PKGS.	DESCRIPTION OF ARTICLES, SPECIAL MARKS, AND EXCEPTIONS	★ WEIGHT (Subject to Correction)	RATE	
00	*Crates Cabbage*	*72,000*		

Fig. 2. Uniform Order Bill of Lading

to make the goods deliverable to the order of the buyer, especially if he buys on credit. The meaning of the language in the order bill is that the carrier engages to deliver the goods either to the person named, or to any person who presents the bill to the carrier with the indorsement (order) of the person named in the bill. In either case, the goods are not to be delivered without surrender of the bill. Thus, if goods are shipped under an order bill, no one is entitled to the goods unless he presents to the carrier the properly indorsed bill of lading. This is why an order bill can be used as security. It can be indorsed and placed in the hands of the creditor, and it gives to the creditor complete legal control of the goods, just as though he had the goods themselves in his possession.

Rule 239. *Order bills are used as collateral in several ways.* Suppose that Wakeman orders from the Binkley Company a car of grain and that the Binkley company, being willing to sell the grain to Wakeman on simple credit on an open account, ships the goods under an order bill of lading to the order of Wakeman. The bill of lading will be sent directly to Wakeman under such circumstances. Now, suppose that the bill reaches Wakeman some two or three weeks before the grain is likely to arrive and that he wishes to make a short time loan to meet current expenses. His bills receivable are such that he expects to receive sufficient money from them within a few days to take up the loan before the grain arrives. Under these circumstances, Wakeman takes his bill of lading to his bank and offers it as security for a loan. If the loan is made, Wakeman indorses the bill of lading in blank by writing his name on the back of it and gives it to the cashier of the bank along with a promissory note for the amount borrowed. This is similar in effect to the simplest kind of pledge transaction. If the loan is not paid when due, the bank may, if it does not wish to renew the loan, sell the bill of lading and keep the proceeds, just as the ordinary pledgee may do.

In a second kind of transaction, the bill of lading is not used as security for a loan at all, but as a means of securing payment for the goods. For example, Groves orders three cars of oil from the X Petroleum Company. The company does not wish to sell to Groves upon credit, and Groves does not wish to pay in advance.

The X company delivers three cars of oil to a railway company and takes three bills of lading (one for each car). The bills are made to the order of the X company; the goods are to be transported to Groves's city; and he is to be notified by the railway agent when the goods arrive. But in this case, the bills of lading are not sent to Groves. The X Company takes the bills to its bank, indorses them in blank, draws a draft upon Groves for the price of the oil, and delivers the bills and the draft to the bank. The bank then forwards the draft and the bills to a second bank in Groves's city for collection. The second bank notifies Groves that it holds the draft and the bills of lading, and, if Groves comes in and pays the amount of the draft, the bills of lading are turned over to him. Since they are indorsed in blank, and since Groves is entitled to the bills because he has paid the draft, he may get the goods from the carrier upon surrender of the bills. In this way, the bills of lading are used as a means of securing the seller against the risks of a credit sale. By the use of them, the seller retains control of the goods until the price is paid, and yet the buyer need not pay until the goods are ready for immediate delivery.

In a third kind of case, the seller is willing to sell to the buyer upon credit, but at the same time wishes to receive a part of the price as soon as the goods are shipped. In such circumstances, the shipper will deliver the goods to the railway or shipping company and take a bill of lading to his own order. The shipper indorses this bill in blank. He draws a draft upon the buyer, calling for payment of the draft ninety days (or whatever the term of credit is) after sight (after demand for the drawee's promise to pay the draft). The shipper deposits this draft and this bill of lading with his own bank, as before, for collection. But this time, the shipper desires an advance from his bank upon the security of the draft and bill of lading. The bank, if it is willing to make an advance, discounts the draft (gives the shipper credit for the amount of it minus interest and other fees), and then sends the draft and bill to the collecting bank. Now, if the buyer *accepts* the draft (promises in writing upon its face to pay it at the time named in the draft), since a promise is all that is required of him at that time, the bill of lading is delivered to him. He may get the goods and sell them and use the proceeds to pay the draft when it falls due. Here, the draft and bill of lading are used to secure a loan from the shipper's bank to the shipper. If the buyer does not accept or if he does not pay the draft when it is due, the shipper, as drawer of the draft, is liable to his bank to repay to it the amount of the draft, thus discharging his debt upon the loan or discount. If the holder of the draft wishes, he may hold the drawee who accepted the draft.[10]

The third kind of transaction is sometimes used as a means of enabling a person to have in transit goods valued at a sum several times greater than the amount of his investment in them. For instance, suppose that Hert was a buyer of potatoes from farmers and truck gardeners. Suppose that a car could hold 1000 bushels of potatoes, that Hert paid the farmers sixty cents per bushel, and that he could sell them to commissioner merchants at $1.20 per bushel. He started with $2000 as capital, in addition to what he must pay for freight charges and other incidental expenditures. He has $2000 to invest in potatoes, enough to buy potatoes to fill three cars and leave $200. He can buy no more potatoes until he has sold the first cars, but the season is short and he wants to handle as many cars as possible; so he buys three carloads, loads them up, takes bills to his own order, and draws three drafts upon commission merchants for the price of the three carloads. The total face value of the drafts is $3600. They are ten day drafts. His bank will advance him $3000 for them and send them on for collection. He then can buy five more cars, and for the drafts and bills upon these the bank may advance him $4500. With this he can buy potatoes for seven more carloads. By this time, some of the first drafts may be paid, the first loan may be cancelled, and if everything goes well, he can borrow on the last lot. With every car sold for which the draft is paid, his own investment in the chain becomes larger. By the use of this device, a business man may have in transit goods valued at several times the amount of his original investment, and yet all of the loans may be adequately protected as long as the goods remain in

---

[10] See **Rule 246** and **Rule 249**.

good condition. Only short time loans are made on perishable goods. Warehouse receipts and storage receipts are often used as collateral in a manner similar to the first of the three just discussed.

Rule 240. *A finder is a bailee.* One who finds lost property is regarded as a bailee and, in general, is subject to the usual duties of care. He must exercise ordinary care to protect the goods from loss or damage; he may not use the goods for his own purposes; and he must return the goods to the true owner upon demand.

Rule 241. *A finder usually has no lien on the goods.* The finder of lost property does not have a right to retain the goods for a reward unless the owner promises a *specific* reward for the return of the goods. If the owner does not promise any reward at all, the finder is entitled to no reward, although, if he expends money upon the care of the goods, he is entitled to recover a reasonable amount of such money; but he is not entitled to hold the goods for the payment of such money. If the owner promises a *liberal* reward or just *a reward,* the finder has no right to retain the goods until a reward is paid. He must deliver the goods on demand and then may recover whatever the courts deem a *reasonable* reward if he cares to sue for it. But, if the owner offers a reward of twenty dollars or any other specific reward, then the finder has a right to retain the goods until such specific reward is paid. Since the latter is the least common of all cases in this field, the rule is as stated: The finder has no lien, as a general rule.

Rule 242. *An installment buyer is usually a bailee.* Since the distinguishing feature of a conditional (installment) sale is that the title is retained by the seller (see Chapter IV, page 113), the buyer is a mere bailee in spite of the fact that he considers himself the owner of the goods. The degree of care probably is not so great as in other mutual bailments, but the bailee-buyer is not entirely free of obligation to exercise care in dealing with the goods involved.

QUESTIONS AND PROBLEMS

1. What is the chief distinguishing mark of a bailment? Can real property be made the subject of bailment? **Rule 214.**

2. Give an instance of each class of bailments from the point of view of which party is to be benefited. **Rule 215.**

3. Is it necessary that a bailor be the owner of goods which are the subject of a bailment? Can a finder be a bailor? **Rules 218, 222.**

4. What is the right of interpleader? In what types of situations is it useful? By whom is it used—that is, by bailor or bailee? **Rule 220.**

5. In the case discussed under **Rule 222,** assuming that the warehouseman acted in good faith without knowledge of the claim of the true owner, why was it that he was held to be not liable? Explain how it was, as you understand it, that he performed his duty as a bailee in spite of the fact that he did not deliver the sugar to the rightful owner.

6. Clark loaned a car to Fox to drive to a neighboring town. While on the way, within the limits of the bailment, Fox collided with another car. The car of Clark was damaged, and he sought to recover the damages from Fox. Fox rested his defense upon the ground that he had used the car and driven it just as carefully as he would have driven it if it had been his own car. Would that be sufficient to excuse him from liability? If not, why not? What do you think he would have to prove in order to escape liability as a bailee? **Rule 223.**

7. In the discussion under **Rule 226,** in the case between Riley and Lowden, a decision which is apparently contrary to the statement of **Rule 226** was reached. Assuming that this decision was a proper one (as it was), explain the apparent contradiction.

8. Compare **Rule 227** with the rule which prescribes the duty of an agent with regard to his skill and care. **Rule 153A.**

9. Ward left a team of horses with Glenn to be shod. There was no agreement as to whether Ward was to pay cash for the work or whether it was to be done on credit. When Ward called for the horses, Glenn refused to allow him to take the horses away until the work was paid for. **Rule 228** states that Glenn was in the right in this. But suppose that Glenn allowed Ward to take the horses without paying for the work. Then, suppose that Ward brought in the same team to be shod again two weeks later and, at the same time, brought in another team to be shod. Without any specific agreement about it, would Glenn have a right (a) to hold the team which was shod twice for the charges for the first shoeing; (b) to hold the team which was shod once, for the charges of the first shoeing; or (c) to hold both teams for the charges of all three shoeings? If not, what could he do?

10. Suppose that under the facts of the first part of question 9, after the first shoeing, Glenn held the horses for the charges. Suppose, too, that during the night, Ward broke into Glenn's stable and stole

his own horses. Would this deprive Glenn of his lien upon the horses? Do you think that Glenn would be able to recover possession of the horses by court action unless his charges were paid? **Rule 228.**

11. In the fifth part of the discussion under **Rule 228**, it is said that if a debtor makes a proper tender of payment, the bailee's lien is lost. Does this mean that the debt is discharged also? Go back to **Rule 99.**

12. Explain the meaning of a sign in a shoe repair shop, *Not responsible for goods not called for within thirty days*. **Rule 228.**

13. How does the liability of a common carrier for the safety of goods differ from the liability of an ordinary bailee for mutual benefit? **Rule 232.**

14. What is the practical significance of the rule that a common carrier is liable as insurer of goods, subject to certain exceptions? Write out the list of exceptions. Do not omit any. **Rule 232.**

15. Suppose that a railway company, having learned that as a common carrier it was liable as insurer of all goods entrusted to it for carriage, required every shipper to agree that the company should not be responsible for the loss of goods, except on the basis of the rules of law which govern the liability of an ordinary bailee for mutual benefit. Then, suppose that a certain shipment belonging to John Smith was lost without the negligence of the carrier, but not due to any of the exceptions named in connection with **Rule 232.** Would the courts hold the railway liable in spite of the agreement of the shipper? **Rule 232.**

16. What is the importance of the fact that a carrier may sometimes be liable as a warehouseman? What is the legal difference between the liability of a common carrier, as such, and the liability of a warehouseman? **Rule 233.**

17. Why is it that a lender of money may be willing to accept as security a mere document instead of the actual goods which are offered him as security? **Rule 236.**

18. Explain carefully why it is that a straight bill of lading can never be used as collateral security. **Rule 237.**

19. Explain how an order bill of lading may be used as collateral by the buyer of goods. How may it be used as collateral by the seller of goods? How may it be used as a device for securing the payment of the price of goods by the buyer? **Rule 239.**

20. Explain why an installment buyer of a piano, for example, is in reality a bailee in spite of the fact that he considers it his piano. **Rule 242.**

Nebraska State Capitol, Lincoln
Underwood & Underwood

Maryland State Capitol, Annapolis
Underwood & Underwood

New Jersey State Capitol, Trenton
Underwood & Underwood

New Mexico State Capitol, Santa Fe
Underwood-Stratton

CHAPTER VIII

THE LAW OF NEGOTIABLE INSTRUMENTS[1]

The basic rules of the law of negotiable instruments were worked out by the merchants of the late Middle Ages and of early modern times. This body of rules was a part of what has become known as the law merchant. Within the past fifty years, the law of negotiable instruments has been carefully analyzed and clarified in the form of the Uniform Negotiable Instruments Law, known and referred to as the N.I.L., which, with some minor variations, is in effect in all jurisdictions of the United States.

Rule 243. *The legal rights of an owner of a negotiable instrument do not necessarily depend upon the rights of the person from whom the instrument was received.* In Chapter III, **Rule 87** states that one usually cannot assign more rights than he owns.[2] The assignee of the nonnegotiable note, which was discussed in that connection, could not collect the note from the maker unless the payee could have collected it. But, if Gates, the buyer of the car, had executed a negotiable promise to pay,[3] the seller of the car could not have collected the amount of the note unless the guarantee had been fulfilled; but, if the bank purchased the note before maturity for value and in good faith (without notice of the guaranty), it could have collected the note from Gates whether the guaranty was made good or not. Thus, the transferee may get a better right to collect the note than the transferor had if the instrument is negotiable.

---

[1] Much of the subject matter of this chapter was adapted from the author's book, *Modern Business Law,* by permission of the publisher, The Macmillan Company, New York.

[2] See also **Rule 119.**

[3] What a negotiable instrument is, is discussed later in this chapter.

This is illustrated in another way by the following case. Suppose that the negotiable note given by Gates to the company was payable to the bearer[4] and that before the note was due, the company to whom it was payable lost it. Suppose it was found by Thompson, or that it was stolen by Fox from the original owner. Now, if Thompson or Fox (as the case might be) sold the instrument to Holden for value before its maturity, and if Holden honestly believed that the seller had a right to dispose of it, he could collect the note from Gates in spite of the fact that Thompson or Fox could not have done so. One who buys a valid negotiable instrument in good faith before its maturity and for value may collect the instrument even though it was given without consideration or was stolen, or even though it had been issued in exchange for work which was never done.

Thus, the law of negotiable instruments is directly opposed to the law of assignment of contracts. The law governing negotiable instruments was worked out to make such instruments usable in place of money. By the use of such instruments, persons in the position of the bank or Holden are willing to advance money on such instruments; and persons in the place of the seller of the car are able to collect their money in advance by borrowing on (discounting) the note before it is due.

Rule 244. *Negotiable instruments are used in place of money.*[5] If Johnson deposits $5,000 in currency in the Acme Bank, it is commonly said that Johnson has $5,000 in the bank. But he is not entitled to any particular $5,000. The bank merely owes him $5,000, which it is obligated by the contract of deposit to pay out in accordance with his orders. Suppose Johnson wishes to pay $2,100 to Palmer for an automobile. He could go to the bank, draw out $2,100 and take it to Palmer; but this would be inconvenient because it would involve a trip to the bank, drawing just the right amount of money, and taking the risk of carrying the money to Palmer. Perhaps, too, Johnson is not certain when he

---

[4] What makes an instrument payable to bearer is discussed later in this chapter.

[5] The discussion is taken from pages 320-321 of *Modern Business Law,* by permission of the Macmillan Company.

goes to see Palmer that he will buy the car. It is convenient for him to give Palmer a written order, directing the Acme Bank to pay Palmer or some person designated by Palmer $2,100 and to deduct the amount from the debt which the bank owes to Johnson because of his deposit. In this way, Johnson is relieved of inconvenience. At the same time, Palmer does not need to take the risk of carrying the money about with him.

More important than the convenience of either Palmer or Johnson, however, is the fact that when written orders or checks are used, a good deal of the work of society can be done without the necessity of actually moving money about. For example, Palmer deposits the check for $2,100 in his own bank, which gives him credit for this amount on its books. Palmer can draw against this credit, giving a check for $400 to Morton for rent. Morton deposits this check in his bank and may draw against it, and so on. Meanwhile, the Acme Bank subtracts $2,100 from the amount due to Johnson, Palmer's bank makes the entries of deposit and withdrawal on Palmer's account, Morton's bank does the same, and so on. Palmer's bank could collect the $2,100 from the Acme Bank, and Morton's bank from Palmer's bank; but, in fact, each bank in a given town has many checks on each of the other banks. Their messengers meet in a clearing house every day and reckon up the differences which the accounts disclose, and the several banks merely pay these differences, often by checks or drafts on other banks, and often by mere bookkeeping operations in the form of entries of balances and credits. More than 85 per cent of retail transactions and 95 per cent of the wholesale transactions are conducted without the transfer of actual money, thanks to the use of checks.

All of this activity and use of paper in place of money is made possible and safe, of course, because of the law of negotiable instruments, which gives every bona fide holder of such an instrument greater rights and security than are provided by the common law in respect to ordinary kinds of property. For example, each bank which takes a check or other negotiable instrument under the proper conditions is entitled to the right of an owner of that instrument, even though it received the paper from one not authorized to collect or sell it. This is one of the facts which make banks and other persons willing to accept checks.[6]

The law of negotiable instruments plays a very important part in the protection of the whole credit system. This branch of the law gives to holders of instruments certain rights which they would not have under the law of contracts, but it gives those rights only when the parties comply strictly with the conditions laid down by the law. What those conditions are is the subject of the remainder of this chapter. They are found in connection with the discussion of the following questions:

1. How can one be sure he is dealing with a negotiable instrument?

2. How are such instruments properly transferred?

3. What are the liabilities of parties who make, draw, or transfer such instruments?

4. What are the legal rights of holders in due course of such instruments?

5. How can one be sure that, as a purchaser of a negotiable instrument, he will acquire the rights of a holder in due course?

Rule 245. *Negotiable instruments are defined very strictly.*[7] Negotiable instruments are of two kinds: bills of exchange and promissory notes. They are called, shortly, bills and notes. A bill is an order upon some person, directing him to pay money; common examples are bank drafts and checks. A note is a promise to pay money; examples are bank notes, municipal bonds, and ordinary notes of hand.[8] The *drawer* of a bill is the person who draws it up (signs it), ordering the payment. The *drawee* of a bill is the person to whom the order to pay is directed. If the drawee promises to pay the amount ordered in the bill by writing

---

[6] Of course, it must be remembered that persons will take such instruments for value only if they feel that they can rely upon the credit (ability and willingness to pay) of the persons whose names appear upon the instruments.

[7] This discussion is taken almost verbatim from pages 323-328, of *Modern Business Law,* by permission of The Macmillan Company. Some of the subsequent illustrations in this chapter are adapted from pages 329-340, of the same book.

[8] Bills of lading, warehouse receipts and stock certificates are negotiable for some purposes by reason of special statutes; they are not affected by the law of negotiable instruments.

his name across the face of the bill, he is said to have accepted it
and becomes the *acceptor*. The person who makes out (signs) a
note is called the *maker*. The person to whose order the payment
is ordered or promised is called the *payee*.

The instrument shown in Fig. 3 is a bill; that in Fig. 4 is
a note. The drawer of the bill is Horton, the payee is Williams,

---

_____*Ten days*_____*after sight, pay to*

_____*John Williams*_____*or order,*_____*$127.50*

One hundred twenty-seven and 50/100 _____ *Dollars*

*George Horton*

To MORGAN AND COMPANY
24 East Park Street
Kansas City, Kansas

Fig. 3.—EXAMPLE OF A BILL

____ *Six months* ____ *after date,* ____ *I* ____ *promise to pay*

*to the order of*_____ *Delbert T. Stone* _____ *$100.00*

One hundred and no/100 _____ *Dollars*

__ *Chas. Pettit.* __

Fig. 4.—EXAMPLE OF A NOTE

the drawee is Morgan and Company. The maker of the note is
Pettit; the payee of the note is Stone. The payee may be the same
person as the maker, the drawer, or the drawee; the drawee may
be the same person as the drawer. That is, a man may draw a
bill upon himself or payable to himself, or both, if he likes. You
may make a check payable to yourself or to the bank on which
it is drawn (see Fig. 5).

Any instrument, to be negotiable and to be subject to this
branch of the law, must conform to the following requirements:

1. A bill must contain an *order;* a note must contain a *promise.*

2. The order or the promise must be *unconditional.*

3. The order or the promise must be an order or promise to pay money.

4. The amount of money payable must be a specific sum; it must be fixed or readily ascertainable by calculation from information (such as interest) given by the instrument.

5. The instrument must be payable either to bearer or to some specific person or bearer, or to some person or order, or to the order of some named person. If it is payable to merely John

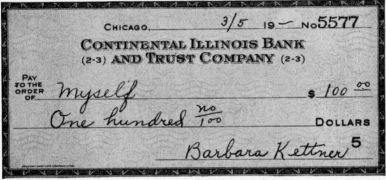

Fig. 5.—EXAMPLE OF A CHECK

Smith, and either the word *order* or *bearer* is not used, the instrument is not negotiable.

6. The parties—drawer, drawee, payee, and maker—must be identifiable.

These are arbitrary requirements, to be sure, but they are for the purpose of enabling one to determine what is and what is not a negotiable instrument; and they must therefore be sharp and definite and rigidly adhered to.[9]

---

[9] It is not necessary, in order that an instrument be negotiable, that it contain the phrase *for valuable consideration,* nor the words *for value received.* Nor is it essential that the instrument be dated. The true date of the instrument may be inserted by any lawful holder; the true date is a matter of fact to be proved upon trial, like any other matter of fact. The fact that the instrument names a date is not conclusive. It should also be noted that certificates of deposit are generally held negotiable in spite of the fact that they do not contain the words *order* or *bearer.*

Rule 246. *The drawee of a bill is not liable until he accepts.* If a drawee of a bill *accepts* the bill by writing his name across the face of it, he becomes liable for the face value of the bill without any further demand upon him for payment. The same result is reached by *certification* of a check by the bank upon which the check is drawn. Without acceptance, a drawee is under no liability at all to the holder of the instrument. If the payee of an uncertified check presents it to the drawee bank, and if the bank refuses to pay the check, the holder has no rights at all against the bank. The holder will be able to recover from the drawer of the check, provided he takes the proper steps (which are discussed subsequently). Or, if one is a holder of a check payable to some other person, and if the check has been properly indorsed, such holder can hold the indorser of the check if he takes proper steps. But in the latter case, again, the holder cannot recover anything from the drawee unless the drawee has accepted or certified the instrument.

Rule 247. *A bearer instrument is transferable by mere delivery.* Whether or not a given instrument is payable to bearer is determined in accordance with any one or more of the following important rules:

1. It must say on its face, *Pay to bearer,* or *Pay to John Smith or bearer;* or

2. The payee must be an inanimate object, such as *cash, petty cash,* or the like; or

3. The payee must not exist and the maker or drawer of the instrument must fairly be presumed to know that fact; for example, *Pay to the order of Julius Caesar,* on a check made today would make the check payable to bearer; or

4. The last indorsement on the instrument must be in blank.[10]

Suppose you own a check payable to bearer for any one or more of the preceding reasons. If you lose it or if it is mailed to your bank and lost before the bank receives it, whoever buys the check in good faith within a reasonable time will get good title to it, even as against you. Of course, the finder (or a thief) will

---

[10] This seems the better view of a conflict between sections 9 and 40 of the N.I.L. Blank indorsement is explained in **Rule 248.**

not get good title, but because of the negotiability, either the thief or the finder can convey a good title. For this reason, if you own a check payable to your order (as most checks are now made), and if you wish to mail it to your bank for deposit, you should not indorse it in blank by merely signing your name on the back of the check. You should indorse it, *Pay to the X Bank* (your bank of deposit), and then sign your name. If you indorse it in that way, no one except your bank can get any title without the indorsement of your bank.

Rule 248. *An order instrument can be transferred by indorsement and delivery and in no other way.* If an instrument is on its face payable to some person or order, it is said to be an order instrument unless indorsed in blank. Such an instrument, payable to order, is not transferable by delivery. It can be transferred only by indorsement (writing) by the payee, and by delivery by him with intent to pass title. Indorsement serves two purposes. It shows that the owner intended to pass the instrument on, and, if it contains more than his name, it shows what he wanted done with the instrument—who was to have it, for example. Indorsement also serves the purpose of binding the indorser to certain contractual obligations to subsequent holders of the paper. What the terms of such contracts are depends upon the kind of indorsement used in a given case.

Blank indorsement is the commonest type. When the owner of an instrument, whether he is the payee or an indorsee of the instrument, writes only his name upon the back of the instrument, this constitutes a blank indorsement. An instrument so indorsed becomes a bearer instrument, and further transfer can be made by delivery without further indorsement, even by a thief or finder, provided, of course, the transferee becomes a holder in due course.[11]

Special indorsement is made by writing on the back of the instrument the transferor's name, following the name of the person to whom he wishes to transfer the paper. Thus, in the case of the instrument shown in Fig. 3, the payee would write on the back, *Pay to the Stockyards Bank, John Williams.* This is called a special indorsement because it names the person to whom the instru-

---

[11] The term *holder in due course* is defined later.

ment is thus made payable. The instrument by this process becomes payable to the order of the person named[12] and is still an order instrument. It can be further transferred by the indorsee only by his indorsement and delivery of the instrument to another purchaser.

Restrictive indorsement is one which in some way shows that the indorser does not intend to bind himself to the usual obligations of one who indorses specially or in blank. For example, if the payee of the instrument in Fig. 3, wished to appoint the Stockyards Bank as his agent to collect the check, but did not want the bank to negotiate the check further, he would use a restrictive indorsement. He might write on the back of the check, *Pay to the Stockyards Bank, for collection, John Williams.* This shows that he does not intend to pass title to the bank, and that he does not assume any obligations to any person who may subsequently take the check. In fact, with a restrictive indorsement on it, an instrument's negotiability comes to an end. An indorsement, *Pay to the X Bank, for deposit,* or simply, *For deposit* will serve the same purpose.

Qualified indorsement is used when the holder of an instrument desires to transfer the title but does not care to assume the liabilities of an ordinary (blank or special) indorsement. If the payee of the check shown in Fig. 3 wished to give the check to the American Red Cross Society, he might not care to undertake an obligation to make the check good if the drawee should, for some reason, refuse to pay the check. In order to escape this obligation (which would rest upon an ordinary indorser in favor of a holder in due course),[13] the payee would indorse the check, *Pay to the American Red Cross Society, without recourse on me, John Williams,* or he might write merely, *Pay to the American Red Cross Society, without recourse, John Williams.* Either indorsement will be qualified. Just how much his obligation is limited by this, is discussed in a following paragraph.

---

[12] *Pay to the order of the Stockyards Bank, John Williams* has the same effect. The words *or order* are not required in a special indorsement, though it does no harm to include them.

[13] A donee in such a case would not be a holder in due course, but the donee might indorse to such a holder.

Conditional indorsement is comparatively rare. It is made in a form similar to the following: *If all work is satisfactory, pay to Henry James, John Williams.* This kind of indorsement limits the liability of the indorser, as well as the passing of title to the indorsee, to the fulfilling of the condition named. Indorsees, of course, are not often willing to take paper so indorsed. It is not negotiable, in fact, because practically no one would give any value to Henry James for this paper since it would be difficult (and sometimes impossible) for a purchaser of the instrument to know whether or not the condition had been performed by the holder or by the payee.

Anomalous or irregular indorsements are quite common. They are made by persons who are not owners of the instruments so indorsed, and therefore do not pass title. Such indorsements are used for the purpose of securing the credit of the owner of the instrument who is passing title, or, sometimes, the credit of the maker or drawer of an instrument. For example, Clay wished to borrow $500 from the Middletown Bank. As collateral security, he wished to deposit a long term note for $1000, payable to Clay. The bank, however, wanted more security. Clay induced Morgan to indorse the note, and Morgan indorsed in blank. It is clear that Morgan did not indorse in order to pass title to the note, since Morgan had no title; he indorsed merely to make greater the probability that the bank would be able to recover the $500 when Clay's debt became due. After this indorsement, the bank could rely upon either the maker of the note, Clay (as indorser), or Morgan (as anomalous indorser). Anomalous indorsers are often called accommodation indorsers, as they assume obligations for accommodation of some party—the borrower, Clay, in this illustration.

Rule 249. *Primary parties are liable without any notice.* The maker of a note is liable unconditionally to pay the note either upon demand or at the date specified in the note. Similarly, a drawee who has accepted is unconditionally liable. These liabilities must exist so that negotiable instruments may be used in place of money. When the due date arrives, the holder of an instrument is not required by law to notify parties who are under this kind of liability, which is called primary liability. Even if an instrument is payable on demand, no actual demand is necessary; the holder may begin suit on such an instrument instantly after he becomes the lawful holder of it. The maker of a note is always under a primary liability, but a drawee is not under any liability at all until he has accepted the bill or draft or check. When the drawee accepts, and thus becomes an acceptor, his liability becomes a primary one and is identical with that of the maker of a note. Neither kind of primary party is entitled to notice when the instrument becomes due. Fig. 6 shows such an instrument.

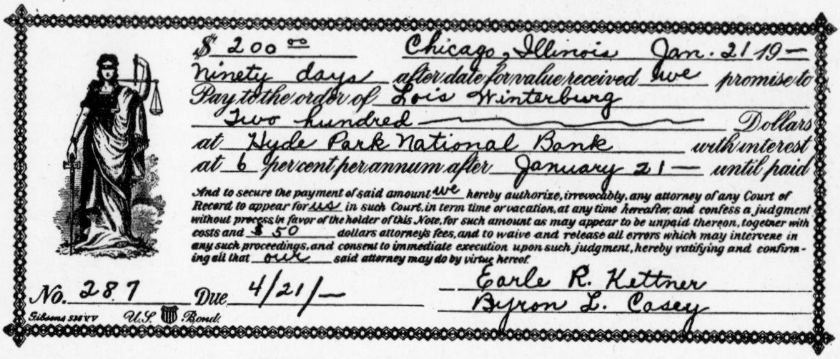

$ 200 00 Chicago, Illinois Jan. 21 19—
Ninety days after date for value received we promise to Pay to the order of Lois Winterburg
Two hundred Dollars
at Hyde Park National Bank with interest
at 6 per cent per annum after January 21— until paid

And to secure the payment of said amount we hereby authorize, irrevocably, any attorney of any Court of Record to appear for us in such Court, in term time or vacation, at any time hereafter, and confess a judgment without process in favor of the holder of this Note, for such amount as may appear to be unpaid thereon, together with costs and $ 50 dollars attorney's fees, and to waive and release all errors which may intervene in any such proceedings, and consent to immediate execution upon such judgment, hereby ratifying and confirming all that our said attorney may do by virtue hereof.

No. 287 Due 4/21/— Earle R. Kettner
Byron L. Casey

Fig. 6.—A Judgment Note[14]

A form similar to this is in common use by banks. The effect of its provisions is that if the note is unpaid at maturity the holder may take a judgment without even notifying the indorsers or the maker. This power is not often used; it is merely an extra precaution. Note that a similar provision applies to the indorsement.

[14] On the reverse side of such a note is found the following indorsement:

FOR VALUE RECEIVED, we, and each and all of the endorsers hereon, jointly and severally guarantee payment of the within note, accepting all its provisions authorizing the maker, without notice to us or either of us, to obtain an extension or extensions in whole or in part and waiving presentment for payment, demand, protest and notice of protest and nonpayment; also agreeing that in case of nonpayment of principal or interest when due, such arrearage may be offset by application of any amount or amounts, whole or in part, which may be due any of us from the holder of such note and suit may be brought by the holder of this note against any one or more or all of us, at the option of said holder, whether such suit has been commenced against the maker or not and that in any such suit, the maker may be joined with one or more or all of us, at the option of the holder.

And I, or we, hereby authorize, irrevocably, any attorney at law to appear for me or us in any court of record in the United States, in term time or vacation, and waive the issue and service of process and confess judgment from time to time against me or us at any time hereafter in favor of the holder hereof, for such amount as may appear to be unpaid or declared due and payable hereon, together with costs and reasonable attorney's fees and to release all errors and waive all right of appeal.

Rule 250. *All indorsers (except qualified or restrictive) incur certain general liabilities.* Every indorser of a negotiable instrument (unless his indorsement is restrictive or qualified) becomes subject to certain obligations imposed upon him by law. First, he guarantees that the instrument is genuine—that it is not a forgery; second, he guarantees that he has a good title to it— the lawful right to indorse and pass title to it; third, he guarantees that he has no knowledge of anything which would impair its validity—that he does not know of any defect in his own rights on the instrument. If any of these defects exist, and if they prevent the collection of the face value of the instrument by subsequent holders, indorsers may be held liable on these warranties, which are really contracts.

Rule 251. *A regular indorser is under an additional obligation.* The most onerous and most frequently used obligation of an indorser of a negotiable instrument is this: If the instrument is presented to the primary party before it is overdue, if the primary party refuses to pay, and if proper notice of the dishonor (failure to pay upon proper presentment) is promptly given to the indorser, then the indorser becomes liable for the face value of the instrument to the lawful holder of the instrument.[15] The obligation of an accommodation or anomalous indorser is precisely the same as that of a regular indorser. Otherwise, there would be no value in his signature.

Rule 252. *Qualified indorsers do not incur the liabilities discussed in the foregoing rule.* The qualified indorser, by indorsing *without recourse,* is considered to state specifically that he does not undertake the liability of a regular indorser. Such an indorser, however, is subject to the liabilities discussed under **Rule 250,**

---

[15] There is a large number of rules concerning waivers of presentment, excuses for lack of presentment, waivers of notice, and excuses for failure to give actual notice of dishonor. These rules are extremely technical and cannot be dealt with in a brief treatment which can give merely an outline of the general principles of law. In general, presentment must be made by exhibiting the instrument and demanding payment or acceptance; notice of dishonor (failure to accept or pay, as the case may be) must be given within twenty-four hours of dishonor; notice may be given orally or in writing, except that if the instrument is a foreign bill—one which was drawn in one state and is payable in another—the notice must be in the form called a protest, which involves the services of a notary public, as a rule.

and one who transfers a bearer instrument by delivery, while he is not liable as a regular indorser, is under the same liabilities as those imposed upon a qualified indorser; but, in the case of one who transfers a bearer instrument by delivery only, his warranties extend only to his immediate transferee, and such a transferor cannot be held on such warranties by any party subsequent to his immediate transferee.[16]

Rule 253. *The drawer's liability is similar to the liability of a regular indorser.* If the drawee of a check or bill does not, upon proper demand, either accept or pay the instrument, and if the drawer is promptly notified of this dishonor, then the drawer may be held liable to the lawful holder for the face value of the instrument.[17] From this, it should be clear that one who issues a check does not, by so doing, pay the debt for which the check is issued. If the check is not honored by the drawee, the drawer can be held upon the original debt, or upon the check, as the holder desires, provided only that the holder complied with the rules of law concerning presentment and notice of dishonor.

Rule 254. *To be a holder in due course, one who takes an instrument must comply with certain requirements.* A holder in due course must (a) be a transferee by negotiation from a former holder, (b) give value for the instrument, (c) buy it before the instrument becomes overdue, (d) have no actual knowledge nor legal notice of any invalidity in the instrument or in the claims of the transferor.[18] The rights of a holder in due course are merely the other side of the obligations of indorsers, makers, acceptors, or drawers, as the case may be. The ensuing illustrations should make clear the general principles involved.

Goode was the owner of a note payable to his order on June 25, 1941. He indorsed the note specially to Wilkes, his nephew, and delivered it to him as a gift. If Goode could have

---

[16] A conditional indorser, of course, may stipulate the precise conditions under which he will be held liable. A restrictive indorser does not incur any liability at all; he does not pass title, but merely appoints an agent to collect the instrument for him.

[17] See footnote 15 under **Rule 251.** The same kinds of rules are in effect in relation to the liability of the drawer.

[18] What constitutes legal notice of such defects is highly technical.

enforced the note against the maker, then Wilkes could do so, since a man may give away (in most circumstances) the rights which he has. But Wilkes is not a holder in due course because he gave no value for the note, and if Goode could not have enforced the note, then Wilkes could not enforce it. No one can enforce an instrument against the primary parties except a holder in due course or someone who acquires his rights through a holder in due course or through some transferor who could have enforced the instrument. Now, remembering that Wilkes was not a holder in due course, suppose that on June 10, 1941, he sold the note for value to Clay, who had no notice of any defect in the rights of Goode or of Wilkes, if there were any such defects. Clay bought the note for value, in good faith, and before its maturity date, and thus became a holder in due course. He could enforce the note against the maker whether or not Goode could have done so, or he could hold either Goode or Wilkes on the note as indorser.

Suppose that Clay did not enforce the note, but that he gave the note to his son, Clay, Jr., after maturity. Clay, Jr., would not be a holder in due course, but he has the rights of such a holder, because he acquired his rights from a holder in due course. Clay, Jr., could hold any prior party on the note.[19] One may acquire the rights of a holder in due course, then, either by complying strictly with the requirements set out under this rule, or by acquiring the instrument from a holder who had the rights of a holder in due course.[20]

Rule 255. *Sometimes, not even a holder in due course can enforce an instrument.* If an instrument were originally forged, if any necessary indorsement were forged, if the instrument were made, accepted, or drawn by an infant, if the instrument were

---

[19] Even if Clay, Jr., knew, when he took the note, that Goode could not enforce the note against the maker, Clay, Jr. would still be able to do so, since he took the position of the previous holder, and the previous holder was a holder in due course.

[20] It must always be borne in mind that no one can take title to an instrument through a forgery. If the instrument is forged in the first place (if the signature of the drawer or maker is not valid), the instrument is a nullity; and if there is a forged indorsement in an order instrument, in general, no holder subsequent to the forgery can have any title nor any rights against any party prior to the forgery.

issued or accepted as a part of an unlawful transaction, or if the
party who issued or accepted it were induced to do so by fraud
as to the nature of the transaction,[21] no holder, whether in due
course or otherwise, could acquire rights against the primary or
original party to the instrument. Such circumstances are said to
be real defenses; they are defenses of primary parties (or a drawer)
against all persons, even against a holder in due course.

Rule 256. *Personal defenses are not good against a holder
in due course.* If an instrument were originally acquired by fraud
in the inducement[22] or without consideration, or if the maker has
a claim which he could set off against a suit by the payee, the
maker would have personal defenses, which can be used only
against some person with notice of the particular defect and cannot
be used against a holder in due course.

Rule 257. *Personal defenses do not operate in favor of indorsers.* Indorsers make certain warranties and undertake to pay
under certain conditions which have already been stated. Even if
an instrument has been forged or made by an infant or issued for
no consideration or under any other similar condition, an indorser
who indorses after the fraud, forgery, or other defect, is liable to
the holder upon the contract of warranty.[23]

Rule 258. *A holder may elect to sue any one of several
personally liable on the instrument.* When several parties are each
liable to the holder upon the same instrument, the holder may
select any one of them from whom to collect. He is not obliged
to sue them in any particular order. Gray was the holder of a
note made by Moore and indorsed by Carter, Clay, Mills, Darr,
Hill, and Burgess, in that order. Gray might choose to sue Moore,
and if he should do so, all of the indorsers would be discharged
because no party can hold liable as a transferor of the paper any
party who signed after the person who was sued signed it. Gray
might sue Mills, in which case Darr, Hill, and Burgess would be
discharged for the same reason. If Mills were compelled to pay,
he could sue any party prior to himself, provided he had the right

---

[21] See **Rule 59.**
[22] See **Rule 60.**
[23] This is the result of **Rule 250.**

of a holder in due course the first time he held the instrument. Otherwise, Mills could hold no one.

These illustrations are intended chiefly to emphasize the fact that an indorser does not end his connection with an instrument merely by passing it on. It may come back to him as a liability at some later time. It must also be remembered that the holder has the rights which have been specified only if he meets the conditions of proper presentment and notice of dishonor.

Rule 259. *Certification of a check may discharge the drawer.* When a check is certified by the drawee bank at the request of

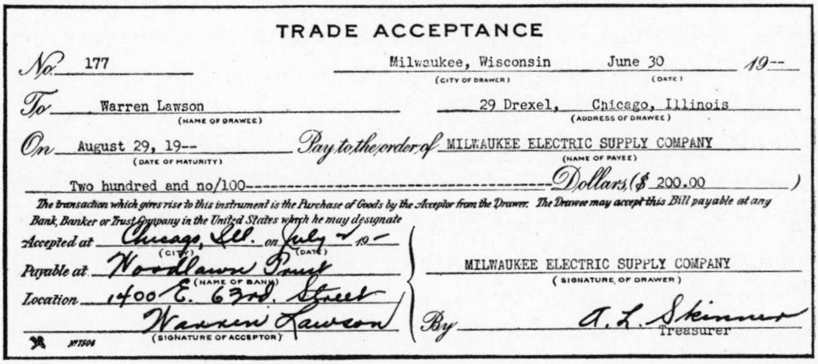

TRADE ACCEPTANCE

No. 177 Milwaukee, Wisconsin (CITY OF DRAWER) June 30 (DATE) 19--

To Warren Lawson (NAME OF DRAWEE) 29 Drexel, Chicago, Illinois (ADDRESS OF DRAWEE)

On August 29, 19-- (DATE OF MATURITY) Pay to the order of MILWAUKEE ELECTRIC SUPPLY COMPANY (NAME OF PAYEE)

Two hundred and no/100 Dollars ($ 200.00)

The transaction which gives rise to this instrument is the Purchase of Goods by the Acceptor from the Drawer. The Drawee may accept this Bill payable at any Bank, Banker or Trust Company in the United States which he may designate

Accepted at Chicago, Ill. (CITY) on July 1 (DATE) 19--

Payable at Woodlawn Trust (NAME OF BANK)

Location 1400 E. 63rd. Street

Warren Lawson (SIGNATURE OF ACCEPTOR)

MILWAUKEE ELECTRIC SUPPLY COMPANY (SIGNATURE OF DRAWER)

By A. L. Skinner Treasurer

Fig. 7.—Trade Acceptance

This is a bill drawn by the seller of goods upon the buyer, so that he may discount the buyer's credit. The seller can borrow money on his book accounts if they are in this form. Of course, to do so, the seller (payee) must indorse, and he then may be made liable if the acceptor (buyer) does not pay the bill. An important feature of the use of the trade acceptance is that if it is in the hands of a bona fide purchaser before maturity of the instrument, the drawer-acceptor is liable upon it even if the goods are not satisfactory or even if they are not delivered.

the holder, the certification discharges the drawer of the check as well as all indorsers who have indorsed before the certification. This is not true of a bill of exchange or trade acceptance (see Fig. 7).

Rule 260. *Material alteration of an instrument renders the instrument void as to the parties to the alteration.* If the amount of an instrument is raised without the consent of parties liable on it before the change, the instrument becomes wholly void, as far as it concerns any party to the alteration. For example, if Hill were the payee of a note for $100 made by Jones, and if Hill raised the amount to $1000, he could not recover anything at all from Jones. If Hill should sell the note to Knox, a holder in due course, Knox could recover from Jones only the original face value of the note. As to the remainder, Knox or any subsequent holder could rely only upon the warranty of Hill or any later indorser. Material alterations having this effect include any changes which alter the apparent liability of any party to the instrument, such as changes in the due date, amount, rate of interest, place or manner of payment, and the like.

SUMMARY

It is possible, in a general textbook, to point out only a few of the more important principles of this branch of the law, which is highly specialized and very technical. The law of negotiable instruments grants to holders of negotiable instruments certain rights and privileges not enjoyed by purchasers of other kinds of property. These privileges and rights can be enjoyed, however, only if the following technical requirements of the law are strictly complied with:

1. The instrument must be strictly in accord with technical specifications.

2. Only holders in due course (or those who take from such holders) enjoy these rights and privileges.

3. The liabilities of those who make, draw, accept, or indorse such instruments are determined by specific rules.

4. The rights of a holder and the liabilities of parties come into effect only if the holder follows the proper procedures.

Unless all of the rules of the law of negotiable instruments are strictly complied with, the ordinary rules of property law will apply to all transfers and to the rights and liabilities of all parties to such instruments.

QUESTIONS AND PROBLEMS

1. In the first case referred to in the discussion under **Rule 243,** why was it that the seller of the car could not have recovered on the note? Since that is true, why is it that the seller still could not have recovered on the note if the note had been negotiable? Under the latter circumstances, why is it that one to whom the negotiable

instrument was properly transferred could have collected on the note, whether the warranty was performed or not?

2. Under **Rule 243,** it is said that the law of negotiable instruments is directly opposed to the law of assignment of contracts. Explain what this means as a practical matter.

3. Give at least two good reasons why the use of negotiable instruments is convenient. **Rule 244.**

4. Define in simple language the following terms: *payee, drawee, drawer, maker,* and *acceptor.*

5. Copy on paper and learn the six requirements which must be met by an instrument in order that its negotiation and the parties handling it shall be subject to the law of negotiable instruments. **Rule 245.** Be sure to read footnote 9.

6. In Fig. 3, page 206, who is the acceptor? Who is the payee? Who is the drawer? Who is the drawee?

7. Read the language of the judgment note in Fig. 6 very carefully. What is the most significant thing about the instrument, in your opinion? That is, how does it differ most from an ordinary promissory note?

8. What is the liability of Morgan and Co. on the bill in Fig. 3, page 206? Explain your answer.

9. Write down the four statements found under **Rule 247,** which indicate different ways in which an instrument may be payable to bearer. What is the important difference between the uses to which one can put a bearer instrument and the uses to which one can put an order instrument, provided both instruments are negotiable and provided that they are both in the hands of a person who is not the owner of either one?

10. What is the commonest type of indorsement used in the transfer of negotiable instruments? What are the legal liabilities incurred by a negotiator of a negotiable instrument if he uses this kind of indorsement? **Rule 248.**

11. What is an anomalous indorser? Why should anyone ever make an anomalous indorsement, since he does not receive any consideration for his signature? How does his liability differ, if at all, from that of a regular indorser (either blank or special)? **Rule 248.**

12. What is the meaning of the term *primary liability?* Give an illustration of a party to an instrument whose liability is primary. When, if ever, is a primary party liable for the face of the instrument, without notice of dishonor, if the instrument is in the hands of a lawful holder in due course? Is the liability of the following primary or secondary: drawee; drawer; payee who has not indorsed? **Rule 249.**

13. Write out the general liabilities imposed by law upon all indorsers except certain designated classes. Also, name in writing the two kinds of indorsers excepted from these liabilities. **Rule 250.**

14. Write out and commit to memory the following statement concerning the liability of an ordinary indorser: If the indorsed instrument is properly presented by the lawful holder to the party primarily liable before the instrument is overdue, and the primary party refuses to pay, and if proper notice of this dishonor (refusal to pay) is promptly given to the indorser by the holder, then the holder can recover the face value of the instrument from the indorser.

15. Why is it that a qualified indorser is not subject to the liability indicated in question 14? What is a qualified indorser? Is such an indorser under any legal liabilities at all to a subsequent lawful holder of the instrument? **Rules 250** and **252.**

16. In the absence of a statement to that effect, does the acceptance of a check by a creditor from the debtor constitute payment of the original debt? If there is a stipulation to the effect that such an act does cancel the original debt, can the drawer be held liable upon the check if the drawee bank refuses to pay it? If so, under what circumstances can this liability be enforced? See **Rules 251** and **253.**

17. Jones was the holder of a negotiable draft payable to the order of himself and drawn by Wilson on the Charter Bank. The draft was payable July 3, 1943. Jones had obtained the draft from Wilson by fraud. (a) Could Jones recover on the draft from Wilson if the bank refused to pay the draft when properly presented on July 3, 1943, and if Wilson had been properly notified of the dishonor? (b) Suppose that on June 25 Jones indorsed the draft in blank to Helm. If Helm presented the draft to the bank on July 3, and payment were refused, what would Helm be required to prove before he would be able to recover from the bank? (c) What would Helm be required to prove to enable him to recover from the indorser? **Rules 254** and **256.**

18. In the last paragraph under **Rule 254,** why was Clay, Jr. not a holder in due course? This being true, why is it that he could still recover on the instrument in question?

19. Write a list of the so-called *real defenses.* What does that mean? Write a list of the personal defenses. What does *personal defense* mean in the law of negotiable instruments? **Rules 255, 256.**

20. Is there any order in which a holder of a negotiable instrument must proceed against indorsers or other parties to the instrument? Is there any order in which he cannot proceed at all? You may need to read **Rule 258** and the discussion of it carefully to find the answer to these questions.

New York State Capitol, Albany
Underwood & Underwood

North Carolina State Capitol, Raleigh
Underwood & Underwood

North Dakota State Capitol, Bismarck
Acme Newspictures, Inc.

Ohio State Capitol, Columbus
Underwood & Underwood

CHAPTER IX

REAL PROPERTY LAW

Rule 261. *In the legal sense, real estate includes more than mere soil.* The term *real estate* or *land,* in the legal sense, includes not only the actual soil and the waters of the earth within the several national territorial jurisdictions, but also such things as buildings, fences, pumps, boilers, windmills, walls, sidewalks, and many other things which are so much a part of the premises to which they are attached that to remove them would bring about an essential change in the character of the property. The term *real estate,* which is synonymous with *real property,* further includes growing things which have their roots in the soil. A stand of timber, for example, is legally part of the land upon which the trees grow. The same is true of minerals and oils in natural deposits.

Still further, real property includes a certain amount of space above the soil. Some hundreds of years ago, it was said that the owner of real property was the owner of all space or deposits downward to the center of the earth and upward to the sky. Since scientists have taught us that there is no tangible sky, and no physical mark by which one could determine when he might reach the sky, the modern interpretation of this old statement would be that a man owns the space above his land upward to infinity. A little over a hundred years ago, this was interpreted to mean that if a balloonist passed over one's land without the owner's assent, the balloonist was a trespasser. Under modern conditions, with the common use of airplanes, it is clear that it is quite impractical to accord an owner of land such extensive rights, thereby giving him the legal right to exclude the passage of planes above his land at a height of three or four miles. Such a passage does not interfere in any sense with the full use of one's land. On the other hand, it is not practicable to make interference with use the sole test of the right of an owner of land to exclude others from the space above the land. For instance, a telephone company, without touching Bacon's land at all, strung a wire across his lot at a height of forty feet. The land was used for farming, and the presence of the wire did not in the least interfere with the use of the land; but, in an action of ejectment to compel the removal of the wire, a court held that the stringing of the wire was a trespass and that the wire must be removed.

For these reasons, and because of other difficult technical considerations, it is impossible to define accurately the term *real estate* or *real property*. The most one can say about it, in general, is that an owner can legally use the space above his land as far as he likes; that no person may, without the owner's consent, erect a permanent or temporary structure above the land of another; and that no person may lawfully project missiles, as by shooting arrows or throwing objects, across the land of another. On the other hand, an owner may not, as a rule, interfere with the passage of airplanes above his land, provided the planes pass at reasonable elevation, and provided they do not actually injure structures which an owner of land has erected.[1] Furthermore, the law defining the extent of an owner's right downward from the surface of his soil has still to be worked out. Under the common law, an owner of land may dig down into the ground as far as he likes, and he may remove and use or sell any natural deposits he finds there. But this right, also, is in the process of modification by laws which regulate the extraction of oil, ores, gas, and, in some cases, water.

Rule 262. *There are different degrees of ownership of land.* One's legal interest in a given plot of land may vary from complete ownership to a mere temporary right of occupancy. The various legal interests in land are known as estates. Those of most practical importance are called ownership in fee simple, life estates, estates for years, estates from year to year, and vested remainders.[2]

---

[1] The matter is affected, too, by city ordinances and state laws which regulate the heights above ground at which flights of planes may be lawfully made.

[2] Estates in tail are very seldom encountered anywhere in this country. In all but one or two states, such estates have been abolished by law.

Fee simple, or estate in fee as it is often called, is the interest in land which is ordinarily known as complete ownership. It is ownership free from any limitations or restrictions as to particular heirs. It is the kind of ownership conveyed by the language used in the old common law deeds, for example, *to John Smith and his heirs forever.* In most states, this language is no longer necessary to convey a fee simple because statutes have provided that unless otherwise indicated, it is to be assumed that a conveyance passes such an estate. Not uncommon are qualified or determinable fees. For example, Massey granted to a certain society a tract of land in fee, subject to the condition that should the society ever be disbanded or should its purposes become other than religious, the fee should revert to the heirs of Massey. The society holds a fee under this grant, but it is a qualified one. (Of course, life estate, estates for years, and remainders may also be qualified.)

Life estate is created when land is conveyed to some person to hold until the occurrence of some stipulated event. This kind of estate gets its name from the fact that, at first, by far the most common event stipulated as a mark of the end of the estate was the death of the person to whom the land was conveyed. Thus, Herbert conveyed land to Fitzhugh for the life of the latter. Sometimes, the conveyance is made to a person for as long a period as another person shall live. For example, a father might leave land to his son for the life of the father's wife. The son would have a life estate. A third kind of life estate is for the duration of something other than the life of a person. Knox may convey land to a certain society for the life of a horse. The society would have a life estate. The most common kind of life estate probably is that known as a widow's dower. When a married man dies, leaving land in his own name, his widow has a life estate in one-third of all such land. This right is known as dower. In many states, a husband has a similar right in the land of his wife.[3] The owner of a life estate, of course, can sell or lease his right, but his lease or conveyance cannot

---

[3] It is necessary to emphasize that dower is a life estate for the life of the widow. When she dies, the land subject to dower goes to the heirs of the husband's estate. In a few states, dower gives a fee simple title. Local authorities must be consulted as to this.

possibly give the grantee or lessee any rights whatever beyond the duration of the life estate. A life tenant cannot grant oil rights or mineral rights unless he himself has such rights (which, ordinarily, he does not have). In fact, it is very seldom that anyone will pay anything for a lease of property which is held under a life tenancy.

Estates for years and estates from year to year. An estate for years is the interest held by a tenant for any definite period of time agreed upon by lessor and lessee. Even if the period is less than a calendar year, the tenant's interest is called an estate for years, just as long as its termination date is set when the tenancy is granted. It is the sort of interest which one holds under a lease for any definite period of time. An estate for years comes to an end automatically and without notice at the end of the stated time.[4] An estate from year to year is characterized by the fact that a tenant of such an estate has an interest which cannot be lawfully terminated by either party (without the other's consent) until the end of some number of full years from the beginning of the tenancy. Thus, if on March 1, 1941, Ingersoll became a tenant from year to year, this relationship could be ended by either Ingersoll or his landlord, only on the last day of February, 1942, or some other year. If the matter is allowed to pass until March 1 of any year, then it cannot be terminated by either without the consent of the other until the last day of February in the next year. This kind of tenancy is important because, in many states, if a tenant for years remains in possession of the land after the end of his term and without the consent of the landlord, the tenancy then becomes a tenancy from year to year (unless, of course, a new agreement created a new estate for years).[5] In some states, statutes provide that if a tenancy from year to year is to be terminated at the end of a given year by either party, such party must give at least sixty days' (or some such period's) notice to the other party.[6]

---

[4] Several states have modified this last rule. See **Rule 296.**

[5] Tenancy from month to month is like a tenancy from year to year, differing only by the length of the period. See **Rule 296.**

[6] The words *tenancy* and *tenant* may be somewhat confusing to some students because the term tenant is often used to refer to lodgers or boarders who are not tenants at all in the true legal sense. Their rights and obligations are based upon contract law as modified by local statutes and ordinances, and not upon real property law.

Remainders. While this term is technically hedged about with difficulties, it has certain aspects which can be rather easily understood for practical purposes. A remainder is defined as *an estate which is limited to commence after the termination of a particular estate previously limited by the same deed or instrument out of the same subject matter.* If the word *created* is substituted for the word *limited,* the meaning is somewhat clearer. As an illustration, suppose that Jones conveys all of his rights, title, and interest in his farm to his wife Anna for her life, and upon her death, to her sister Gertrude Wales and the latter's heirs and assigns forever. The estate of Gertrude is not to begin until the termination of a previous estate (Anna's) which has been created by the same instrument from the same property. Gertrude's estate is a remainder. The holder of such an estate is called a remainderman. The use of the term remainder always implies that some other estate in the same property precedes or has preceded the remainderman's rights, and a remainder must take effect immediately upon the termination of the preceding estate. There may be remainders after remainders, as in a conveyance to Mary for her life, then to Jean for her life, and then in fee to Albert. A remainder may follow a life estate or an estate of years, but no remainder can follow an estate in fee because, upon the conveyance of a fee, nothing remains.[7]

Rule 263. *There are two classes of remainders.* If a remainder is to come into effect upon the occurrence of an event which is certain to take place, and if the owner of the remainder is in being and designated so that the remainder cannot possibly terminate before the preceding estate terminates, the remainder is said to be a *vested* remainder. But if it is possible for the remainder to terminate before it comes into effect, then the remainder is said to be a *contingent* one. Suppose that Welch made a conveyance to Ella, his wife, for her life, with a remainder to John, his son, for his life, and a second remainder to Hannah, his daughter, in fee. Now the

---

[7] Sometimes reversion is confused with remainder. A reversion is an estate which comes back (reverts) to the grantor or to his heirs upon the termination of some estate previously created in the same instrument. For instance, King conveyed land to Bates for life, then to Hill for life, and then in fee back to King and his heirs. This means that Bates has a life estate, Hill has a remainder for life, and King has a reversion in fee.

estate of Ella will terminate when she dies. Ella's death is an event
which is certain to take place; it must occur before the estate of
Hannah takes effect. Also, John is certain to die, and his death,
too, must occur before Hannah's estate takes effect. But Hannah's
estate cannot terminate before John's death nor before Ella's because Hannah's estate in fee will run on forever in someone. Hannah, therefore, has a vested remainder. The practical significance
of vested remainders is that, once created, they cannot be destroyed
without the consent of the owners or the heirs of the owners.

In the same example, John's estate is contingent because John
must be alive upon the death of Ella in order to take the life estate
given him. John's estate may therefore terminate before the preceding one does. If John dies before Ella dies, then the fee goes at
once to Hannah upon the death of Ella; and if both Ella and John
die before Welch, then upon Welch's death, the fee goes at once
to Hannah or to her heirs if Hannah is not living at that time.
This example is given here for the sole purpose of indicating the
complex character of such estates. To attempt the creation of any
such estates without the advice of competent counsel is to invite
disaster and to bequeath trouble.

Rule 264. *The creation of estates is subject to the rule against
perpetuities.* Here is another warning signal to the layman. The
creation of contingent remainder is very considerably limited by the
so-called rule against perpetuities. This rule is regarded by some
authorities as the most complex and difficult to understand of all
the rules of property. Here is an example of its working. Hawkes
conveyed a plot of ground to the Battle Creek Church on condition
that the minister of the church reside in a certain house, and upon
the further condition that, should this house not be occupied by
the minister of the church, then the said land should descend to
John Hancock and his heirs. This may seem to the layman to be a
simple and straightforward matter, but the conveyance to Hancock
is wholly void because it violates the rule against perpetuities. The
estate cannot vest in Hancock or his heirs until the occurrence of
the event named—the failure of the minister to occupy the house—
and that might not take place until a very long time after the making of the conveyance. Now, in general, the rule against perpetui-

ties provides that no estate is valid unless it must come into possession of the grantee, either within the life of some person who is alive when the grant is made, or within twenty-one years after the death of some person who is alive at the time of the grant. The grant referred to in the foregoing example does not meet these requirements since it might be a hundred years or more before the minister of the church no longer lived in the designated house. The contingent remainder being void, the title of the Battle Creek Church is a title in fee. This is only one aspect of this rule. Such grants are always likely to encounter difficulties.[8]

Rule 265. *Vested remainders may be conveyed.* Since vested remainders are property, they may be conveyed, or attached by creditors, or, sometimes, devised by will. If Jones grants land to Link for life, and then to Sims in fee, Sims has a vested interest. Sims may mortgage his interest, or he may devise it by will, or he may sell it, or it may be attached by his creditors. But the interest of Link may never come into existence in fact at all. If Link should die before Jones does, Link's heir would have no right at all to the property. A contingent interest cannot be attached nor sold nor devised by will.

Rule 266. *The same property may be owned by more than one owner.* Some particular estate in land is frequently owned by more than one person at the same time. Co-owners may be brother and sister, husband and wife, partners, or any other persons. There are several types of co-ownership with different legal effects, but for practical purposes it is necessary to discuss only two of them, tenancy in common and joint tenancy.[9]

Tenancy in common. When two or more persons are entitled to the same land in such a manner that each has an undivided interest in the whole and that each may convey his interest, but no

---

[8] A number of books and many articles have been written about the various aspects of the rule against perpetuities. Since the authors of these discussions do not always agree as to what the rule means and what its effects are, it should be clear that no one should be trusted with such matters but an expert of the very highest qualifications, who is not unlikely to advise against attempts to create some kinds of contingent interests. The ordinary lawyer in general practice, as a rule knows little or nothing of this branch of the law.

[9] Remember that these are technical terms and that they do not mean the same thing at all.

one of them is entitled to exclusive possession of any particular part
of the land, such persons are said to hold the land by tenancy in
common. Such a tenancy may be created in real or personal property. It may be created by deed, by bill of sale, by will, or by
descent under administration. While any tenant in common can
give good title to his own share, he cannot convey the share of any
other tenant in common. No tenant may act for the other tenants
in common without specific consent. Whenever two persons are
made co-owners of the same property, it is generally assumed that
they are tenants in common; and if one of two or more tenants in
common dies, his share passes to his heirs or in accordance with
his will, just as any other property does. All this is what one might
expect to be true of co-ownership, but much of it is not true of
joint tenancy.

Joint tenancy. In an estate of joint tenancy, the several tenants hold the property in equal shares, but if one joint tenant dies,
the surviving joint tenants take the whole of the title. This is in
sharp contrast to tenancy in common. Suppose, for example, that
A, B, and C were tenants in common of a plot of ground. Upon
C's death, one of his heirs will become entitled to his share. The
tenants in common would then be A, B, and the heir of C. But if
A, B, and C were joint tenants, upon C's death A and B are the
remaining joint tenants, and C's heirs are entitled to nothing. Then,
upon the death of B, A would become the sole owner of the land,
leaving B's heirs nothing. Joint tenancy by husband and wife is
an excellent device for avoiding delays and expenses due to administration of estate, for, if the husband dies, the wife as joint tenant
automatically becomes sole owner, and no record is needed beyond
the record of the husband's death. No will is necessary and no
period of probation or administration is necessary.[10]

Another aspect of joint tenancy is that if A and B are joint
tenants, but are not husband and wife, then the spouses of A and B
are entitled to no dower rights in the property. In most of our
states, in order to create a joint tenancy, very precise language must

------

[10] Of course, where an estate is very large, it must be remembered that
joint tenancy cannot, in most states, be used as a means of evading the inheritance tax laws.

be used so that there can be no doubt as to what is meant. In some states, the statutes prescribe the very language which must be used in order to create such a tenancy. In Illinois, for example, the statute provides that such a tenancy may be created only by the use of the words *as joint tenants and not as tenants in common,* following the names of the grantees. Under such a statute, the use of the mere words *joint tenants* would create a tenancy in common. A joint bank account should be made in the name of *A or B or the survivor* in order to avoid the processes of administration upon the death of either. From such an account, either owner may withdraw funds without the consent of the other. Under joint ownership of land, however, no conveyance of the land will be valid without the signature of all joint tenants then living (or their authorized agents).[11]

Rule 267. *Ownership of real estate includes easements.* An easement is defined as a privilege, which the owner or lessee of one plot of land has, to make use of another plot of land without profit. The land to which the privilege belongs is called the dominant piece, and the land over which the privilege is held is called the servient piece. Every true easement must meet the following qualifications:

1. Every easement must be incorporeal.

2. Every easement must be imposed on corporeal property.

3. No easement confers a right to profits.

4. Every easement must be imposed for the benefit of corporeal property.[12]

Here are some examples interpreting these requirements. Carey leased his pond to an ice company for securing ice. He also granted them a privilege of hauling ice over other land between the pond and the highway. The latter grant was an easement. The pond was the dominant piece, and the land where the hauling was

---

[11] Tenancy in partnership resembles joint tenancy more nearly than it resembles tenancy in common since neither partner may convey the firm's property without the express or implied consent of the other partners, except in the ordinary course of the firm's business.

[12] Because of failure to meet the fourth requirement, licenses fail to constitute true easements, though many licenses are erroneously called easements. Licenses are discussed subsequently.

done was the servient piece. The privilege was incorporeal in that the ice company had merely a privilege of passage and could not build any structures there nor prevent the use of the land by others. The privilege was imposed upon corporeal property—the land where the hauling took place. The easement was for the benefit of corporeal property—the ice on the lake, and did not give the ice company the privilege of taking profits from the land where the hauling was done.[13] In another case, Horn sold a lot to Palmer, granting him the right to draw water from a well on land still owned by Horn. This right also was an easement.[14]

Rule 268. *Easements may be in gross or appurtenant to land.* An easement in gross is a privilege which belongs to a person, but which is not for the benefit of corporeal property. This is a definition of an easement which is not a true easement because it does not conform to the fourth requirement indicated under **Rule 267.** Some authorities go as far as to say that, because of the failure of such a privilege to comply with the fourth requirement, an easement in gross is not an easement at all. Logically, these authorities are correct, but the courts have recognized such privileges and have called them easements in gross. For example, Willis agreed to build a fence around a race track in exchange for the exclusive privilege of posting advertising matter upon the fence. Now, this privilege was a personal one which belonged to Willis. It was not connected with any land which Willis owned and, therefore, did not attach to any dominant piece of land. This easement is an unusual kind, which is called by a court an easement in gross, meaning precisely that it is personal. Easements in gross are looked upon with disfavor by the courts in some states, and, in practically all states, they are not transferable and cannot pass by will or by inheritance. An easement that is appurtenant, however, does conform strictly to the requirements listed above. In the case, for example, in which Horn granted Palmer the right to draw water from the well, the easement was appurtenant to the lot bought by

---

[13] Profit, in this sense, does not mean mere gain or advantage; it means something taken from the land such as crops and the like.

[14] Some privileges which are not easements will be given in connection with the discussion of licenses.

Palmer. Should he sell the lot to Smith, the easement would be transferable with the lot, and Horn could not prevent such a transfer. Thus, when an easement is appurtenant to land, it is said to run with the land, meaning that it runs with both the servient and the dominant pieces. On the other hand, Palmer could not sell the water privilege to Smith unless he sold Smith the lot also or an interest of some kind in the lot; and if Horn should sell the servient piece to Walsh, it would still be subject to the easement.

Rule 269. *Easements are usually created by a specific grant.* When an easement is created by a grant, the grant should be in writing and conform to other requirements of valid deeds of conveyance because otherwise it may not be good against subsequent purchasers of the servient piece. Easements are not good against the purchasers of the servient piece if such purchasers buy without notice of the existence of the easements. Thus, if Hicks granted an easement over his land to Brown, a neighbor, and if such grant were by deed, the easement would not be valid in favor of Brown against Jackson, a purchaser of land from Hicks, unless Jackson knew of the easements, or unless the deed granting the easement were properly recorded in the county where the servient piece lay. (See **Rule 293.**)

Rule 270. *Some easements arise by implication.* Suppose that Hicks had sold to Brown a lot which did not border upon any public way and that Hicks had neglected to grant an easement of access. Brown would have a right of access by necessary implication, and from the lay of the land. A subsequent purchaser of the servient piece from Hicks would be held subject to the easement by implication. Such an easement is, of necessity, appurtenant to both pieces, and Brown's conveyance of his dominant piece would carry the easement along whether or not his conveyance mentioned it. (See **Rule 272**, last case.)

Rule 271. *Easements sometimes arise by prescription.* The technical requirements of easement by prescription are very seldom complied with and are very widely misunderstood. In order to establish an easement over another's land, one must not only use this land openly for twenty years (in most states), but he must also use the land under an asserted claim of a right to use it. Thus, if

Johnson cuts across Gorman's lot every morning for twenty-five years on his way to the nearest suburban station, Johnson could never acquire an easement unless he had claimed a legal right to cross there and unless he had claimed the right for twenty years or more. Even if Johnson had the express permission of Gorman to cross the ground, no easement could arise because there would be no open claim of legal right to do so since Johnson would have a mere license which is revocable at will by the licensor.

Rule 272. *Easements may be extinguished in several ways.* The dominant owner may execute a specific release of the easement. A release may be either written, oral, or implied from conduct such as long continued failure to use the easement. In one case, Wade was owner of an easement to take water from a spring. He gave oral assent to the owner of the spring to board it up and put a lock on the boarding. This was held to be a valid termination of the easement. Most important is the termination of easements by so-called merger of the dominant and servient estates. For example, Baker owned a lot, appurtenant to which was a strip of land, on which he had an easement, leading to the beach of a lake. Baker bought the strip leading to the lake. When Baker later sold the original lot to McCay, but did not grant an easement, it was held that McCay did not acquire an easement. The easement was ended when the dominant and servient pieces came into the ownership of the same man, Baker. Another case shows termination of an easement by the cessation of the purpose for which it was created. Jones bought from Knight a strip of land across the back of Knight's lot. Since there was no other access to a street, Jones was entitled to an easement of necessity across Knight's lot to the street; but when a new street was opened up, abutting on the strip which Jones owned, his easement over Knight's land was terminated because the necessity no longer existed. (See **Rule 270.**)

Rule 273. *A license is less formal than an easement.* For practical purposes, a license is an express or implied permission to use or occupy land. Curry was the owner of a piece of land on the shore of Lake Michigan. He permitted several neighboring residents to cross his land and to use the beach which he owned. These persons were licensees, but they were not holders of easements. The difference is very important. For one thing, a license can be terminated at any time. If the license has been granted in return for some kind of payment, its revocation may be a breach of contract; but if it is revoked, the former licensee cannot enter upon the land without being a trespasser. He will have to resort to an action for breach of contract to get any satisfaction. Also, the holder of a license cannot transfer it to anyone else. If one of Curry's neighbors should sell his lot, he could not transfer his license with it. A license is personal and does not run with the land. Also, the holder of a license cannot share it with other persons without the consent of the owner of the land subject to the license. Again, a license may be given by an owner to anyone whether or not such licensee owns any property. Still further, a license can be granted only by one who has full control of the estate over which the license is granted. A joint tenant or a tenant in common cannot grant a valid license without the consent of his cotenant.

Rule 274. *Licenses may arise by implication.* The driver of a milk wagon walks through Gunther's back yard each morning to deliver milk to a neighbor. Since Gunther does not object to it, the driver probably is a licensee by implication, but he cannot become the holder of an easement no matter how long he is permitted to take this short cut. A storekeeper licenses prospective customers and salesmen; the management of a business licenses persons in search of employment; one who sells at auction, on a farm, for example, licenses prospective bidders to cross his land to attend the sale; all of these licenses, together with many similar ones, exist by implication. Any of these licenses may be modified or revoked at any time by the owner of the land. If any licensee, either by expression or implication, uses the land for any purpose other than that for which the license exists, he becomes a trespasser *ab initio* (from the beginning), that is, his license becomes void and he may be treated as though he had been a trespasser from the first entry. The licensor, on his part, owes to the licensee a duty to warn him of hidden dangers such as vicious dogs and dangerous pits. Some duty of this kind is owed even to peddlers and solicitors of various kinds, though probably there is no such duty to beggars or tramps.

Rule 275. *Mutual rights of adjacent owners should be established by execution of cross-easements.* In order that the privileges involved be perpetual, when the owners of adjoining plots of land build mutual driveways or party walls, the parties should see to it that they create true cross-easements, and that such easements are made appurtenant to the respective pieces of land. This should be done by the execution of formal instruments, which should then be properly recorded. If this is done, then no purchaser of either piece of land can successfully claim that he had no notice of the existence of such easements. If it is not done, the respective rights of the parties may at some time be held to be mere licenses and, as such, revocable. In that event, one or both of the parties might be compelled to remove his part of the wall or to relinquish the use of his part of the driveway.

The law with respect to easements and licenses has been considerably modified by statutes in some of the states, and no one should attempt to adjust such matters for himself without the advice of competent legal counsel.

DEEDS OF CONVEYANCE

Rule 276. *Deeds of conveyance of real estate are of two kinds.* Land conveyances must be made in written form in order that the conveyances can be recorded.[15] Such conveyances are either quitclaim deeds or warranty deeds. While the language used in such documents may vary in some details in different localities, such language generally follows that of the forms which are reproduced in the ensuing pages of this chapter. Printed forms can be obtained from banks, real estate dealers, trust companies, or publishers of legal forms.[16] The forms also include space for the attestation of a notary public, which is required in practically all states before a deed can be recorded. A few states require other witnesses (usually two) of the signature of the maker of the deed, and in those states, the proper form includes two or three blank lines for

---

[15] Recording of deeds is discussed later.

[16] One well-known publisher is *The Chicago Legal News,* 111 West Washington Street, Chicago, Illinois.

the signatures of such witnesses. The witnesses must be parties other than the grantor and the grantee.[17]

WARRANTY DEED—LONG FORM

This indenture, Made this *13th* day of *August* in the year of Our Lord One Thousand Nine Hundred *Thirty* BETWEEN *George Fowler Brown* of the *City of Chicago* in the County of *Cook* and State of *Illinois* party of the first part, and *William Konesty* of *Chicago* in the County of *Cook* and State of *Illinois* party of the second part.

WITNESSETH, That the said party of the first part, for and in consideration of the sum of *Twelve thousand* Dollars in hand paid by the said party of the second part, the receipt whereof is hereby acknowledged, and the said party of the second part forever released and discharged therefrom, ha*s* granted, bargained, sold, remised, released, conveyed, aliened and confirmed, and by these presents does grant, bargain, sell, remise, release, convey, alien and confirm, unto the said party of the second part, and to *his* heirs and assigns FOREVER, all the following described lot , piece , or parcel of lands, situated in the County of *Cook* and State of *Illinois* and known and described as follows, TO WIT: *Lot 42, Block 16, Wilsdon's Subdivision on the E$\frac{1}{2}$ of the N. W. $\frac{1}{4}$ of Sec. 36 Township 9, North, Range 15 East of the 3rd Principal Meridian, Known as 1438 South Claymore Avenue, Chicago, Illinois.*

TOGETHER WITH ALL AND SINGULAR The hereditaments and appurtenances thereunto belonging, or in anywise appertaining, and the reversion and reversions, remainder and remainders, rents, issues and profits thereof; and all the estate, right, title, interest, claim or demand whatsoever, of the said party of the first part, either in law or equity, of, in and to the above bargained premises, with the hereditaments and appurtenances: To HAVE AND TO HOLD the said premises above bargained and described, with the appurtenances, unto the said party of the second part, *his* heirs and assigns, FOREVER.

AND The said *George Fowler Brown* party of the first part, for *his* heirs, executors and administrators, do*es* covenant, grant, bargain and agree, to and with the said party of the second part *his* heirs and assigns, that at the time

---

[17] The grantor is one who signs the deed. The grantee is one to whom a conveyance is made. The grantor is usually called the party of the first part, and the grantee the party of the second part. The chief reason for this is to make possible the printing of the whole instrument, except for the single insertion of the names of the parties and other essential matter.

of the ensealing and delivery of these presents,   *he is*   well seized
of the premises above conveyed, as of a good, sure, perfect, absolute
and indefeasible estate of inheritance in law, in fee simple, and has
good right, full power, and lawful authority to grant, bargain, sell and
convey the same in manner and form aforesaid, and that the same are
free and clear from all former and other grants, bargains, sales, liens,
taxes, assessments and encumbrances, of what kind or nature soever:
and the above bargained premises, in the quiet and peaceable possession of the said party of the second part,   *his*   heirs and assigns,
against all and every other person or persons lawfully claiming or to
claim the whole or any part thereof the said party of the first part
shall and will Warrant and Forever Defend.

AND The said party of the first part hereby expressly waives and
releases any and all right, benefit, privilege, advantage and exemption, under or by virtue of any and all Statutes of the State of
Illinois,   providing for the exemption of homesteads from sale on
execution or otherwise.

IN WITNESS WHEREOF, The said party of the first part
hereunto sets   *his*   hand and seal , the day and year first above
written.

George Fowler Brown [Seal]

WARRANTY DEED—SHORT, OR STATUTORY FORM

THE GRANTOR,   *John Doe*   of the
City of Chicago in the County of   *Cook*   and State of
Illinois   in consideration of the sum of
Two Hundred   dollars, in hand paid, conveys and warrants[18]
to   *Richard Roe*   of the   *City of Chicago,*   County of
Cook , and State of   *Illinois*   the following described
Real Estate, to wit: *Lot one, in Block two of Section one, Township
two, North, Range three, East of Third Principal Meridian,*
situated in the   *City of Chicago* in the County
of   *Cook*   and State of   *Illinois* , hereby releasing and
waiving all rights under and by virtue of the
Homestead Exemption Laws   of the State of
Illinois,
DATED, This   *19th*   day of   *October* , A.D.,
1912.

John Doe   [Seal]

---

[18] The word *warrants* in this form refers to the warranties which are
printed in full in the long form. In some states, as in Illinois, the use of the
short form conveys the same rights as the use of the long form.

QUITCLAIM DEED

THIS INDENTURE WITNESSETH, That the grantor, *John Doe*, of *Chicago,* County of *Cook,* and State of *Illinois,* for the consideration of *Two Hundred* dollars, conveys and quitclaims to *Richard Roe* of *Chicago,* in the County of *Cook,* and State of *Illinois,* all his interest in the following described Real Estate, to wit:

Lot one, in Block two, of Section one, Township two, North, Range three, East of Third Principal Meridian, situated in the County of *Cook,* State of *Illinois,* hereby releasing and waiving all rights under and by virtue of the Homestead Exemption Laws of the State of *Illinois.*

WITNESS the hand and seal of the said grantor, this *19th* day of *October,* A.D., *1912.*

John Doe   [Seal]

The attestation clause or acknowledgment is sometimes printed on the face of the instrument and sometimes on the back. Its location on the document is not important. Such clauses run as follows:

State of Illinois⎫
              ⎬ ss.
County of Cook⎭

I *Harold Gray,* a Notary Public in and for *Cook* County, Illinois, hereby certify that *John and Martha Howe* personally known to me as the person*s* whose name*s* *are* signed to the above instrument, appeared before me on this day in person and acknowledged that *they* signed, sealed, and delivered this instrument as *their* free and voluntary act for the purposes therein set forth.

Given under my hand and seal on this *27th* day of *February,* A.D., *1964.*

Harold Gray,
Notary Public

This form may be adapted for use by a justice of the peace, a military or naval officer, or any other person authorized to administer an oath. In some states, when the acknowledgment is executed by a notary, he is required by law to indicate when his commission expires, and he usually does this by the use of a rubber stamp. He must also affix his official seal.

Rule 277. *Warranty deeds contain warranties and covenants which are legally binding upon the grantor, and, sometimes, restrictions which are legally binding upon the grantee.* Agreements or promises which are included in deeds of conveyances are known as covenants, some of which may be warranties. They impose obligations upon the grantor. Covenants may relate to warranties of title, quiet enjoyment, freedom from incumbrances, or other sorts of assurances. Thus, a deed of conveyance serves not only to convey title and as a record of that fact; it also serves as a means of recording promises which have been made by the grantor as a part of the transfer of title, and restrictions which may be placed upon the grantee as to the use of the land.[19]

Rule 278. *Covenants in warranty deeds usually run with the land.* Most covenants are such that the right to enforce them or the liability to perform them will pass from the grantee to his assignees or to his heirs. Such covenants are said to run with the land. This phrase means that whoever is the owner of land (subject to such covenants) at any time subsequent to the conveyance containing the covenants, will be subject to or able to enforce (as the case may be) all such covenants. For example, Carr was grantee of a mill and a water right through which he was to acquire water with which to run the mill. As a part of the grant to Carr, Carr agreed to keep the mill and the millrace in good repair. Carr sold the mill to Thomas. It was held that the water right passed with the mill, and that the duty to keep the mill and the millrace in repair also ran with the land, and that Thomas was bound by this restrictive covenant made by Carr. Furthermore, the restriction ran with the land in another sense: Carr was no longer bound by the obligation of repair after he had conveyed the land to Thomas. In order that a covenant run with land, it must be made a part of a deed of conveyance, as a rule, and it

---

[19] For example, when land was granted by A to B in fee, subject to the restriction that the land never should be used as the site of a saloon, this was a restriction upon the rights of B. It was a restrictive covenant, binding also upon B's successors in title.

must be made between the parties to a conveyance and between parties who have estates in the land concerned by the covenants. For instance, two millowners, owning separate mills, each drew water from the same dam. By mutual covenants they agreed as to the amount of water each should take from the dam. One of these owners sold his mill to Clayton, who had no notice of the covenants about the water. It was held that, while these covenants may have been binding between the two original owners, they did not run with the land because they concerned land which the parties did not own—the site of the dam. The covenants were not part of any deed of conveyance, and both of the covenanting parties did not have estates in the site of the mill which was sold; only one of them had such an estate.

Rule 279. *Warranties of title and quiet enjoyment run with the land.* Jones conveyed certain land to Knipe by warranty deed. Knipe then conveyed a part of the land to Hill by a quitclaim deed which did not contain any warranties at all.[20] Now, if Hill should be ousted from the land by a party with a title superior to that of Jones, he could not hold Knipe liable because Knipe did not warrant the title; but he could hold Jones liable because Jones's warranty ran with the land and could be enforced by any subsequent holder. This is a further illustration of the rule that one may transfer as much right as he himself has.[21] Knipe had been entitled to the warranty of title from Jones, whose warranty Knipe transferred to Hill even though he did not give his own warranty to Hill.

A word of caution is necessary in connection with warranties of quiet enjoyment. Such warranties do not mean that the warrantor promises that the grantee will not be disturbed; such warranties mean merely that the grantor promises that there will be no interference with the grantee by any party who has a better title to the land than the warrantor, nor by any party who derives his title from the warrantor. For example, in the instance just given, if Hill's possession is disturbed by someone whose title is superior to Jones's, or by someone who derives a valid title from Jones,

---

[20] See the discussion of quitclaim deeds later in this chapter.
[21] See **Rules 87** and **243**.

Hill may recover damages from Jones; but if the enjoyment is disturbed by someone who is a stranger to the title, Jones cannot be held liable because the warranty does not cover such disturbance. Thus, a warranty of quiet enjoyment is a part of the warranty of title.

Rule 280. *Building restrictions sometimes take the form of covenants.* Ames was the owner of two adjoining lots. He sold and conveyed one of the lots to Bass, taking Bass's covenant, which was in the deed, to the effect that Bass would not build any structure nearer than five feet to the boundary line between the two lots, and that he would not construct any automobile driveway on that side of the lot which was nearest to the remaining lot of Ames. Bass sold the lot to Cooper, who erected a house on the lot during Ames's absence from home. When Ames returned, it was found that the eaves of the house projected to a line within three and one-half feet of the boundary line. Ames brought a proceeding to compel the removal of the projection. It was held that Bass's covenant ran with the land. Cooper was therefore bound by it, so that the order to remove the projection was issued.

Oftentimes, city subdivision lots are sold under restrictions forbidding the erection of houses nearer than twenty feet to the sidewalk or under other like restrictions. These, if they appear in deeds, are regarded as covenants which run with the land and are enforcible unless they are contrary to public policy. They are usually enforcible either against the assignees of the grantee or in favor of the assignees of the grantor. Purchasers of property will do well to examine the record of former conveyance in order to ascertain whether there are any such covenants outstanding against the property, or to take covenants from the seller warranting that there are no such outstanding burdens upon the property.

Rule 281. *A quitclaim deed does not contain any covenants or warranties.* Turn to the form of quitclaim deed shown on page 237. It should be noted that this instrument merely assigns the grantor's interest, whatever it may be, *as is* to the grantee. The instrument does not warrant the title of the grantor; it does not promise anything at all. Such an instrument is very rarely used between buyer and seller because a buyer is not willing to take the risks involved[22] in using such an instrument as his sole evidence of title. Of course, if the grantor's title is entirely valid, then the grantee's title is good even under such a deed; but the grantee (if he is a buyer) usually will not take the risk.

There are, however, some situations in which a grantor may find a quitclaim deed very useful and in which the grantee is interested in acquiring only the rights of the grantor. For example, suppose that an owner of land wished to dedicate it to a city as a park and that this owner were willing to permit the city to dispose of the land at some later time. This owner should realize that if he made a covenant of warranty, and that if the city should ever sell the land, the grantor could be held liable on warranties of title, should the title fail. This grantor does not wish to assume this risk as a part of a transaction in which he is presenting a gift to the city. He therefore executes a quitclaim deed, which contains no warranty. The city does not object to this form because it is desirous of taking the gift.

The quitclaim deed is useful in another type of transaction. Adah Carson, a widow with three grown children, was the owner of a city lot. The lot had been sold under contract to Gray, but title was to pass only upon the payment of three-fifths of the price. Before this amount had been paid, Mrs. Carson became ill and wrote out a document which she intended as a will, stating that she wished the title to the lot to descend to her daughter, Helen. Soon afterward, Mrs. Carson died. The will was not valid because it was not witnessed by two witnesses.[23] Under the law of descent, the lot would descend to the three children. Now, Howard and George, the other two children, were quite willing that Helen should have the lot in accordance with their mother's wishes. Gray, the purchaser, did not care to whom the title went, but it was to his interest to know to whom the payments should be made. He made the payments to Helen, taking a receipt from her as trustee or agent for the other two heirs. This protected Gray, but when the time should come for the conveyance to him, he must have the deed executed by all who own interests in the

---

[22] An exception is given later under this same rule.
[23] See **Rules 312** and **313**.

property. It may be more difficult to get the signatures of three or four than it is to get the signature of one. Because of this difficulty, it is to the interest of Gray as well as to the interest of Helen that she be given the sole title to the lot. She therefore induces her brothers to convey to her their interests in the property. Suppose, however, that they conveyed by warranty deed and that some flaw should develop in their mother's title. In that case, the coheirs, who had in reality donated their interests to their sister, might find themselves liable upon those warranties. For this reason, they may object to making the conveyance, but if they use a quitclaim deed, they run no such risk.

A third type of situation in which the quitclaim deed is useful is the following. Vance was the owner of a lot three hundred yards from the shore of Lake Michigan. He had been granted a license to pass over certain land of Smith to gain access to the beach of the lake. Vance wished to sell his lot to Brown, but he was unwilling to warrant his title to the license to pass to the lake or to warrant that he could convey it with the land. He, therefore, executed a warranty deed which covered the title to the lot, but he executed a quitclaim deed to the right to pass over the land of Smith to the lake. Under this arrangement, if Smith should succeed in an action to prevent the use of the passageway by Brown, Brown would have no remedy against Vance because the quitclaim deed contained no warranty.

Rule 282. *A deed of conveyance must contain words of proper import to pass title.* No particular form of language is necessary to pass a valid title to land. The words most often used are *grant, sell, convey* and *confirm,* all used together in the same deed, but any language which is clearly intended as a conveyance will be adequate. Even an indorsement on the back of a deed may be held sufficient. Porter was the owner of certain land conveyed to him by deed in 1891. In 1904, Porter, in order to convey the land to Wilson, indorsed on the back of the deed, *I hereby assign the within title to this land to George W. Wilson and his heirs forever,* and signed his own name. This was held to be a valid conveyance, but it is not recommended as common practice. Each conveyance should rest upon its own deed. Printed forms are easy to acquire, and it is even easier to fill them out than it is to write a homemade form.

Rule 283. *A deed must accurately describe the property conveyed.* The description of the property should be precise although it may be accomplished by reference to some document where the description can be found. For example, a deed purporting to convey title to *my farm in Lake County* might not be valid in some circumstances because there are Lake counties in many states; but if the state were named, and if the grantor owned no more than one farm in Lake county of that state, the description might be sufficient. The best kind of description is one in which property is described in terms of the government survey. If the property does not lie within the limits of such survey, then it may be described in the most convenient way; however it should be described clearly. In conveyances of city property, it is usual and desirable to add to the technical description the designation of the property in accordance with the street numbering system, although the latter is not essential.

Rule 284. *A valid deed must bear the signature of the grantor.* The signature of the grantor must appear in order to make the deed valid and also to make possible the acknowledgment. The signature should correspond exactly with the name in which the title stands recorded. For instance, if the title to a plot of land is in the name of Arthur Graham Parker, a grant from him should be signed in the same way. A. G. Parker would not be a proper signature on a conveyance from him. A valid signature may consist of any initials or mark, however, provided it can be shown that the initials or mark were affixed with the intent of signing.

Rule 285. *Some states require the presence of a seal on every valid deed of conveyance.* It is commonly held that a seal is essential to the validity of any conveyance of land. However, the marks which are commonly used as seals are of such character that almost any kind of scrawl or printed device will usually be recognized as a valid seal if it has been used with the intent that it should be so regarded. In many states, statutes which regulate the conveyance of land make the use of seals unnecessary. In other states, the requirement of seals is more or less rigidly adhered to. When a seal is required, one seal is sufficient for one deed; it is not necessary that each party to the document affix his own seal. Legal forms furnished by stationers include the word *seal* on or near the lines left blank for signatures. This is practically always regarded as a sufficient seal in every state.

Rule 286. *Acknowledgment is required for recording.* Acknowledgment is sometimes called attestation or witnessing. It is not required, under common law, to make a conveyance valid as between the parties, but some states have enacted statutes which require acknowledgment to make any deed valid. In practically every state, however, no deed may be recorded without an acknowledgment before a notary or some other officer authorized to administer oaths. To be on the safe side, therefore, every deed should be acknowledged in proper form before a notary.

Rule 287. *It is not necessary to recite consideration in a deed.* When no consideration is expressed in a deed of conveyance, consideration may be proved by evidence outside the document, if necessary; and, on the other hand, the fact that a deed does recite consideration is not conclusive. In fact, a deed of gift may be made without any consideration at all and with no mention of consideration. But covenants and warranties are neither valid nor enforcible without valuable consideration because they are contractual in their nature. Thus, the recital, *one dollar and other valuable consideration,* is mere surplusage so far as the validity of a deed is concerned. If there is consideration, it is unnecessary to say so; if there is no consideration, saying that there is consideration is not conclusive; and no consideration at all is necessary in deeds of gift.

Rule 288. *Delivery is necessary to the validity of a deed.* No deed of conveyance of land is ever regarded as complete, even between the parties, unless and until it has been delivered to and accepted by the grantee; and once such delivery has been made, the conveyance cannot be revoked, no matter what becomes of the instrument itself. Even an unconditional delivery of a properly signed deed to a third person for the grantee is valid when made. This is called *delivery in escrow* and cannot be revoked by the grantor unless there is a failure of the condition upon which the third person is to turn over the deed to the grantee.

Rule 289. *A deed cannot be used as a substitute for a will without delivery by the grantor.* This rule is a special case of **Rule 288.** It is illustrated by the following cases. Miller executed a deed which purported to convey his land to his son, Arthur. The deed was duly signed and attested, but Miller kept it in his possession. It was in his possession at the time of his death. The deed was delivered by the administrator of the estate to the son, Arthur; but it was held, upon petition of two other sons, that the deed was not valid since it never was delivered by the grantor. The estate was ordered to be disposed of in accordance with the statutes of descent. In another case, an owner of land made a similar deed, purporting to convey land to one who was not an heir. After his death, the deed came into the possession of the grantee, who sold the property to a purchaser in good faith. It was held that the grantee took no title because the deed had not been delivered by the grantor. The grantee never acquired title, and, therefore, the purchaser received no title from her. The heirs were entitled to a disposition of the property under the processes of administration. In the language of one court, "It must appear, in order to constitute a good delivery, that the grantor intended to part with the title to the property and that he parted with the deed by placing it beyond recall." Even if the deed should be recorded, the presumption that it was delivered may be rebutted by proper evidence. Voluntary delivery is absolutely essential to the validity of a deed.

Rule 290. *A deed usually takes effect from the time of delivery.* This rule is a corollary to **Rule 288.** It is the common law rule, although in some states statutes provide that deeds are not effective to pass title until they have been recorded or filed for record. Thus, under the common law rule, if a deed were executed and delivered on a Sunday in a state in which it is unlawful to convey property on a Sunday, it would not be valid, while if it had been delivered on a secular day, the deed would be valid. The time of delivery is the time of the effectiveness of the deed unless a statute provides otherwise, as indicated previously.

In a state in which a deed does not take effect until it has been recorded, it is sometimes advisable that the purchaser of land see to it that the terms of his contract do not require payment by him until the recording has been done. If he does not insist upon this, it is possible, though not very probable, that after the price has been paid, but before recording, the grantor might convey the land to a second purchaser in good faith. If that should be done, and if the second purchaser in good faith should record his conveyance before the first one does, the title would go to the second purchaser, and the first purchaser would have only a right of action for his money against the grantor. This is another instance in which a transaction in real estate should be made under the supervision of competent advisors.

Rule 291. *An owner's rights are not necessarily lost by the loss of his deed.* If a deed has been recorded, there is no difficulty in establishing title since the purchaser depends upon the record rather than upon the deed by which title came to the seller. Also, if a deed has been recorded, an owner is entitled to a copy of it from the recorder's office upon the payment of a very small copying fee. In fact, any person may have a copy of any instrument which is a matter of public record, in most states, merely by paying a small fee. If a deed has not been recorded and is lost, proof of title after the loss may be difficult; and in those states which require recording to make the deed valid, loss before recording will prevent the recording. But even in the latter case, the loss of the instrument did not affect the owner's title because he never had any title; and the failure of the title is due to the failure to record, and not to the loss of the document. Of course, an owner who has lost his deed is entitled by law to another one; but it may be difficult to get one, in some cases, especially if the grantor is dead or insane or has left the jurisdiction of the grantee. All such difficulty can be avoided by prompt recording. No grantee should ever delay, even for a day, the recording of his documents of title.

Rule 292. *Mistakes in deeds should be corrected at once.* When an error is discovered in any deed of conveyance, the grantee should at once see to it that the old conveyance is destroyed and a new one executed. He should then record the new deed. His title will take effect as of the date of the delivery (or recording, as the case may be). Other devices to correct errors may not be effectual. For instance, Hayes executed a deed to convey land to Nelson and delivered it to him. Nelson sold the land to Gates, but, instead of making a new deed, he merely changed the name of the grantee to that of Gates. Even though this deed was delivered to Gates, it did not pass title to him. If a deed is altered after delivery, it is not effective. There must be a new execution, including delivery. The safest method of changing a deed is to destroy the old one and execute a new one.[24]

THE RECORDING OF DEEDS

The object of the statutes which provide for recording of deeds is to make available a public record which any purchasers of land may consult in order to determine who holds title to any parcel of land which they may desire to buy. In order that such purchasers may rely upon the records with complete confidence, it is also provided by the statutes that purchasers are held to have notice of all matters which appear upon the record. Incumbrances on title which are not on the face of the record and which are not known to purchasers do not affect the rights of purchasers. Suppose that Wade is the owner of a lot and that he has recorded his title deed. Ball wishes to buy the lot. He inspects the record, which shows that Wade is the owner. If Ball does not know of any incumbrances and if the record does not show any, Ball may safely buy the property. If Hill were the holder of a mortgage against the land, not known to Ball and not recorded, Hill's claim against the land would be lost by the sale to Ball.

Rule 293. *Contracts of purchase should be recorded.* However, if the property is occupied by someone other than the seller, the buyer is charged with legal notice of the claim of the occupant. This situation arises frequently when the occupant is a purchaser under contract (from a seller like Wade). If the buyer under contract is not in possession, of course, a purchaser in the position

---

[24] In certain circumstances which involve technical matters, courts will sometimes *reform* an instrument when they are convinced that the intent of the parties is not represented by the instrument as it stands.

of Ball will not be charged with notice of the buyer's contract
unless (a) Ball actually knows of the contract, or (b) the contract
is recorded. Therefore, all purchasers of land under contracts, if
they do not get title, should record their contracts, just as deeds
are recorded.

Rule 294. *There are two systems of recording in the United
States.* The older and more common system of recording is called
the *registration of deeds* or *recording of deeds*. Where this system
is in effect, an officer is designated as *register of deeds* or *recorder
of deeds* or by some similar title. He maintains an office at the
county seat of his county. Persons may leave with him docu-
mentary evidence of their claims to or against property in the
county. He transcribes these documents, sometimes by hand and
sometimes by photography, into books provided for that purpose.
The books are arranged by a system of indexing which permits
examination of the whole chain of title to any particular plot of
ground. This device is an excellent one for the protection of persons with interest of the sort which was discussed in the previous
paragraph. Holders of mortgages, too, find it extremely valuable
because it enables them to serve public notice of their claims. But
the system is not as efficient as it might be. In some localities,
every time a new purchaser is desirous of acquiring an interest in
a particular piece of property, it is the practice to search the whole
record of title of this piece of property from the original grant from
the government of the United States down to date. In most cases,
there is no flaw in the ancient conveyances or other parts of the
record, so that much of the expense and labor involved in making such searches is useless. A much more efficient device was in-
vented in New Zealand some years ago and has been adopted in
some of the states in this country.

The other system of recording is called the Torrens System
of Registration of Land Titles. Under this scheme, the record of
title to a particular parcel of ground is thoroughly searched once.
The result of the search is presented to a court. The court holds
an open hearing to determine the validity of the conclusions of
the search as to who owns the property. Anyone who believes
that he has any claim against the land is free to present his claim

to the court. When the court has concluded the hearing, it decides
in whom the title rests and issues a certificate of ownership to him.
The certificate shows all mortgages, liens, or other claims which
should be recorded. One copy is deposited with the recorder or
register of deeds, and another copy is given to the owner. If a
purchaser wishes to inspect the title to a given piece of land, the
recorder will show him the certificate. When he buys the property,
the old certificate and the duplicate are destroyed and new ones
issued—one to the recorder and one to the new owner. Thus, at
any time, only one document need be inspected in order to learn
the identity of the owner and the status of the title of any piece
of property which is registered under this system. The cost of
such registration is nominal. The statutes which install the system
provide against mistakes in registration. From the fees collected for
registration, a fund is set up from which persons who may have
been injured by mistakes in the first registration may be reim-
bursed. If, for example, a holder of an unrecorded mortgage
should have been for some reason legally unable to appear at the
hearing, his claim would not have been recorded upon the certificate. If the property has since been sold to another who bought
in good faith, the certificate, being final, cuts off the mortgagee
from his right to use the property as security for his claim. It
does not extinguish his claim, of course; it only deprives him of
the use of the land as security. Now, if he can convince a court
of all this, he may be awarded proper damages from the fund
set up from the registration fees; but he cannot go back of the
certificate, once it has been issued.

PARTY WALLS AND FENCES

A party wall is a wall which stands in part upon each side
of a common boundary line between two parcels of real estate.
In a number of states, statutes provide that, if the line between
two contiguous lots is unoccupied by any structure, the owner on
either side of the line may erect a wall standing equally upon
both pieces of land, and that the other owner, whenever he desires,
may make the wall a party wall by contributing to the cost of
erection; and, of course, owners of adjoining lots may, by agree-

ment, contract for the erection of party walls. Whenever buildings
have party walls, conveyances by either owner pass to the purchaser a title to one half of the wall and an easement for its support
by the owner of the other half. That is, once a party wall is erected,
either by statutory permission or as the result of an agreement,
neither party may remove it without the consent of the other.
Each owner, of course, may join his building to the party wall in
the customary way.

Fences are often treated in much the same way as party walls,
that is, they may be built upon the dividing line, and once they
are so built, they may not be removed without the permission of
the adjoining owner. Of course, a partition fence built wholly
upon the land of one owner is a part of his land, and it may be
removed at his pleasure. The removal of fences, however, is regulated by statute in most of the states, and one cannot be sure of
his rights with respect to fences unless he consults a competent
attorney. In most states, such statutes include provisions which are
interpreted to mean that an owner of livestock is not required to
fence his own livestock so as to keep it from the unfenced land of
others unless such animals are vicious or diseased. If one wishes
his land kept free of animals which belong to others, he must fence
it off, though if they enter his land, he may drive them away at
the point at which they entered, whether his land is fenced or not;
but, if he wilfully or carelessly injures the animals in driving them
away, he may be held liable for such injury. Other statutory provisions regarding fencing of both farm and city property are very
numerous and varied, so that no brief, general statement can be
made about them. Even the statutory regulations which govern
the erection and maintenance of railway right-of-way fences are
different in the different states, though there are general provisions
in most of the states, under which railways are required to fence
their right-of-way lands and maintain cattle guards at crossings.
In some states, these rules apply to both private and public
crossings.

Rule 295. *A landowner owes a duty of lateral support to
adjacent land.* Somewhat related to the matter of party walls is the
so-called right of lateral support. Every landowner is said to have a

right to have his land, in its natural state, supported by the adjacent land. That is, one has no right to dig an excavation upon his land without providing against the caving in of his neighbors' lands; and, if he does so, he has violated their right of lateral support and may be liable for the damage thus caused. This right does not extend to the support of buildings, at common law; but, in most of the states, there are statutes which either require the exercise of care and skill to prevent caving of buildings into excavations or impose a duty of support of buildings. Here, again, there are so many differences in detail that they can be understood only as a result of a careful study of local law.

LEASES OF REAL PROPERTY

Rule 296. *A lease of land is a contract and a conveyance.* A lease is a conveyance because it conveys from the grantor (or lessor) an estate in the land to the grantee (or lessee). It is, therefore, usually regarded as taking effect at the moment of delivery to the lessee and acceptance by him. A lease is also a contract since it states the obligations and rights of the parties as between themselves; and, as a contract, a lease is subject to the general law governing other contracts. In the absence of statutory regulations, lessors and lessees may insert into their leases any terms which seem suitable to them, just as parties may do with other contracts; and, since both lessor and lessee are holders of estates in land in the premises subject to the lease, they may transfer their interests by deed or by will.

Rule 297. *A lessee may assign his interest without the lessor's consent.* Unless there is a specific provision in the lease-contract to the contrary, a lessee may either assign the whole of his interest or sublet any part of it without the consent of the lessor. Most modern leases, especially of business buildings and apartments, contain restrictions upon the powers of the tenant to assign or sublet the premises or any part of them[25] without the lessor's consent.

---

[25] Lodgers, boarders, and roomers in rooming houses are not usually considered as holders of leases, and such occupants do not usually have any power to assign or sublet their interests. These kinds of occupants do not have estates in the premises; they have merely contractual rights with the keepers of the houses.

Rule 298. *Leases must be distinguished from contracts to lease.* A *contract to lease* is merely an agreement under which the landlord is bound to make a lease; it does not give the other party any estate in the land until the lease is actually executed and delivered, nor any right to enter into occupancy. For example, Case and Warner agreed that Case might occupy Warner's store premises and that Warner would execute the lease within a few days. Case moved into the building. No lease was executed. After about six months, Case left the premises. Warner brought suit to recover damages for the remainder of the year, but he was not entitled to them because there was no lease: there was only a contract to make a lease for a year. Also, if the contractual feature of this transaction is noticed, it will be clear that Warner could not enforce the promise of Case to remain in occupancy because Warner had not performed his part of the agreement.

On the other hand, if Case had desired that a lease for a year be executed, he could have had a court decree ordering execution of a lease, in most states. Some of the covenants made in leases may also be enforced specifically. Some illustrations are covenants to furnish light and heat, covenants to renew the lease at the tenant's option, covenants to decorate, and other covenants of similar character.[26]

Rule 299. *No special form is required for leases.* While it is probable that most leases are executed by filling out standard printed forms, the use of such forms is not necessary. Any language which shows clearly the terms of the agreement will suffice. In fact, at common law, it was not even necessary that a lease be in writing to be valid. In most of our states, the Statute of Frauds requires that contracts for the disposal of interests in land for more than one year must be in writing. This requirement includes leases for more than a year.[27] Even in cases where this rule applies, how-

---

[26] These cases are exceptional. Most courts do not favor the remedy of specific performance if any other remedy is adequate. In most cases, a right to recover damages is apt to be regarded as an adequate remedy for breach of such covenants.

[27] Tenancies at will are not discussed here because they are quite rare. At common law, such tenancies can be terminated without notice by either lessor or lessee. Under statutes in some states, termination is not permitted without some sort of notice.

ever, no particular form of writing is required; but in some states, leases for more than a year must be executed in writing, acknowledged, and recorded in the same manner as deeds must be, in order to be valid.

Rule 300. *A lease for years may become a lease from year to year.* A lease for years is a lease for any stipulated period, whether for a week, a month, or any other definite time. A lease for years, under the common law, came automatically to an end with the expiration of the stipulated period. Under modern statutes and in most states, however, unless the lessor or lessee shall give notice to quit and unless the notice is given at some specified time (not less than sixty days, for example) before the expiration of the lease, the tenancy will be changed from a lease for years to a lease from year to year. A lease from year to year is terminable only at the end of some year—not a calendar year, but a lease-year. And a lease from year to year is terminable only by adequate notice, which is usually sixty days before the expiration of any lease-year. Thus, Held leased land to Thorn for two years. The statute required that notice to quit must be given not less than sixty days and not more than ninety days before the end of the term, and that if it were not given, a tenancy from year to year should begin at the end of the term of years. The lease expired May 1, 1927. Notice was not given until March 3. This was too late, so the tenant became a tenant for another year, and neither he nor the landlord may terminate the lease from year to year except by mutual consent and on the first day of May in some year after 1927, preceded by proper notice. Statutes regulating leases and tenancies in this manner vary considerably in detail in the different states, of course, so here is yet another kind of problem with regard to which parties must resort to knowledge of local law.

Rule 301. *The landlord is not usually required by law to keep the premises in repair.* Under the common law, it is not the duty of a lessor to keep the premises in repair; nor is it his duty to do so under modern statutes, in most states, unless there is some specific undertaking to that effect in the terms of the lease.[28]

---

[28] Most apartment leases contain such provisions.

At the same time, however, it is held in most states that it is the duty of a landlord to maintain the premises in a healthful and inhabitable condition. Thus, when a landlord leased the upper story of a building and failed to repair drains so that water accumulated in the basement and rendered the whole premises unhealthful, it was held that this was a violation of the landlord's duty and it entitled the tenant to leave the premises without any penalty.[29]

Rule 302. *Covenants to keep in repair are contractual.* When a tenant covenants to keep premises in repair, it is held in most states that he must even rebuild if the premises are destroyed by fire or other calamity.[30] When a landlord covenants to keep the premises in repair, the tenant's remedy for breach is usually confined to a right of action for damages. The tenant is not entitled to continue in occupancy, rent free. For instance, Knox leased the upper floor of a building to Long, covenanting to keep the building in repair. The electrical connections operating an elevator failed, and the failure was not repaired by Knox. Long continued to use the premises but refused to pay any rent. In an action for the rent, it was held that Long was still obligated to pay the rent; but, since he was entitled to damages for breach of the covenant to repair, the amount recoverable was diminished by the amount of the damage due to the failure of the elevator.[31]

Rule 303. *Improvements on the premises belong to the lessor.* When a tenant installs permanent fixtures, unless there is a specific agreement to the contrary between lessor and lessee, these fixtures cannot lawfully be removed from the premises by the tenant, either before or after the expiration of the term of the lease. Such additions are regarded as real property and belong to the owner of the land upon which they have been affixed. For example, when boilers, heavy machinery, smokestacks, or any kind of per-

---

[29] Mere failures of plumbing, leaking of roofs, and the like need not be repaired by a landlord unless he has agreed by contract to do so.

[30] In the absence of a covenant to repair by the tenant, if the premises are destroyed without the tenant's fault, the lease is regarded as terminated, and his obligation to pay further rent comes to an end.

[31] Upon failure of the elevator, Long, the tenant, could have left the premises without any penalty or obligation for rent subsequent to the time he left.

manent structures are installed by a tenant upon leased land, such things are very likely to be regarded as *fixtures* (real property) which cannot be removed by the tenant without the landlord's consent. Any tenant who installs such equipment should, therefore, obtain in advance the landlord's permission to remove it. If he does not take this precaution, he may lose his equipment.[32] Similarly, a tenant is not entitled to reimbursement for improvements which he may make upon the premises, such as painting and decorating, unless the landlord has agreed to pay for such improvements and repairs.

Rule 304. *A lessor may assign his reversion.* The interest which remains to a landlord under a lease is known as a *reversion.* The sole control of the property will revert to him upon the termination of the tenancy. A transfer of the reversion is not a legal wrong to the tenant. The tenant is liable for the rent after the assignment, just as he was before; but, after the assignment, the payment should be made to the new owner, provided the tenant has notice of the assignment of the reversion. For example, Blake leased a farm to Lincoln and then assigned the reversion to Smith. Neither Blake nor Smith notified Lincoln of the assignment, so Lincoln paid the rent to Blake. This was held a valid payment; but if Lincoln had been notified of the assignment before he paid the rent, payment to Blake would have been improper without the assent of Smith.

Rule 305. *A lessor has no general right of entry to the premises.* A landlord has a right to enter the leased premises without the lessee's consent only (a) if the landlord reserves such right in the lease, or (b) if entry is necessary to make repairs or to make inspection as to the need of repairs if the lessor is bound to make them, or (c) to perform some other legal duty which the lessor owes to the lessee. The tenant is regarded as the owner of an estate in the land which entitles him to exclude even the lessor unless one of the above conditions is complied with. A lessor who enters upon leased premises in violation of these rules

---

[32] The definition of such property is extremely hazy, and no chances should be taken. It is very easy to provide for such matters in a lease.

may be treated by the tenant as a trespasser.[33] Even when a lessor has a lawful right of entry, he may exercise it only at reasonable hours and at reasonable intervals.

REAL ESTATE MORTGAGES

Rule 306. *Mortgages are conveyances in form.* In general, there are two types of real estate mortgages in common use. Both kinds are in the form of conveyances. One kind (perhaps less common now than the other) is that in which the mortgagor conveys the premises to the mortgagee. In some cases, there is nothing in the instrument to indicate that it is a mortgage; but such a conveyance will be treated by the courts as a mortgage if the courts are convinced that the instrument was executed as a security. In other cases, the body of the instrument is exactly similar to any other conveyance, but an additional clause provides: *This conveyance shall be void upon the payment of the sum of dollars by the grantor to the grantee. Otherwise, the conveyance shall be in full force and effect.*[34] Such an instrument, of course, shows on its face that it was intended as a security. The other and perhaps more common kind of mortgage is that in which the mortgagor conveys the property not to the mortgagee, but to a third person, called a *trustee*. This kind of mortgage indicates that the grantee is a trustee, and, in many instances, the instruments also indicate the terms upon which the mortgage is to be released.

Rule 307. *A mortgagor has an equity of redemption.* Under modern law, when a mortgage is foreclosed, the property subject to the mortgage is sold under supervision of an officer of a court. If the proceeds of the sale are great enough to pay the costs of the sale and the debt which was secured by the mortgage, the mortgagor is entitled to whatever money remains. This right of the mortgagor is known as his *equity of redemption.* More recently, it has come to be called merely the mortgagor's *equity.*

Rule 308. *A surrender of the equity of redemption is void.* If a mortgage contains a clause which provides that the mortgagor

---

[33] Most modern leases provide for entry by the landlord for inspection at reasonable times.

[34] Different language with similar meaning may be used.

will not enforce his equity, such clause is uniformly held invalid by the courts in this country, and such a promise is not binding upon the mortgagor.

Rule 309. *A power of sale mortgage is valid at common law.* Some mortgages contain clauses which provide that, upon default of payment of the debt by the mortgagor, the mortgagee himself may sell the property. Where such clauses are regarded as enforcible at law, when the debt is unpaid, a mortgagee need not resort to the courts for foreclosure. Such provisions were regarded as valid under the rules of the common law, but, in a few states, legislation now provides that such provisions are not valid under any circumstances.

Rule 310. *The foreclosure of a mortgage does not necessarily discharge the debt which was secured by it.* If the foreclosure sale does not produce enough money to pay the legal costs of the sale and the secured debt, the proceeds of the sale are used, first, to pay the legal costs of the sale, and, second, to pay as much as possible of the debt. Then, the court which has jurisdiction of the case will issue what is called a *deficiency judgment* against the debtor. This is a court order stating that the debtor still owes to the mortgagee the balance of the debt, and ordering the mortgagor to pay this amount. With a deficiency judgment, the creditor may proceed to levy upon property of the debtor, just as a creditor may do with any other kind of judgment.

Rule 311. *A mortgage should be recorded by the mortgagee.* Since a real estate mortgage constitutes an incumbrance upon the title of the mortgaged premises, and since such an incumbrance is not good against a purchaser of the property who buys in good faith without notice of such mortgage, the mortgagee should record the mortgage immediately upon its execution. The recording of a mortgage, like the recording of a deed, serves as notice to everyone that the mortgage has been executed; and after the mortgage has been filed for record, no one can buy the property without legal notice of the mortgage. Similarly, as soon as a debt has been paid, the mortgage securing it should be released at once, and the release also should be recorded. When this has been done, the title is again clear; but, until the release is recorded, no purchaser will be likely to take the risk of the apparent cloud upon the title.[35] Mortgages must be acknowledged in order to be recorded, just as deeds and other instruments.

THE LAW OF DECEDENT ESTATES

The property of a deceased person can be lawfully distributed only under the supervision of the courts. For the control of such distribution, two bodies of law have been developed. There is the law of *testamentary disposition,* which controls the disposition of land and goods under valid wills; and there is the law of *intestate succession,* which controls the disposal of property which is not subject to the terms of a valid will.

Rule 312. *The law of wills is entirely statutory.* A will is an instrument in which the owner of property expresses his desires as to the disposal of his property upon his death.[36] The privilege of making a will is not a common law privilege. It rests entirely upon state statutes. Therefore, no will can be enforced in the courts unless the testator, in making his will, has very carefully followed the formalities prescribed by the law of the state which controls the disposal of his property. If a testator fails in any material particular to conform to the requirements, his will cannot be held valid and his property will be disposed of just as though he had made no will at all.

Rule 313. *The statutory requirements are not hard to follow.* The statutes of wills in the several states are quite similar in their provisions, which are fairly simple. As an illustration, consider the Illinois Statute. This law provides that the testator must be at least twenty-one years old to make a valid will disposing of real estate; every will disposing of real estate must be in writing, signed by the testator or by his agent in the testator's presence, and signed also by at least two witnesses;[37] at least two of the witnesses must be able to testify that they either saw the testator (or his lawful

---

[35] It is necessary once more to point out the broad general character of the rules stated in this book. The law of mortgages is another technical branch of the law in which expert advice should be sought and followed.

[36] One who makes a will is called a *testator* or, if female, a *testatrix.* One who dies without making a will is said to have died *intestate.*

[37] Some states require three witnesses.

agent in the testator's presence) sign the will, or that they heard the testator acknowledge that this was his last will. Two or more witnesses must be able, also, to testify that they believed at the time of signing (and still believe) that the testator was of sound mind and memory at the time he signed the will. The statute further provides that no *necessary witness* can take any bequest or devise under the will. Thus, if there were three witnesses to a will in a state which required but two, a bequest to any one of them would be valid since only two are necessary. On the other hand, if a necessary witness is also a person who would receive some of the decedent's property if the will were not valid, such witness may take such share, but not to exceed the amount named in the will.

These requirements seem more complicated, perhaps, than they really are. Let the testator simply see to it that the witnesses are not persons named as beneficiaries of the will, that there is the required number of witnesses,[38] and that they know that it is a will they are signing; then, if the testator is legally competent, the will probably will be held valid.

Rule 314. *Some states enforce holographic wills.* A holographic will is one written entirely in the handwriting of the testator and without witnesses. In those states in which such wills are recognized as valid, the instrument must be dated.[39] Very few states will enforce holographic wills.

Rule 315. *In some states, oral wills are valid as to personal property.* Oral wills are recognized in some states only if the proper procedure is very carefully followed, and even then such wills are not valid for the disposal of real property. Such wills are known as *nuncupative* wills. In Illinois, in order to make such a will valid, the terms of the disposition of the property must be dictated by the testator in the presence of two disinterested witnesses. These witnesses must write down the terms of the will within ten days of the time of the testator's death and not more than twenty days after the dictation; and two other witnesses, also disinterested, must be able to swear that the writing was made within the required time. Nuncupative wills are provided for as emergency measures

---

[38] Three will always be sufficient.

[39] A date is not legally required to make valid an ordinary will.

to be used in case of accidental injury or sudden illness. They are very seldom used.

Rule 316. *Valid codicils may be made only in the same way as wills are made.* Any addition to a will is called a codicil. It may be an amendment, an alteration, or an addition. But every codicil, to be valid, must be signed and attested by witnesses, just as if it were a new will. Any alterations in a will are entirely disregarded unless they have been made in strict compliance with this rule of law.

Rule 317. *A testator may alter or revoke his will at any time before his death.* A will does not take effect until the testator's death. Hence, he may revoke it or make changes in it at any time. A revocation of a will, however, cannot be made orally. Revocation is effective only if it consists of intentional obliteration, cancellation, destruction, or some other act of the testator, with intent to revoke the will. Of course, the making of a new will in due form will operate as a revocation of all former wills of the same testator; but the destruction of a later will does not revive earlier wills. If a will is lost or destroyed without intent to revoke, it will be regarded as valid if its terms and its proper execution can be proved. For this reason, it may be wise for a testator to prepare several copies of his will and to have them kept in different places.

Rule 318. *In general, the making of a will is not difficult.* As a general rule, the greatest difficulty which a testator encounters is the task of deciding to whom he wishes his property to be distributed. Once he has made the decision to his own satisfaction, there is the second task of making a clear and unmistakable statement as to what he wishes to be done. When this has been accomplished and the simple formalities have been observed, the will is pretty sure to be held valid.

Rule 319. *There are four types of restrictions upon the making of wills.* There are four types of things which a testator cannot do in the making of his will. In the first place, he cannot deprive his widow of her right of dower.[40] In the second place, no devise or bequest can be distributed until all of the testator's creditors

---

[40] See **Rule 262.** Note that in some states a husband has dower in his wife's property.

have been paid in full or have waived their claims. In the third place, certain kinds of charitable gifts are restricted;[41] and, finally, there is the rule against perpetuities.[42] Aside from these restrictions, the testator may order the disposal of his property as he sees fit, and his orders will be regarded as final and binding by the courts if he has complied with the law for the making of wills.[43]

Rule 320. *Wills are executed under court supervision.* The executor of a will may be a beneficiary, or any other person, subject to the provisions of the law of the state.[44] The executor is required to post a bond unless the will provides otherwise. Upon the testator's death, the person who has the will in possession should at once deliver it to a court of probate jurisdiction. The executor named in the will, or any other interested person, may request that the court appoint an executor and that the will be filed for probate (which means accepted by the court for testing its validity). When the executor has been appointed, and the will admitted to probate (which means declared to be valid), the will is delivered by the court to the executor. If the will is not admitted to probate (that is, if it is declared invalid), or if there is other property not within the terms of the will, all property not subject to a valid will is distributed in accordance with the law of intestate succession. Many persons hesitate to make wills because they are afraid of the litigation that may arise. However, there is much more likelihood of litigation if no will is made. Only a very small percentage of wills produce lawsuits beyond the simple procedure of execution; but the procedures and litigations arising from intestate succession are very numerous and often are drawn out for a long time. Every person with property should determine how he wants it to be disposed of and then see to it that his wishes are incorporated into the form of a will. The procedure is simple and the results are quite secure.

Rule 321. *The law of intestate succession also is statutory.*

---

[41] This group of restrictions is extremely technical and complex.

[42] This is the rule referred to in **Rule 264.**

[43] A testator, for example, is not required by law to leave anything at all to his wife (aside from dower) nor to his children, as a general rule.

[44] Many states require that executors, to dispose of real estate, must be residents of the state where the land is attested.

At common law, the property of an intestate[45] descended to his next of kin or to his heirs. Heirs and next of kin were not always the same persons, and some confusion arose out of this fact, as well as from the fact that there were different ways of determining in some cases who next of kin were. Under modern law, the disposal of intestate property is regulated by *statutes of descent*. These statutes differ in their details in the several states, but they are similar in their general outlines. The following is a summary of the provisions of the Illinois statute.[46]

1. If a husband or wife and direct descendants remain, the spouse takes one third of personalty and realty (unless dower is elected). In the latter case, the spouse takes dower and one third personalty. Children take equal shares of the remaining property. The descendants of each deceased child take collectively equal shares of the property which the deceased child would have taken if alive.

2. If descendants only survive, each child takes an equal share of all property. Descendants of each deceased child take equal parts of his share.

3. If spouse and no descendants remain, spouse takes all personalty, one half of realty, and dower in remaining one half of realty. Parents, brothers, sisters, take equal shares in remaining one half of realty, but subject to dower. If only one parent survives, such parent is entitled to a double portion.

4. If spouse, but no descendants, no parents, brothers, or sisters or descendants of any of them survive, spouse takes all personalty, one half of realty, and dower in the other half, and next of kin in equal degree (cousins, grandparents, etc.) take equal shares in the half of realty which is subject to dower.

5. If no spouse or descendants remain, then parents, brothers, and sisters take all in equal shares, except that if only one parent survives, such parent takes a double share. Descendants of deceased brother or sister take their deceased parent's share in equal shares among them.

---

[45] An intestate is one who dies without having made a valid will.

[46] Remember that this statute applies only to property which is not subject to distribution under a valid will.

6. If no spouse, descendants, parents, brothers, or sisters, or descendants of the same remain, the next of kin in equal degree take all of the property.

7. If husband or wife alone survives (no descendants, no next of kin, no brothers and sisters), surviving spouse takes all the property.

8. If there is no surviving spouse or relatives, the property vests in the county in which the property lies.[47]

Even a rather hasty reading of these provisions should serve to indicate the desirability of the making of a will by every person for the disposal of his property. This is true, not only because of the complexities of the statute, but also because of the fact that, to achieve a proper distribution of property under the laws of intestate succession, some of the property must be sold; and such sale may be a source of loss to the estate because it is a more or less forced sale, which does not always bring the best price for property sold under such circumstances.

Rule 322. *Intestate property is distributed by an administrator.* The person charged with the handling of intestate succession is called an administrator. Like an executor, an administrator must be satisfactory to the court by which he is appointed, and he must do his work under the court's supervision. His duties are closely prescribed by law, and, in some instances, if he violates those duties, he may be compelled to make reparation out of his own pocket to any persons injured by his mistakes in not following the law.

QUESTIONS AND PROBLEMS

1. After reading the discussion of **Rule 261** very carefully, state in writing why it is that one could be held liable as a trespasser solely upon the ground that he had thrown a stone across his neigh-

---

[47] In most states, a public administrator, or other county or state officer performing that function, takes and disposes of the property of persons who die intestate and who leave no families or next of kin.

Under the Illinois statute, a legally adopted child inherits as a natural child; half sisters and half brothers take equally with those of the full blood; a stepchild takes nothing from a stepparent (unless legally adopted), nor from stepbrother or stepsister ; and an illegitimate child takes by descent only through its mother.

bor's land without the neighbor's consent, even though the stone did
not touch either the land or anything upon the land.

2. What is the commonest kind of life estate? Can the owner
of a life estate issue a valid mortgage on his estate? Can he issue a
valid lease on such an estate? **Rule 262.**

3. If a landlord leased a farm to a tenant, stipulating that the
lease was to end on the first day of July, 1947, but that the rent was
to be paid monthly, would this lease be a lease for years or from month
to month, and why? **Rule 262.**

4. State briefly what you understand to be the rule against perpetuities. It is not expected that you will give a technical definition.
Use your own language. Why is the rule against perpetuities important
to the student of commercial law? **Rule 264.**

5. Explain clearly the distinction between tenancy in common
and joint tenancy. Point out at least one advantage which each has
over the other. **Rule 266.**

6. Name one of the dangers of a *joint* bank account. **Rule 266.**

7. What is the distinction between easements in gross and easements appurtenant? Why is this distinction important? If you wished
to create an easement over your property in favor of some friend of
yours, which kind of the two do you think would be most likely to be
upheld by the courts in case a dispute should arise? **Rule 268.**

8. Knott and Fisher were neighbors occupying adjacent lots.
They wished to provide a driveway between their houses, so that neither would be obliged to take the whole of the space for a driveway
from his own lot. They decided to install a *common* driveway. What
legal device should be used for this purpose, in order that no serious
legal complications might arise in later years? **Rule 275.**

9. Why must deeds conveying land be recorded for practical
purposes? Which party is the grantor? Which is the grantee? Which
one signs the deed? Which is usually the party of the first part? Why
are the terms used: *party of the first part* and *party of the second
part?* **Rule 276.**

10. Since the short-form deed is said to be just as effective as
the long-form deed, what reason can you find for using the long form,
even in a state in which the short form has been specifically made
proper by statute? Read the two forms through carefully before you
answer.

11. If an easement is appurtenant to the land—runs with the
land—what is the importance of this to the successors in title to the
servient piece? What is its importance to the successors in title to the
dominant piece? **Rule 278.** (See also **Rule 267.**)

12. Smith conveyed to Jacobs a certain plot of land, warranting

quiet enjoyment. The quiet enjoyment of the land was disturbed by certain gay parties which were held by Henry, a next door neighbor. Does or does not this come within the warranty made by Smith? Why? **Rule 279.**

13. In the discussion of the case under **Rule 280,** Cooper was then successor in title of Bass. If Cooper did not know of the building restriction, how is it that he could be held liable for allowing the eaves of his house to project too far?

14. Name five essential features which must be found in a deed, in order that it be valid and that it be subject to recording. **Rules 282-288.** Read these rules carefully.

15. Compare **Rule 289** with **Rule 313.** State in your own language why it is that a deed of gift cannot be substituted for a will; that is, why will the courts not consider valid a deed which has been properly made, properly attested, and even recorded, if it has not been delivered by or for the grantor *within his lifetime?* **Rule 290** might give you some help on this.

16. Does the loss of one's title deed affect his title in any way at all, in most states? If there is any doubt about this question in the mind of any person, what simple thing can he do which will protect his title, even if he loses his deed? **Rule 291.**

17. Explain fully why it is that a purchaser of land, under contract, should record the contract just as soon as possible after the contract is made, unless he is an occupant of the property. Explain, also, why the exception is made. **Rule 293.**

18. Explain the duty of lateral support. Who owes this duty, and to whom does he owe it? **Rule 295.**

19. Is a lease of land a contract? Who makes most of the promises in a lease-contract—the grantor or the grantee? **Rule 296.**

20. If Hill leased a house and lot to Gale, may the latter sublet part of the premises to Finley if the lease-contract does not provide to the contrary? Why is it important to know this? **Rule 297.**

21. Explain carefully how it is that a lease for years may become a lease from year to year upon the happening of a certain event. What is the significance of the difference between these two kinds of leases? **Rule 300.**

22. If a lessor of a building covenants to keep the premises in repair and does not do so, the lessee has a choice of two legal remedies. What are they? **Rule 302.**

23. Mack owed a debt of five thousand dollars, which was secured by a mortgage upon his small country place. When the debt was due, Mack was unable to pay it, and the mortgagee foreclosed the mortgage. The mortgage sale produced only forty-five hundred dol-

lars. The expenses of the sale were two hundred and fifty dollars. What will the courts usually do about the remainder of the debt? Is it discharged by the foreclosure of the security? **Rule 310.**

24. By whom should every mortgage be recorded, and for what reasons? Similarly, what steps should be taken by the mortgagor as soon as the mortgage debt is fully paid? **Rule 311.**

25. Write out a short sample will, disposing of all of your property, real and personal, to some fictitious person. Fill in the names of fictitious witnesses, making sure that they are not the names of any beneficiaries. Is it necessary to acknowledge a will before a notary public? Will such acknowledgment make a will valid? **Rules 312 and 313.**

26. What is a holographic will? Is it wise to make such a will? Explain your answer briefly. **Rule 314.**

27. What is a codicil? What precautions must be taken to make a valid codicil? Suppose that a will were made in valid form and that the testator wanted to make some additions to it but did not require the signature of witnesses, nor did he require the former witnesses to sign again. Would the codicil be valid? If the codicil to a will is invalid, how does that invalidity affect the validity of the will itself? **Rule 316.** This rule is not discussed at length because it is believed that you can easily work out such problems as this without much discussion in the text.

28. When does a will take effect: when it is made; when it is witnessed; when it is delivered to a court; when the testator dies; when the court declares the will valid; or when the bequests are made? **Rule 317.**

29. Name the four types of restrictions upon the making of wills. State what the maker of a will should do about these restrictions. **Rule 319.**

30. Give as many reasons as you can why every person who owns property should make a valid will. Read all of **Rules 312-322**, inclusive, again before you try to answer this question.

Oklahoma State Capitol, Oklahoma City
Underwood & Underwood

Oregon State Capitol, Salem
Underwood & Underwood

Pennsylvania State Capitol, Harrisburg
Harrisburg Chamber of Commerce

Rhode Island State Capitol, Providence
Underwood & Underwood

CHAPTER X

LAW OF INSURANCE

Rule 323. *Insurance contracts are not required by law to be written.* Insurance contracts are essentially governed by the general law of contracts whether they concern property, life, health or accident. Parties must be competent; there must be consideration; and the agreements are voidable if they are contrary to law or public policy. Also, unless they are subject to some statutory regulations, contracts of insurance need not be in writing to be enforcible.[1] Such exceptions are very rare. To be sure, the parties to insurance contracts often agree that there shall be no contract of insurance between them until written memoranda have been signed. This is true of nearly all contracts for life insurance and some automobile insurance. Many fire insurance contracts, however, as well as many other kinds of property insurance contracts, are made orally. Such contracts are valid unless they come within one of the rare exceptions already indicated.

Rule 324. *Standard policy statutes do not require written form.* In several states, there are statutes called standard fire insurance policy acts.[2] These acts stipulate that all fire insurance contracts entered into in the state where the statute is in effect must be made in the terms named in the statute. This does not mean that the parties must sign a form containing the terms prescribed in the statute; it means merely that no contract can be made for

---

[1] Two such provisions are found in the Statute of Frauds. One requirement is that a contract to answer for the debt of another must be in writing to be enforcible. This includes fidelity insurance or surety bonds. Another is that if there is a contract to provide insurance, and if such insurance is not to take effect for more than a year after the making of the contract to insure, the Statute of Frauds requires such agreement to be in writing. The latter does not refer to policies of insurance, but only to *contracts to insure.*

[2] See **Rule 47.**

fire insurance coverage in that state, except in the terms set out in the statute; and the practical effect of it is that, no matter what the parties say or write, and no matter what any printed blank which is used may contain, the terms of the contract of fire insurance in those states are set out in the statute book. So, if any contract of fire insurance is made in any of those states, the terms of the contract are set by the law, and not by the agreement of the parties. All that the parties can do is to agree that they will be governed by the terms of the statute.

Rule 325. *Every contract of insurance must be based on an insurable interest.* If an insurance agreement is made by a person who has no insurable interest in the life or property covered by the policy, such agreement is regarded as a wager and not enforcible because wagers have long been regarded as contrary to public policy. Insurable interest is not precisely definable; and since it does not mean quite the same thing in relation to life insurance as in fire (or other property) insurance, it is necessary to discuss the two types separately.

Rule 326. *In property insurance, there must be an insurable interest in the beneficiary of the policy at the time of the loss.* Property insurance is a device for providing protection against loss. Such insurance is valid, therefore, only if the beneficiary of a policy actually sustains a loss due to damage to the property concerned. One of the best definitions of insurable interest in property is: "A person has an insurable interest in property when he sustains such relations with respect to it that he has a reasonable expectation, resting upon basis of legal right, of benefit to be derived from its continued existence, or of loss or liability from its destruction."[3] An owner has an insurable interest in what he owns, of course. A bailee of personal property, a lessee of real property, a mortgagee of either real or personal property, and even a stockholder of a corporation have insurable interests in the property concerned. The interest, however, must exist at the time of the loss. For example, if Jones insured his house against fire and then sold the house to Smith without transferring the insurance (with the company's consent), Jones could not recover on the policy if the house should be

---

[3] Vance: *Law of Insurance* (second edition), page 124.

destroyed. One who has a reversion in real property (see **Rule 304**) or a vested remainder (see **Rule 263**) has an insurable interest; but one who has a contingent remainder (see **Rule 263**) has no insurable interest. The reason for the latter is that if the property is destroyed while his remainder still is contingent, he cannot show any loss as of that time because he has not yet become the owner.

Rule 327. *In life insurance, there must be an interest in the insured by the party who makes the contract at the time the contract is made.* Life insurance is not regarded as an indemnity or compensation, as property insurance is regarded. Every person has an insurable interest in his own life, and he may name as beneficiary anyone at all, so far as the law is concerned; and, in general, near blood relationship is enough to give one an insurable interest in the life of another. In a few cases, even a right to look to the insured for support (as a stepchild may look to a foster parent) is probably a sufficient basis for an insurable interest so that the stepchild could make a valid contract of insurance on the life of the foster parent. Thus, a stranger could not collect upon a policy taken out by him on the life of the world's champion heavyweight; but one who controls the contract of the fighter could take out such a policy which would be valid; and if the champion himself should take out a policy, and if he should name the Tuskegee Institute as beneficiary, the institute would be entitled to recover on the policy in case of his death. The problem of insurable interest does not arise very often in other than property or life insurance because scarcely anyone ever takes out insurance unless his claim to an insurable interest is so strongly based that no one would ever raise any question about it. Those who take out property insurance are nearly always owners, bailees, or lessees, or people who have some other kind of legal interest which gives them an insurable interest.

RISKS COVERED BY INSURANCE

Rule 328. *Losses due to negligence of the insured or beneficiary are covered unless specifically excepted in the policy.* Suppose that Gray's house, which is insured against loss by fire, should be damaged as the result of his negligence in using a worn electric cord in connection with some electrical appliances; or suppose that he had left an electric heating pad in a folding bed and closed the bed, causing a fire. In either of these cases, the damage would have been due to Gray's negligent conduct. In many similar cases, insurance companies have declined to pay losses suffered under such conditions, but the courts have uniformly held that losses due to the negligence of the insured (or beneficiary) are covered by fire policies, life policies, and accident policies unless such losses are definitely excepted in the particular policy.[4]

Rule 329. *Fire insurance covers only losses directly due to hostile fire.* Practically all fire insurance policies contain provisions to this effect. There is some disagreement among the courts in this country as to what is meant by *directly due to fire.* Probably the best practical explanation is that there must be some unbroken connection between the loss complained of and a *hostile* fire, and that the loss must be the kind of loss which is a natural consequence of fire. For example, a fire occurred in a powerhouse, causing a short circuit. The short circuit overloaded a dynamo, which was driven by a belt. With the increased load, the belt broke. This took all the load from the driving pulley of the engine which turned the dynamo, and the speed of the engine increased so that the flywheel broke into pieces, causing considerable damage to machinery and buildings. In another case, Building A was insured against fire. Fire broke out in building B, adjacent to A. As a result of the fire, the walls of B fell upon A. There was no fire in building A, but there was damage done to A by the falling of B. In both of these cases, the loss was held to be directly due to fire.[5] Destruction of property by firemen or police (in the line of duty) to prevent the spread of a fire which is burning at the time of such

---

[4] It should be clear that intentional damage is not usually covered by insurance. But see **Rule 330**, regarding suicide.

[5] In the second case, a provision in the policy which covered A provided that there should be no liability for damage due to falling walls. However, in the particular case, the falling of the walls was directly due to fire, and the loss was covered. This is the universal interpretation of the *falling wall* clauses. If the walls of an insured building fall before a fire or if the fall is not due to fire, the loss caused by the fall is not covered by the policy, even though the fall should be the cause of a fire.

destruction is held to be directly due to fire, and covered by a fire policy which does not provide specifically to the contrary; and the loss or theft of goods which have been set out of a burning building is also said to be directly due to fire and covered by policies insuring such goods.

The distinction between *hostile* fires and *friendly* fires is commonly defined as arising from the fact that a friendly fire is burning in a place where it is supposed to burn for some legitimate purpose, as in a stove, a furnace, or a fireplace, while a hostile fire is one which is burning outside its intended or legitimate place. For example, a great deal of smoke in a building brought about the coming of firemen. The firemen caused some damage by the use of water and axes before they discovered that there was no fire at all outside the stove. All of the smoke came from a leaky flue. The damage was not due to a hostile fire, and it was not covered by the policy of insurance. The burning of loaves in a baker's oven, the peeling of varnish on furniture set too near to a radiator or hot stove, damage to a boiler which was fired while there was no water in it, damage to jewelry which was hidden in a stove when a fire was lighted, damage done by smoke from a lamp chimney—all of these were due to friendly fires and were not covered by the respective policies. On the other hand, when fire in a chimney ejected smoke and soot which damages walls and furniture, when flames escaped from a crack in a smoke-pipe and set off a sprinkler which caused damage by water to goods underneath, or when furniture near a hot stove was actually charred or took fire, then the loss was due to a hostile fire.

Rule 330. *In life insurance, suicide is usually covered if the policy does not specifically provide otherwise, and if the beneficiary is a person.* If a life policy states that there shall be no liability if the insured takes his own life within three years of the date of the policy, and if the insured takes his life after such time, his beneficiary will be entitled to the face value of the policy; and, if the policy says nothing about suicide, the beneficiary can recover the face value of the policy, no matter when the suicide takes place.[6]

---

[6] If it can be shown that the policy was taken out with intent to commit suicide, the policy is voidable on the ground of fraud.

The preceding statements represent the law when the beneficiary of the policy is not the estate of the insured. If the insured's estate is named as beneficiary, in most states, the estate cannot recover if the insured takes his own life, even if the policy contains no stipulations at all about suicide.[7] This question has produced so many lawsuits that most life policies now state clearly either that the policy does not cover loss of the insured's life due to suicide, whether he is sane or insane during some period named in the policy, or that it does cover death from any but certain stated causes, not naming suicide.

Rule 331. *Accident policies should be read with the greatest care.* Accident policies vary a great deal in their terms, especially as to risks which are to be covered by them. Because of this fact, it is impossible to make accurate general statements as to the risks covered by accident policies. In addition, there is no satisfactory answer to the question: What is an accident? Every holder of an accident policy should scrutinize the terms of his policy with great care before any loss occurs. In no other way is it possible to tell what risks are covered by the policy. Some accident policies cover disease, and some do not; some cases hold that *accident* includes the consequences of a hemorrhage suffered while shaking down the ashes in a furnace, or the consequences of a cold bath, or an ear infection from a nasal spray, while other policies deny that such events are accidents. The practical effect of this is the necessity of emphasizing the rule at the head of this paragraph. The best policy, in this sense, is the policy which is most specific, both as to what an accident is and as to what consequences of accidents are, and what are not, covered by the policy.

AMOUNT OF RECOVERY

In life and accident insurance contracts, questions do not often arise as to the amount of recovery because the amount of payment to be made upon the occurrence of certain events is definitely stated. But, in fire insurance, automobile insurance, and other

---

[7] In three or four states, it has been held that in the latter type of case, the policy covers suicide while the insured is insane, but that it does not cover suicide while he is sane.

property insurance, the question of the amount of recovery is often an important one.

Rule 332. *Under an open policy, recovery is limited to the amount of the actual loss.* An open policy is one in which the amount named is regarded as merely the upper limit of the insurer's liability, but it does not follow that the amount named can be recovered, even if the property is wholly destroyed. For example, suppose you insure your building and receive a policy which states that in case of total loss, the insurer shall pay not to exceed $12,000. Of course, if the building is damaged in an amount less than total value of the property, and also less than $12,000, you may recover the value of the loss, or, under many policies, the insurer may discharge his obligation by restoring the property to its former condition. Furthermore, if the building should be totally destroyed, the insurer under an open policy, may show, if he can, that the value of the property is less than the amount named in the policy. Thus, if the insurer should be able to convince judge or jury that your building was worth only $9,000 when it was destroyed, if it were wholly destroyed, you would be able to recover only $9,000 in spite of the fact that you had a $12,000 policy. If a policy is an open one, the holder runs the risk of this kind of result.

Rule 333. *Under a valued policy, one may recover the stated value in case of total loss of the property.* In a valued policy, the insurer agrees that the value of the property is some stipulated sum. For instance, if a policy states, "Insure the said property, valued at $12,000," etc., total destruction of the property would entitle the insured to collect the full amount of the policy. Under a valued policy, the insurer is not entitled to introduce any evidence of value at all in case of total loss.[8] In some states, under so-called valued policy statutes, practically all fire insurance policies are valued policies because the statutes so require.

Rule 334. *Under valued policies, partial loss must be paid in full.* Suppose that a building, valued at $25,000, actual value,

---

[8] Of course, an insurance contract can be avoided for fraud, just as any other contract. Therefore, an insurance company may always be permitted to show that the difference between the value of the property and the amount stated in the policy is so great as to be fraudulent; but not many cases are won on this ground.

were insured under a valued policy of $10,000. If a fire should damage the building to the extent of $15,000, some insurers have contended that, since the property was insured for only two-fifths of its value, the insurer should bear only two-fifths of the loss. But the courts will allow recovery for the loss, in such cases, up to the full amount named in the policy.[9] Some policies provide that, if insurance is not carried up to 80 per cent of the full value of the property, then, in case of partial loss the insurer shall be liable only proportionately. Such clauses are called 80 per cent clauses. Under them, the rule of proportionate liability is enforced. All policies should be read carefully with these points in mind. It should also be kept in mind that policies which contain 80 per cent clauses are very often open policies, except in those states where they are made valued policies by valued policy statutes.

Rule 335. *Options of an insurer to rebuild are held valid.* In many fire insurance policies, the insurers reserve the right, by specific provisions, to choose whether they will pay the loss or rebuild the damaged property. Under such a clause the insurer may pay a part and rebuild a part, this choice being left entirely to him. If he elects to rebuild, he must notify the insured to that effect within thirty days of the time of notice of the loss (under a standard policy); and, once he elects to rebuild, he can be compelled to complete the reconstruction, even if completion should involve higher costs than his liability under the policy.

Rule 336. *Automobile insurance is subject to rules similar to those concerning fire policies and should be examined with equal care.* Many automobile insurance policies are open policies whether they relate to losses due to fire, theft, collision, or other causes. That is, the amount named is treated as an indication of the maximum liability of the insurer; and the question as to the actual value can always be raised upon total loss. The result is that some automobile owners are not so well covered by insurance as they would be under valued policies. It is true that the amount named in a valued policy is usually somewhat lower than the amount

---

[9] A different rule is in effect in marine insurance where the rule of proportionate liability is enforced. But marine insurance is not within the province of a general book on commercial law.

named in an open policy; but the valued policy, as has been pointed out, has the advantage for the insured that, when total loss occurs, he is entitled to recover the full amount named in the policy, always excepting fraud, of course. Automobile theft policies also include, as a usual rule, obligations to pay for partial loss or damage due to theft.

In this connection, there are certain matters peculiar to automobile insurance. In the first place, such policies as cover loss by theft apply only to theft as interpreted to mean the same thing as the term *larceny* in the criminal law. That is, there is no theft unless the car has been taken with intent to steal. This is usually true of burglary and bank insurance too. For instance, a car had been left for repairs and greasing at a certain garage. During the evening, some employees of the garage took the car out for a joy ride. They were involved in an accident, and, while the owner might have a right against the garage owner in most cases, the loss was not covered by his theft policy because the men intended to bring the car back to the garage; they did not intend to steal it.[10]

In the second place, practically all theft policies provide that they shall be void if there are any incumbrances other than those noted in the policy. This provision is strictly enforced. The owner who mortgages his car to secure a loan must notify the insurer of the incumbrance if the insurance against theft is to remain in effect. This information is useful not only to car owners, but to those who lend money upon this kind of security.

In the third place, collision insurance is often of less value than the insured believes. It has been held many times that the term *collision* restricts the right of the insured's recovery to those cases in which the car actually runs into some obstacle upon the road or elsewhere. It does not cover damage due to upsetting, the falling of walls or trees upon the car, or skidding into a ditch. Some courts have gone so far as to say that the term means some contact between the car and some other object upon the same plane or level. Thus, when a driver turned down into a grassy field to detour around a broken culvert and tried to come back upon the road at a right angle, and one of his front wheels collapsed and

---

[10] In some states, the rule is modified by statute.

broke down upon the shoulder of the road, it was held that this was not a collision within the meaning of his policy. Another driver accidently drove his car down a bank and into a river. The court said that this was not a collision, using the following language: "To bring the case within the policy, there must have been, first, a collision; second, the collision must have been with another automobile, vehicle, or somewhat similar object; and, third, it must not have been with any portion of the roadbed, meaning the ground on which the machine was running or attempting to run." The term is a very uncertain one when used without qualification; and one should, if possible, acquire a policy which uses the term in the sense that it covers more than mere collision as the term is usually defined by courts. Such a policy as is desirable would so define the term *collision* as to include coverage of skidding, losses due to striking holes in pavement, and other common perils of the road. It is, in fact, the common perils against which one most needs insurance. There are policies which cover such perils, even down to punctures and blowouts. If the premiums are somewhat higher upon such policies, they are worth the difference; and if one does not feel the need of complete coverage, there is always available the fifty- or one-hundred-dollar exemption policy, which, while it covers the same kinds of risks as the full coverage, does not cover those losses which are small in amount.

In the fourth place, liability insurance usually confines the liability of the insurer to those losses which are legally chargeable to the insured; it does not often extend to all losses in which insured is involved. Such liability also usually covers losses or damage legally chargeable to any person (generally not less than 16 years old) who is lawfully operating the car with the insured's consent. The same things are true, in general, of property damage insurance. These two latter kinds of insurance, but especially liability insurance, are useful not only because they relieve one of the danger of many financial losses; also, one of their principal values lies in the fact that they relieve one of the strain, inconvenience and harassment attendant upon the necessity of defending claims brought by those who may feel that the insured is responsible for the claimant's injuries or losses.

Perhaps it is worth while to emphasize once more the fact that the contractual character of insurance policies renders it of the very first importance that the holder of insurance of all kinds should examine his policies with extraordinary care, so that he may know what assurances and promises of indemnity he gets for his money. Large sums are lost every year because holders of automobile insurance policies do not know how much, or how little, their policies actually cover of the risks which thé insured parties have assumed to be covered. Read your policies today and see what protection they promise you.

THE RIGHTS OF BENEFICIARIES OF LIFE INSURANCE

Rule 337. *If a life policy is payable to the estate of the insured, it is subject to the claims of his creditors.* If a life policy is payable to the insured, personally, or to his administrator or representatives, it is regarded as an asset of his estate upon his death, and, as such, it cannot be distributed to his heirs or next of kin along with other assets until all creditors' claims have been met. From this, it follows that when a policy is so payable as to be considered an asset of the estate of the insured, the insured may use the policy during his life as collateral for any debts or obligations; and, should an insured die after having made such a pledge, the pledgee is entitled to full satisfaction of his claim from the proceeds of the insurance before any of those proceeds can be used for any other purpose.[11]

Rule 338. *When a life policy is payable to some person other than the insured's estate, it is not subject to the claims of creditors.* If a policy is payable to the wife of the insured, for example, it cannot be made available to the creditors of the insured. It is not regarded as an asset of the estate. It is the property of the beneficiary. In most states, if the policy is payable to the heirs of the insured, it is not regarded as payable to the estate, but as payable to those persons who are determined by law to be the heirs of the insured, and the creditors of the insured have no claims

---

[11] There are a few states in which policies so payable are exempt from creditors' claims. This is another matter of local law.

against it. Every person whose life is insured should investigate this aspect of his policy and see to it, if possible,[12] that the matter is adjusted as he wishes it to be.

Rule 339. *The beneficiary of a life policy is the owner of a vested interest in the proceeds, of which not even the insured can deprive the beneficiary.* Under the typical *old line* or *reserve* life insurance policy, when the beneficiary is designated by name, he is said to have a vested right. This means that once such a policy has gone into effect, the insured cannot change the beneficiary without the latter's consent. For example, Patterson took out a policy of this type, naming as beneficiary Miss Alice Lemon, his fiancee. The policy was delivered to Miss Lemon's brother for safe keeping. Sometime later the engagement was broken off, and Patterson induced Miss Lemon's brother to surrender the policy. Patterson turned the policy over to the company and took in its place another policy in which his own brother was named as beneficiary. This was done without the consent of Miss Lemon. When Patterson died, the insurance was paid to his brother; but, in a suit by Miss Lemon against the company, it was held that the company must pay the amount of the policy to her. That is, as beneficiary of this old line policy, she had a property interest of which the connivance of the insured and insurer could not deprive her. Of course, if the premiums had not been paid, or if any other condition of the policy had not been performed, Miss Lemon would not have been entitled to receive anything. However, she is the vested owner of the rights under the policy because the rights, such as they are, cannot be taken away without the beneficiary's consent. This rule applies in just the same way whether the beneficiary has received his right as a part of a contract or whether he is a gratuitous beneficiary; and the same rule is extended to endowment and personal accident policies, as the law is interpreted in most states.

As a consequence of this rule, the beneficiary, not the insured, is the owner of the policy. Even if the insured should refuse to pay premiums, it is the legal right of the beneficiary to be permitted by the insurer to pay the premiums himself and so protect his interest.

---

[12] Sometimes changes cannot be made, as indicated in the discussion under **Rule 339.**

It follows, too, from this rule, that the policy may be assigned by the beneficiary, and not by the insured, and that the policy, as a part of the estate of the beneficiary, is subject to attachment by the beneficiary's creditors; and, in most states, if the beneficiary of such a policy dies before the insured does, the policy belongs to the estate of the deceased beneficiary. Another result of this rule is that, if the beneficiary of a policy should be the spouse of insured, divorce does not affect at all the rights of the beneficiary under the policy.

Rule 340. *One who insures his own life may reserve the right to change the beneficiary.* If a policy contains a clause which reserves for the insured the right to change the beneficiary, the beneficiary under such a policy does not have a vested interest until the death of the insured takes place. A great many modern policies contain such provisions. Under such clauses, the insured is able to use the policy as collateral for his own debts, since, in order to do so, it is necessary that he only change the policy so that his creditor becomes the beneficiary. The change is effective only if made with the consent of the insurer. The right to make such a change is one which is personal to the insured, and it cannot be used on behalf of his creditors, nor does it pass to his estate upon his death.[13]

Rule 341. *Beneficiaries of fraternal policies do not have vested interests, as a rule.* Under a fraternal policy, the insurer may change the identity of the insured at any time, subject only to the provisions of the rules of the society. Also, the insured does not have any property interest in the policy. The policy, therefore, cannot be used as collateral for loans by the insured.[14] Under modern conditions, very few of such policies remain. Nearly all of the fraternal societies have, during recent years, converted their insurance

---

[13] If one is thrown into bankruptcy while he is insured under a policy which provides power to change the beneficiary, the power passes to the trustee in bankruptcy.

[14] There are some exceptions to **Rules 340 and 341** which are based upon technicalities of local law in some states. For example, in most states, if a beneficiary of a fraternal policy has paid the premiums, or if the fraternal insurance has been taken out in performance of an antenuptial contract, the insured may not change the beneficiary without the latter's consent.

policies to the reserve type. The reason is that, due to the rapidly
falling rate at which new members have joined such societies, the
number of assessments (per annum) levied upon the members has
materially increased. In these fraternal societies, under the old
plan of insurance, each member is assessed his *pro rata* share of the
amount paid out upon the policies of deceased members. Under
this plan, if deaths of insured members average ten persons in a
thousand per year, each member will be required to pay each year
a little more than one one-thousandth of the value of the policies
held by those who have died. This means that each member will
pay in assessments something like ten dollars per thousand dollars
of insurance. Due to a decrease in the rate at which new members
join a given society, the average age of the members rises every
year, and the death rate per thousand may become double or treble
or even quadruple in a comparatively short time. And since the
assessment rate must rise with the death rate, the cost of such
insurance can very easily, and in a short time, rise much higher
than the cost of old line or reserve insurance. The conversion of
insurance from fraternal to reserve, therefore, is entirely sound,
and its cost to the members is certainly less than the eventual cost
would be to the surviving members if the conversion were not made.

INSURANCE AGENTS

Practically all modern insurance is written in the name of
incorporated companies, which, by their very nature, must carry
on their businesses through the instrumentality of human beings.
These persons are agents, in the legal sense, so far as they represent
their companies in contractual transactions; but some representatives of insurance companies are not agents at all.

Rule 342. *Fire insurance salesmen are usually agents.* In
the making of a fire insurance contract, as a general rule, the contract is made between the customer and the insurance salesman.
At the instant the salesman and the customer come to an agreement, there is a contract between the customer and the insurance
company. Thus, if one calls an insurance agent and says, "Insure
my garage for seven hundred dollars from noon today," and if the
agent answers, "All right," there is a contract. This is true in spite

of the fact that the insured does not know the amount of the premium, nor even the name of the company which the agent represents. Of course, as was pointed out under **Rule 152,** if a legal issue should arise as to the authority of the agent, the burden of proof is upon the customer (in such a case) to show the agent's authority. He may do this by showing either that there was actual authority or that there was an implication of authority; but the latter must be based upon some act of the company to be valid.

Suppose that Stone has carried a fire policy for some years with the Glimmer Company. He had always made his arrangements through the Wells Realty Company. Stone made premium checks payable to the Glimmer Company. The checks were returned through Stone's bank, duly indorsed by the Glimmer Company, but no correspondence was ever exchanged between Stone and the Glimmer Company. Now, suppose that Stone asked the Wells Company to renew his policy and they agreed to do so; but before the policy was issued or the premiums paid, the insured building was destroyed by fire. Upon proof of loss, the Glimmer Company refused to pay upon the ground that the Wells Company had never been authorized to act as agent for it. In spite of this objection, the Glimmer Company is liable on the policy. The indorsement of the checks would be regarded as a practically conclusive estoppel of the Glimmer Company to deny the authority of the Wells Company.[15]

This rule extends even to sub-agents. In most large cities, fire insurance companies commonly appoint district managers who make comparatively few contacts directly with customers. They parcel out the work of writing policies to real estate men, bankers, automobile salesmen, and the like. In many cases, these appointees are not really agents of the insurance companies. In fact, it is often true that the insurance companies do not even know the names of such appointees; but the insurance companies do, as a rule, know that this is the kind of arrangement in use. The customer, on the other hand, often knows nothing about the arrange-

---

[15] Of course, if the checks were indorsed under such circumstances that it was not fair to assume that the indorser knew why the checks came to it, the estoppel would not lie; but such circumstances are rare.

ment. The customer merely knows that he deals with his banker or real estate acquaintance and that the policy and bill for premium follow in due course. This custom is so widespread, that insurance companies are usually bound by transactions entered into by such appointees of general agents.

For example, in January of 1928, Cardy paid a twenty-four dollar premium on a three-thousand dollar fire insurance policy covering household goods. He made his check payable to the Olson Land Company, through which he had procured several other policies in the past. In November of 1928, Cardy received a letter from the X insurance agency, stating that the X agency was general representative for the M insurance company and that a policy issued by the M company would be cancelled unless he should pay the twenty-four dollar premium at once. Cardy at once wrote the X agency, stating the facts of his side of the matter and asking them not to cancel the policy. He also called on the Olson Company who had indorsed his check, but it was in arrears on some thousands of similar transactions for which they had not remitted premiums either to the X agency or to the M company. In the particular case, the amount involved was small and no great damage could have been done unless the insured property had been damaged by fire during the time of the dispute. But there is no doubt at all that the M company could have been held liable under the policy, had a loss occurred. The fact that the M company had done business in the same way through the same Olson Company in the past raises the presumption that it has authorized the Olson Company to continue acting for the M company in the same way.[16]

Rule 343. *An insurance agent may bind his company within the apparent scope of his authority.* A principal is bound not only by contracts made by his agents, but also by his agents' frauds and representations. For example, Kraus was induced by fraud to take out a policy of insurance with the X company. The fraud

---

[16] When this was pointed out to the manager of the Olson Company and the X agency, and when they were advised that, unless the policy were at once reinstated, Cardy would place the facts before the M company and before the Insurance Commission of the state, the policy was reinstated within twenty-four hours. As a matter of fact, as has been pointed out, the policy was valid all the time.

consisted of a statement that similar insurance in the same company had been taken out by over half of the farmers in the county. When Kraus learned that this was not true, he was entitled to rescind the policy and recover his premium. The fraud of an agent within the scope of his employment is chargeable to the principal, whether or not the principal knows of the fraud. In another case, a policy was written covering a peculiar kind of risk which the agent had been told by his company not to accept. This was not known to the policyholder. After the company had learned of the facts, it discharged the agent; but it could not avoid the agreement because the knowledge of an agent (as to any transaction) is chargeable to the principal.

Rule 344. *An insurance company is bound by waivers made by agents.* Most policies stipulate that they shall not be valid whenever certain stated conditions exist, such as the keeping of explosives on the insured premises, the riding of the insured in nonscheduled airplanes, the use of insured premises for certain purposes, and the like. It often happens that the insured desires to do some of these things and that he asks the agent who wrote his policy what can be done about it. It often happens, too, that the agent believes that the proposed action will not invalidate the policy, and the agent often says, "You go ahead. I will take it up with the company, and if you don't hear from me, you will know that it is all right." If the agent, under such circumstances, does not subsequently advise the policyholder to the contrary, the company is almost always held to be bound by the so-called waiver of conditions by the agent. The reason is that such waivers are regarded as being within the agent's apparent authority. For this reason, many modern policies contain distinct limitations upon the powers of agents. It is very often provided that no agent may waive conditions in a policy unless he does it by writing upon the policy. These stipulations, of course, are generally restrictive of the powers of the agent who makes the agreement with the customer; such provisions also apply to the general officers of insurance companies. But, since it is sometimes difficult to be sure whether such restrictions refer to all agents or only to those who make the normal daily contacts with customers, some companies try to avoid misunderstandings by providing that waivers of conditions are valid only when made by the home office, or by some designated officer of the company.

Rule 345. *Life insurance agents are not agents, in the legal sense, as a general rule.* The ordinary life insurance *agent* does not make contracts on behalf of his principal. He merely solicits applications for insurance. These applications provide specifically that no contract will exist until the application has been approved in writing by the home office of the company. But the solicitor of life insurance does make representations and promises; he sometimes waives conditions; and he sometimes makes fradulent representations. Under all such circumstances, although he is not strictly an agent, his actions are binding upon his company, so far as such actions are within the apparent scope of his authority; but, in general, the apparent scope of the authority of such an "agent" is rather limited. He is a salesman solicitor, not really an agent.

QUESTIONS AND PROBLEMS

1. Does the law, in most states, require that contracts of insurance be in writing in order to be valid? To understand the footnote to **Rule 323,** reread the discussion of the Statute of Frauds, **Rule 46.**

2. Read the discussion under **Rule 324** very carefully a couple of times. Do you understand that, in a state where the standard policy law is in effect, every kind of policy is subject to the statute? If not, which kinds are so subject? Do you understand that the parties cannot make a valid contract of fire insurance in such states, except in the terms of the standard policy?

3. Suppose that Wilson, an alumnus of Y College, insured all of his property, naming as the payee or beneficiary of the policies the board of trustees of Y College. If the buildings should be destroyed by fire within the time limit of the policies, would the trustees of the college be able to recover the amount due under the policies? If this were the wish of Wilson, and if the insurance company agreed to it with knowledge of all the facts, what legal objection could be made to the recovery? **Rule 325.** See also page 167.

4. Hill was the owner of a house and lot, which he mortgaged to Glendin as security for a debt. The title was registered in the name of Hill, but the mortgage was a conveyance in form, as discussed in Chapter IX. Suppose that Hill insured the property in his own name and then transferred the policy to Glendin with the assent of the in-

surance company. If a loss occurred to the property before the expiration of the policy, would Glendin be allowed to recover under it, at least to the extent of his debt? **Rule 326.**

5. If, upon the same general facts as those given in question 3, the policies were life policies, would your answer be affected at all, and if so, how? **Rule 327.**

6. Read the discussion of the case in the first paragraph under **Rule 339.** That discussion says nothing about insurable interest. Comparing it with **Rule 327,** what seems to you to be the source of the insurable interest in the case in **Rule 339?** Or do you think the matter was overlooked in the Lemon case?

7. Link was the owner of a car, which was insured against loss by fire. Link negligently set fire to the car by dropping a lighted cigarette behind the seat and not looking for it at once. He assumed it would go out. Would the insurance policy be held to cover a loss due to such a cause? **Rule 328.**

8. What is the distinction between losses directly due to fire and losses remotely due to fire, as nearly as you can state it? What is the distinction made between hostile fire and friendly fire? Give an illustration not found in the text. **Rule 329.**

9. What is the general rule about the liability of insurance companies upon life policies if the insured commits suicide and if the policy makes no provisions with respect to suicide? In order to avoid questions of this kind, what is the usual policy of insurance companies in recent years? **Rule 330.**

10. What general statement can be made about the character of the risks covered by accident policies? Why does the discussion under **Rule 331** warn the reader to be sure to read very carefully any accident policy which he may hold?

11. What is an open policy of insurance? To what kind or kinds of insurance is the term usually applied? If, under an open policy, there is a total loss of the property covered and the amount named in the policy is $11,000, what is the insured entitled by law to recover? **Rule 332.**

12. What is a valued policy? In connection with what kinds of policies is this term used? If, under a valued policy in which the amount named is $11,000, there is a total loss of the property covered, what is the insured entitled by law to recover? **Rule 333.**

13. What is an *80 per cent clause* in a contract of insurance? What is its significance? **Rule 334.**

14. There is no statement in the text as to the amount recovered in case of partial loss under an open policy. From a careful reading of the discussions under **Rules 332-335,** write out a statement of your

opinion as to the answer to the question: How will the courts determine the amount of recovery for partial loss under an open policy? The answer is probably related most closely to **Rule 332** and the discussion under it.

15. Is an option of an insurer to rebuild upheld? **Rule 335.**

16. Give at least two reasons why an owner of an automobile should prefer an open or a valued policy covering his car against losses by fire, theft, and collision. Read the whole discussion under **Rule 336** and choose the best reasons you can find there. You will not find them in so many words, perhaps, but you can work them out.

17. Discuss on paper the meaning of the term *collision,* as used in automobile insurance policies. Is the meaning of the term clear? Does the word mean what you would expect before reading the text? Does it mean, in most policies, all that you think the ordinary car owner would wish it to mean? What should the car owner do about the confusion which you find here as to the meaning of the word? **Rule 336.**

18. If you have any insurance policies at all, get them out and read them through. See how many things you find which you do not understand. Note the things which you do understand, in the light of your reading this chapter. If your policies contain clauses which you do not like, have them changed through the agent or solicitor who wrote them for you.

19. Jensen was insured under life policies aggregating $25,000. Of this amount, $15,000 was payable to his wife, $5,000 to his estate, $4,000 to his daughter, and $1,000 to one of his creditors, the F Bank. Which of these policies could be attached by the creditors of Jensen, other than the F Bank? Which could be attached by the F Bank? **Rule 338.**

20. Under an *old line* policy of life insurance, who is the real owner of the policy—the insured or the beneficiary? What can be done to change this situation? When must it be done, if at all? **Rules 339 and 340.**

21. Why is it true that life insurance *agents* are usually not agents at all in the true legal sense of the word? **Rule 345.**

22. Read the case discussed in the last paragraph under **Rule 342.** Then read **Rule 343.** Is this insurance law, or is it the law of agent and principal? If it is the latter, to what principle in that law are these two discussions related? See **Rules 142** and **160.** Read them again, carefully and entirely.

South Carolina State Capitol, Columbia
Underwood & Underwood

South Dakota State Capitol, Pierre
Underwood & Stratton

Tennessee State Capitol, Nashville
Underwood & Underwood

Texas State Capitol, Austin
Underwood & Underwood

CHAPTER XI

EMPLOYERS' LIABILITY FOR INJURIES TO EMPLOYEES[1]

Rule 346. *At common law, the liability of an employer for injuries to his employees, in their employment, was based on the law of negligence.* In 1888, when the common law in this field was still in effect, James was a railroad brakeman. The coupling devices in common use at that time were extremely dangerous, and, while coupling some cars together, James was seriously injured. The coupling devices on the particular cars were up-to-date, but one of them was defective. However, the only kind of action which he could bring, in those days, was an action of negligence. Success of the plaintiff in such an action depended upon showing that the defendant (the railroad company in this case) had failed to exercise ordinary care in the furnishing and inspection of equipment which the employee used. In our case, James was unable to show lack of ordinary care on the part of the company, and so his action failed.

In the course of its opinion, the court pointed out that, under the common law, it was the lawful duty of an employer (a) to furnish a reasonably safe place and reasonably modern equipment, (b) to exercise ordinary care to keep the premises and the equipment in safe condition, (c) to give warning of dangerous conditions which a reasonably careful inspection by the employer should have exposed, (d) to exercise ordinary care in the selection of workmen to work with his other employees, and (e) to exercise ordinary care in the work, whenever the employer should work alongside his employees. This was the extent of an employer's duty to his

---

[1] This chapter rather closely resembles a part of the author's *Modern Business Law,* by permission of the MacMillan Company, publishers.

men, so far as injury was concerned, unless he should, by contract, assume greater obligations. The latter were very seldom assumed.

Rule 347. *The common law rules put serious risks upon employees in industrial and mechanical employments.* The common law doctrine of liability for negligence is attended by three important corollaries:

(*a*) *The doctrine of assumption of risk* assumes that when a man accepts employment, he understands the types of risks which he is taking; that he is able to note and evaluate any risks which are peculiar to the particular job; that a part of his pay is given in return for his assumption of those risks; and that he is free to accept the job, as it is, with all its risks, or to reject it. All this is logical enough if we assume that the law of negligence is a proper foundation for the determination of liability. Because it puts so much of the risk of loss on the workers, the real question is whether or not the law of negligence should be taken as the basis of liability. The doctrine of the assumption of risks has, in hundreds of cases, produced results similar to those in the following cases. Hill was a locomotive engineer. Once, when his locomotive was running about forty miles per hour, some part of the engine frame gave way, some parts fouled the wheels, and the engine was derailed. Hill's leg was broken, and he suffered several weeks' loss of work in addition to the expenses of treatment. He was unable to show that the accident was due to negligence of the company in inspection or otherwise, and he was unable to recover any part of his loss. He was held to have assumed the risk of this kind of accident, just as James was held to have assumed the risks due to the kind of couplers in use. Such risks were regarded as a regular part of those kinds of work.

(*b*) *The doctrine of contributory negligence* assumes that no one should be allowed to recover for the negligence of another if the plaintiff's own negligence was a part of the responsible cause of his own injury. For example, Hurd was employed in a factory in which there were a number of overhead racks upon which hung tools and equipment. The racks were old and weak, and Hurd, noticing their condition, spoke to his foreman about the matter. The foreman replied, "Those racks have been there a long time and they have never fallen down. They may be getting old, but I guess they are all right. If you don't want to work under them, you can go to the paymaster and get your money. I can't take time to fix them now." Hurd continued to work, and a few days later one of the racks gave way and some of the equipment fell upon Hurd, injuring him. When he sought recovery for eleven weeks' disability, it was clear that the employer was negligent because he had been warned of the condition; but it was held, as in many other cases of this sort, that, since Hurd knew of the danger, he was negligent in continuing to work under such conditions. He was denied recovery on the ground of contributory negligence since his own negligence was a part of the cause of his injury. In a similar case, the foreman promised to remedy the defect; but even then, it was held that, while the employer was negligent, the employee was prevented from recovering because of his contributory negligence. Here, again, the real question is whether or not the basis of liability should be the law of negligence, which places so large a risk on the workers.

(c) *The fellow-servant rule* provides that if an employee is injured due to the negligence of a fellow servant, the injured employee cannot recover anything from the common employer of the two fellow servants. Coyne was a member of a gang of workmen who were unloading rails from railroad cars. The time was near when their work train must go to a siding to permit the passing of another train. The men were hurrying to complete the work of unloading the last car. Gray, one of the men working with Coyne, released his hold upon a rail too soon, and as a result the rail fell and crushed Coyne's foot. Gray was clearly negligent, and since the negligence of a servant is imputed to his master, Coyne brought suit against the employer in an action of negligence. He was unable to recover because of the fact that Coyne and Gray were fellow servants, and the fellow-servant rule denied recovery.[2]

These three corollaries of the law of negligence place upon an employee the risks of injury due to the nature of the work,

---

[2] If Coyne could have shown that the employer was negligent in hiring Gray or in continuing to employ him, Coyne would not have been prevented from recovering by the fellow-servant rule.

the risks of the employee's own failure to use proper care, and the risks of the carelessness of those who are employed to work with him. In the days of simple employments, when these doctrines of negligence were first used, perhaps not much hardship was caused. Workers in those days were more often than not members of their employer's households, and injuries were not very serious, in most cases. But, under the conditions of modern industrial production, the workman encounters massive machinery, powerful electric currents, chemical preparations, and many other things with regard to which he cannot fairly be expected to accept the risk; and even if he does see all of the dangers, he usually cannot afford to leave a job merely because it has become more dangerous than he at first thought it to be. Also, under complex modern conditions of production, fellow servants are not always able to judge the perils due to their working together because they may be miles apart. It must also be remembered that, in order to escape the charge of contributory negligence, a man must sometimes expose his fellow servants by disclosing their carelessness to the employer; and, in other cases, if there is no remedy for the condition of which he complains, he can escape the consequences of the rule of contributory negligence only by leaving the job. The choice is not always between a safe job and an unsafe job; it is, very often, a choice between an unsafe job and no job at all.

In spite of the fact that the law of negligence placed by far the larger part of the risks of injury upon the employee, some employers attempted to escape all liability by requiring their employees to agree, as a part of the contract of employment, that the employer should not be liable for any injuries suffered by the employees, no matter what the cause. Such agreements were declared invalid because they were contrary to public policy.[3] But, when such agreements were signed by employees, they were often effective because an employee thought such an agreement was valid and did not bring suit.

In addition to these risks, another element of uncertainty is often involved. Suppose that the employer is clearly liable in a given case, but that he refuses to pay damages until he is com-

---
[3] See **Rule 55.**

pelled to do so by a court judgment. In such circumstances, the injured man must undertake an expensive law suit, which may be delayed for a long time and may eventually result in a failure of his claim.

All of these risks of loss fall not only upon the injured employee, but also upon his family and even upon society as a whole. A man may, in some cases, be unable to resume his former employment, his children may have to leave school, and the man himself may be reduced to beggary or even tempted to crime. Taking the whole matter together, it has seemed socially desirable that the costs of industrial accidents should, as far as possible, be borne by the industries in which they occur; and beyond that point, they should be put upon society in the form of increased prices due to increased costs of production.

Rule 348. *Workmens' Compensation Acts have made important changes in the law.* Shortly after 1890, legislatures in this country began to realize the inadequacy of the common law rules for dealing with the results of industrial accidents, and some states set about trying to provide legal remedies for this defect in the common law. A few of the states adopted Employers' Liability Acts which abolished the fellow-servant rule in some cases and the doctrine of contributory negligence in others; but nothing very effective was done by legislation until after 1910. During a few years following that date, Workmens' Compensation Acts were adopted in all but four or five of the states. In general, these statutes provide that every injury received by an employee as the result of "an accident arising out of and in the course of his employment" shall be compensated for by his employer, in accordance with carefully worked out schedules. To make sure that all required payments will be made, employers are required to deposit bonds or to maintain insurance funds or to contribute to funds maintained by the state.[4] Under these acts, whenever an employee is injured in the course of an employment which is subject to the act, it is the duty of the employer to pay the scheduled compensation. If he does not, the injured man may submit his case

---

[4] Several sentences immediately following this point are taken from *Modern Business Law*.

292 FUNDAMENTAL BUSINESS LAW

to an industrial commission which has power to decide the matter. The only question to be argued before the commission is whether or not the injury was due to an accident arising out of and in the course of employment; and appeals may be taken to an ordinary law court, not upon questions of fact, but only upon questions of law. The acts apply to all accidents except in certain specified employments, such as agriculture, domestic service, and a few others. They do not apply, typically, to injuries which are due to the injured person's intent or to those received while the employee is intoxicated. In some states, the acts apply to industrial diseases as well as to accidents. It is evident that these acts, in one way or another, practically abolish the fellow-servant rule, the doctrine of assumption of risk, and the application of the contributory negligence rule in all the cases which come within the terms of the acts.

Rule 349. *Federal statutes have made other changes in the law.* Under the Constitution of the United States, Congress is authorized to regulate interstate commerce. In 1893, in the exercise of this power, Congress enacted the Safety Appliance Act. This statute (with its several subsequent amendments) provides that certain kinds of coupling devices, brakes, ladders, grab irons, boilers and boiler equipment, and the like, must be placed upon all cars and trains which carry passengers or goods or which otherwise operate in interstate commerce. The act provides penalties for failures to maintain the standards set by it. In 1908, again exercising its power over interstate commerce, Congress passed the Federal Employers' Liability Act. This statute provides that, whenever any railway employee is injured while he is engaged in interstate commerce, provided such injury is due to the failure of his employer to observe the requirements of the safety appliance act (or any of its amendments), the employer shall be liable in damages without regard to the common law rules of negligence or its corollaries, the fellow-servant rule, contributory negligence, or assumption of risk. These acts, of course, apply only to railway employees who are engaged in interstate commerce at the time they are injured.[5]

Rule 350. *Both state and federal acts have improved the legal and economic position of workers with regard to risks of*

[5] Taken from *Modern Business Law*.

injury. The details of the acts named in the previous paragraph, whether state or federal, cannot be considered here. The important feature of the Safety Appliance Act is that it produces a reduction of the number of actual injuries by requiring the use of equipment of a high standard of safety. The important features of the Liability Act and the Compensation Acts are that they make the procedure of compensation more expeditious, more certain, and less expensive than common law procedure was; that they put the risks of loss due to accidents in industry upon the industry itself or upon its customers; and, apparently, that they exert a pressure which tends to reduce the number of accidents, by making it financially worth the employers' while to try to prevent accidents. It is probable, too, that the effect of the acts upon workmen, generally, is to increase their feeling of economic security,[6] and, thus, to increase their value as workmen and as members of society. Certainly, these acts reduce the dangers of pauperism, so far as the latter may be due to loss of employment by reason of injury, and they also give an important measure of protection to the families of injured workmen. Some authorities believe that this type of legislation was very largely responsible for the "Safety First" movement because these statutes made safety profitable to employers generally. The fewer accidents, the less the losses and the lower the rates for insurance covering such losses.

Rule 351. *These acts do not apply to all injuries.* The Liability Act and the Compensation Acts, of course, apply only to injuries which are within the terms of these acts; but within the terms are included practically all employees in those industries where the risks of injury are high, where they are concealed from the ordinary worker, and where the worker has no way of defending himself against apparent risks except by quitting the job. The common law rules continue to apply, generally, to domestic workers and farm workers because those employments are specifically excepted from the terms of the Compensation Acts; and the common law also applies to employees of those who employ only a very few workers—usually less than four or five—the number varying in the different states.

---

[6] From *Modern Business Law*.

QUESTIONS AND PROBLEMS

1. In the case of James under **Rule 346,** why was it that under the common law, in spite of the fact that the equipment was not in good order, the company was not liable for the injury to James when he was injured in the performance of his ordinary duties?

2. Before you try to think through the next three or four questions, be sure to read carefully the whole of the discussion under **Rule 347.** If you do not do that, you will miss some of the important points covered.

3. State in your own language the common law doctrine of the assumption of risks by employees. Give an illustration from your own experience or from that of an acquaintance. **Rule 347.**

4. What is the doctrine of contributory negligence? Note that it applies not only to the matters discussed in this chapter, but also to every kind of case in which one party's negligence is a direct cause of another's injury, and in which the negligence of the injured person is a contributing factor to his own injury. Keep in mind, also, that negligence is not a synonym for carelessness; it is failure to use the care which a man of ordinary prudence would have used in the circumstances. See **Rules 346** and **153A.** Do you believe that Hurd was contributorily negligent in the case discussed under **Rule 347** (*b*)? Give a reason for your answer.

5. What is the *fellow-servant* rule in the common law? **Rule 347** (*c*).

6. Write a brief summary of reasons why the common law rules would be, in your opinion, inadequate to protect employees in modern industrial employment against carrying an undue share of the risks of injury.

7. What is a Workmen's Compensation Act? To what does it apply? What are the main provisions of such an act? How widespread has been the enactment of such laws in this country? What kinds of employments are usually covered, and which are usually not covered, by such acts? **Rule 348.**

8. What are the Federal Safety Appliance Acts? How long have such acts been in effect? What is the extent of their application, as far as types of employment are concerned? **Rule 349.**

9. Explain how the social order, in general, is probably affected by the enforcement of Workmen's Compensation Laws, in addition to the benefits accruing to workers themselves. **Rule 350.**

Utah State Capitol, Salt Lake City
Underwood & Underwood

Vermont State Capitol, Montpelier
Derick Studios

Virginia State Capitol, Richmond
Underwood & Underwood

Washington State Capitol, Olympia
Underwood & Underwood

CHAPTER XII

INTERPRETATION OF CONTRACTS[1]

THE MEANING OF DOUBTFUL LANGUAGE

Even though the parties to contracts are careful to write out their contracts, and no matter how careful they are in the execution of such instruments, it still is probable that some disputes may arise afterward, as to the exact meaning of some of the language used. When such disputes do arise, it is necessary that there be some basic principles upon which the courts (or the parties or advisors) can proceed to interpret any language, the meaning of which is uncertain. A knowledge of these principles is important to those who enter into contracts in writing, not only because they wish to interpret their own agreements accurately in case of dispute, but also because such knowledge is an important aid in the drawing of contracts, since, by the careful use of such knowledge, a great many disputes can be avoided.

Rule 352. *As a rule, interpretation is governed by the law of the state in which the contract is made.* The basic rules by which the courts interpret doubtful language are about the same in all of the states, in a general way; but in some kinds of cases there are differences in detail. Therefore, the same language might possibly have different meanings in the opinions of different courts.[2] Whenever that is true, it is necessary to determine, in some way, which state's law will be applied to the particular problem. For instance, McDow in Massachusetts wrote to King in Illinois, offering to buy a certain patent right for one thousand dollars. The

---

[1] This chapter is adapted by permission of Longmans, Green & Co., from Chapters XXII and XXIII of *The Law of Contracts and Sales*, which contains a somewhat fuller treatment and additional illustrations.

[2] Remember that this applies only to those cases in which the meaning of the language is not clear to begin with.

offer was accepted by mailing a letter, so the contract was made
in Illinois.[3] If a dispute should arise under this agreement, there
are three possibilities as to which law will be applied. It would
be possible to apply the law of Massachusetts, where the offer
originated, or the law of Illinois, where the acceptance was made,
or, if the case came before the federal courts,[4] federal law might
control. In some contracts of this class, the parties provide that
the contract is to be executed in another state, and, in such a case,
it would be possible to apply the law of the state of performance.

In a still different group of cases, suit might be brought under
such a contract in still another state.[5] In the latter case, some of
the questions involved would be solved by the law of the state in
which the suit was brought. To be sure, the laws of the different
states are not all different on all points; but they are not all the
same. When there is a conflict of this sort, the fundamental rule
is this: The law applicable to the interpretation of contracts is the
law of the place where the contract was made unless the parties
agree, in making the contract, that the law of some other state is
to be applied, or unless the parties have agreed that the contract is
to be performed in some state other than that in which it is made.
In either of the two latter types of cases, the law of the designated
state will be applied. In the patent rights case referred to first, the
law of Illinois would prevail because the contract was made by
acceptance in Illinois. No matter what law is applied to the interpretation of contracts, the principle outlines of the rules of interpretation are quite similar in spite of some differences in detail.
These outlines follow the pattern indicated in the discussion of the
following rules.

Rule 353. *The parol evidence rule is applicable.* Whenever
the parties to a contract put their agreement into written terms,

---

[3] Acceptance is complete when it is mailed, properly stamped and addressed. See **Rule 26.**

[4] The case might come before the federal courts either because the
parties are citizens of different states or because the patent laws might be
involved.

[5] For example, a resident of Michigan makes a contract with a resident
of Missouri, which is to be performed in Illinois. Suit on this contract might
be brought in Ohio if the defendant were subject to that state at the time of the
filing of the suit, or it might be brought in the federal courts.

the courts will presume that the document contains all of the terms of the contract, and neither of the parties will be permitted to introduce evidence tending to show that they meant something different from the expressions used; nor will the parties be permitted to show that the agreement was to contain any additional terms. This presumption is known as the *parol evidence* rule. This rule is applied only when it is fairly clear that the parties intended the instrument to embody the final terms of their agreement; but the parties may show in court, if they can, that the instrument was not intended to be a final draft. It is wise to include in every contract language to the following effect: "The parties hereto assert and acknowledge, by their signatures hereto, that this instrument constitutes and contains all of the terms and conditions of the agreement of which this is a memorandum, and that this is to be regarded as the final form of their agreement." Even in the absence of such a statement, however, the courts presume a written instrument to be final and all inclusive;[6] and it is usually very difficult to overcome this presumption. No one should sign an agreement until he is certain that the paper contains just what he wishes it to contain. If a dispute arises, one is almost certain to be bound by what the paper says, and not by what he thought it said.

When the language used in a document is ambiguous, self-contradictory, apparently meaningless or vague, the courts usually follow certain so-called primary and secondary rules of interpretation. Neither group of rules is more important than the other. The so-called primary rules are usually more general in character than the secondary rules of interpretation. The four rules next given are so-called primary rules for the interpretation of contracts.

Rule 354. *Words are assumed, if possible, to be used in their normal meanings.* A fire insurance policy provided that, if the goods covered should be sold, the policy would be void. The policy covered a dealer's stock; and upon the occurrence of a loss,

---

[6] Of course, many agreements contain references to other instruments. Such references are said to incorporate the other instruments into such contract *by reference*. For example, a building contract need not contain all of the specifications in order to include them. It is necessary only to make reference to the specifications in some definite way. Such reference can be used to make the minutest details a part of the contract.

the insurer sought to avoid liability on the ground that some of the stock had been sold after the policy had taken effect. The sales had taken place over the counter in the normal course of the business. To allow this construction would be absurd since it would invalidate many such policies. It is true that the goods were sold; but the court held that, in this case, the language meant that the policy would be void if the whole stock of goods should be sold to the purchaser of the business. No other sensible interpretation could have been put upon this language. Again, if a lease provides that the premises shall not be used for a *saloon,* the lessee cannot avoid this restriction by calling his place of business a *tavern* or an *inn* or a *refreshment parlor* since the word *saloon* includes any place in which intoxicating liquor is sold to the public over the counter.[7]

Rule 355. *Technical terms are given their technical meanings, as a rule.* If an actor is engaged at a *weekly* rate, it is probably fair to assume that the employment is to run through the current theater season, even though no definite number of weeks is named. When the word *divide* is used in a partnership contract, it is assumed to mean *in equal shares* unless the agreement clearly states otherwise. When any technical language is used in a contract, there should be a statement somewhere within the instrument itself as to whether or not such language is to be understood in its technical sense; and, if it seems desirable, the technical meaning should be explained.

Rule 356. *Every agreement is construed as a whole and in the light of its general purposes.* If an instrument contains obvious typographical errors, they will be disregarded. For example, a son agreed to pay his father's debts. In exchange, the father gave the son a mortgage on some land. The mortgage provided that it should be void if the son failed to pay the father's debt, and if he should permit the debtors to bother his father. The son did not pay the debts, but the debtors did not bother the father, nor even ask him for payment; they sued the son. In an action on behalf

---

[7] Probably the term, in such a case, would also be held to include bottled liquor which was not to be consumed on the premises. This is somewhat doubtful, however, and, if a lease were to cover such a situation, it should be made entirely clear.

of the father to rescind the mortgage, the court held that it was the probable intent of the parties that the mortgage should read *or* instead of *and,* and that the mortgage, properly construed, meant that the mortgage should be invalid if the son *either* failed to pay the debts *or* permitted his father to be bothered about the debts. The mortgage was held invalid. In another case, Jones promised to pay a debt of Brown unless Brown should not pay it himself. This was clearly an error, and the word *not* should be disregarded by a court in interpreting the document containing such a promise.

Rule 357. *One may always show the circumstances under which an agreement was made if they reflect light upon the meaning of the terms.* This rule is applicable whether the terms are ambiguous or not. It is the object of the rule to enable a court to determine the fair meaning of any contracts which may come before it for interpretation. For example, a telegram which stated, "Will accept your offer at forty," might be shown to mean one-hundred and forty, if the previous dealings of the parties had been such as to make that seem reasonable, or if the current price of the commodity in question would make it reasonable to suppose that *forty* in reality meant *a hundred and forty.* Again, when Anderson agreed to paint some buildings for Mackey and the price agreed upon was two cents per square foot, a dispute arose as to whether or not this price included the doors and windows. It it could be shown that such openings were included by general custom, the contract would be so interpreted whether Mackey knew of the custom or not.

The primary rules of construction are, for the most part, merely common sense. The courts, in interpreting uncertain language, are doing only what is sensible. They follow normal meanings of words unless it seems absurd to do so; they follow the general intent of each instrument as a whole; and they do not adopt technical meanings unless it seems fair to do so under the circumstances of the particular contract. The following secondary rules are more specific than the so-called primary rules.[8]

Rule 358. *The main purposes of an instrument will be given effect.* This rule is similar to **Rule 354,** but it is usually applied

---

[8] No attention should be paid to the order in which these rules are given.

only where some part of an agreement is directly contrary to the whole. For example, one clause of an insurance policy provided that no gasoline might be stored on the insured premises, while another sentence stated that not more than five gallons of gasoline might be stored there.[9] The latter provision would prevail since it is the usual purpose of insurance to protect property in its ordinary uses, and it is fair to assume that the latter phrase was intended to operate as an exception to the general statement.

Rule 359. *An instrument will be construed so as to be effective if that is possible.* Suppose that an agreement, signed by both parties, contained a promise of the seller to deliver 375 pounds of butter at thirty-two cents per pound. The instrument did not contain a specific promise of the buyer to buy any butter. But it probably would be construed as an agreement because this seems to be the only fair inference to be drawn from the fact that both parties signed the instrument. Again, an agreement was entered into for the sale of certain farm products to be delivered during the autumn of 1940. In August, a government order forbade the delivery of such goods during October, but not during September or November. It would be possible to hold the whole agreement invalid because of the impossibility of making delivery throughout the whole of the autumn; but most courts would hold that there was still an obligation to make deliveries during the other autumn months, even though none could lawfully be made in October.[10] Another case which illustrates this rule is an English case in which a bond states that the bond would be void if the amount stated in it should not be paid. This language, if taken literally, would make the bond void. It would mean that A promised B that if C did not pay a certain debt, then A would pay it, but that this promise would be void if C did not pay. The word *not* was disregarded in order to give the bond effect.

---

[9] Both provisions were printed. Neither one had been stricken out.

[10] This agreement probably would be interpreted to even affect the total amount to be delivered. If, for example, it was agreed to deliver 1000 tons, but about all that could be handled within a month was some 300 tons, it might be that the agreement would be construed so as to require the seller to deliver and the buyer to take and pay for some 600 tons or less during the *autumn*, exclusive of October.

Rule 360. *Ambiguous language is construed against the party who uses it.* This rule is very important. Under it, the party who chooses the language for the agreement is compelled to assume the burden of either making the language clear or being bound by the meaning least favorable to himself. This rule has often been applied to insurance policies. Early insurance policies contained a considerable amount of language which was obscure, doubtful, or ambiguous. Many cases arose which showed that the insured had been led to expect something which the insurer had not intended to promise. Such language was uniformly construed in favor of the insured. As a consequence of this rule, so far as it is known, parties usually do not intentionally use ambiguous language; and the language of insurance policies has now been well standardized by standard policy laws and by court interpretation. But the rule is still in effect and is applied whenever necessary to any type of contract, including leases and contracts of employment.

Rule 361. *Written provisions prevail over printed provisions.* Frequently, the parties to a contract make use of printed forms, but insert written additions or alterations before signing. Oftentimes, some of these additions are contrary to certain printed provisions; and when such is the case, the courts take the view that the fact that a provision is written upon a printed blank should be taken as an indication of an intent that the written portions should prevail over contradictory printed statements in the same instrument. For example, a house painter made use of a printed form which contained in clear type the statement: *The price shown herein does not include the painting of storm sash.* In the margin of the document was written in ink the following: *16 storm windows to be painted for the price agreed upon.* If the court which was called upon to interpret this contract should be convinced that this written provision was on the instrument when it was signed, such court would disregard the contradictory printed statement.[11]

Rule 362. *Writing prevails over numerals.* Whenever contracts contain statements as to amounts of money, quantities of

---

[11] Of course, there is the difficult question of proof, which exists in all such cases. In fact, one of the principal tasks of the lawyer is the task of proof—convincing the court that his view of the facts is the view which should be accepted.

goods, or measurements of any kind, and whenever these statements are made both in written or printed words and in figures,
it sometimes happens, by mistake, that the writing and the figures
do not agree. This happens rather frequently in the drawing up of
negotiable instruments. In such cases, the written statements are
held to be effective, and not the figures. The reason is that it
seems less likely that errors will be made in writing out an amount
in full than it is that mistakes will be made in making figures.

Rule 363. *Corporation charters are construed in favor of
the public interest.* Corporation charters are regarded as contracts,
with the corporation on one side and the state which grants the
charter on the other side. Such charters confer powers upon corporations, and, since the language is sometimes ambiguous, necessity frequently arises for interpretation. For example, a corporation
was enfranchised by the state of Massachusetts to erect and operate
a toll bridge across the Charles River in the city of Boston. After
the bridge had been in operation for several years, the state authorized the construction of another bridge, which was near the first
one and which was designated as a free public bridge. The corporation operating the first bridge sought to prevent the operation
of the second one. The first corporation's charter did not specifically grant it the right to operate an exclusive bridge, but it was
argued that the erection of a free bridge would destroy the value
of the old bridge and that this would be a violation of the contract
(in the charter). But the Supreme Court of the United States
decided that an ambiguous charter of a corporation should be construed in favor of the public, saying that corporations "can claim
nothing not clearly given them by the charter." This rule of interpretation is now followed in all of the states.[12]

SUMMARY

The foregoing rules of interpretation of contracts are embodied in the following suggestions which should be followed by
contracting parties after they have reached agreement and before
any instrument is signed:

[12] It must be kept in mind that the above rules can never be used to enable
a party to escape a bad bargain. They are used by the courts only to determine
the meaning of what was said.

1. *Be sure that the instrument contains everything agreed upon.*
2. *Use simple, exact language.*
3. *Do not use any words with double or doubtful meanings.*
4. *If you use technical terms, be sure to state what they mean or where their meanings can be found.*
5. *Check figures and writing.*
6. *Check for contradictory statements.*
7. *Make sure that you do not promise more than you intend to promise.*
8. *If necessary for certainty of meaning, use illustrations.*
9. *If you have any doubts, consult an attorney or other experts.*
10. *If you have no doubts, beware!*

THE MEASURE OF DAMAGES FOR BREACH OF CONTRACT

After a contract has been broken, and even after the breach has been acknowledged or determined by a court, it often happens that the parties are unable to agree as to how much money should be paid as compensation for the loss caused by the breach. If one knows something about the manner in which the courts deal with this kind of problem, not only will he know, in some cases, what he is entitled to demand from others for breach of contract, but he will also be able to compromise disputed claims with results which at least approximate his legal rights.

It is only in comparatively rare cases that courts will order a party to a contract to perform exactly what he has promised.[13] In all other cases, one who is injured by breach of contract must, so far as the law is concerned, be satisfied with money damages. Money damages at best, however, are only partial compensation for losses sustained as a result of breach of contract. This is not generally understood because there is not a widespread knowledge of the rules by which damages are determined by the courts.

The basic rule for the determination of the amount of damages arising from breach of contract was laid down by an English

---

[13] For exception, see **Rule 138**, concerning specific performance. For an apparent exception, see **Rule 131**, concerning the legal remedy available to the seller when the title to the goods has passed to the buyer.

Court in 1854 in the case of *Hadley* versus *Baxendale*. The case
is an old one, to be sure, but no one has ever been able to work out
a rule which seems more sensible to the vast majority of authorities
in the field of contract law. In that case the facts were that the
plaintiff had shipped to the defendant a broken mill shaft for
welding. The plaintiff's mill could not be operated while the repairs were being made. The defendant did not know this and
neglected to do the work promptly. The mill was idle for several
days longer than might have been necessary if the defendant had
acted more promptly. The plaintiff brought suit for breach of contract, supposing that he would be entitled to damages to compen-
sate him for loss of his profits while the mill was idle due to the
delay in the work. The court, while deciding that the contract of
repair had been broken, laid down the following rule for application in such cases:

When two parties have made a contract which one of them has
broken, the damages which the other party ought to receive in respect
of such breach of contract should be such as may fairly and reasonably be considered as arising naturally, i.e., according to the usual
course of things, from such breach of contract itself; or [such] as may
reasonably be supposed to have been in the contemplation of both
parties to the contract, at the time when they made it, as the probable
result of the breach of it.

The court thought that it was not reasonable that the defendant should have expected that the mill could not run without
this shaft. Since that was regarded as true, the defendant was not
liable for the loss due to the delay because it does not seem that
both parties contemplated loss from such delay. In like circumstances, the plaintiff should advise the other party as to the circumstances, namely, that the shaft was necessary to the operation of
the mill.

It is worth emphasis that this rule is in two parts. One may
recover (a) for such losses as are the usual, probable, ordinarily-
to-be-expected consequences of a breach of contract, or (b) for
losses which, though unusual, may fairly be thought to have been
expected by both parties when they made the contract.[14]

Some other illustrations of the application of each branch of

---

[14] Note how this rule excludes losses which are remote or uncertain.

this rule should help make clear its significance. In one case, Bloom had sold a shipment of shoes to Snyder & Co., who had stipulated that the shoes must be delivered by a certain day or they would be rejected. Bloom delivered the shipment to the *Y* railway in plenty of time for delivery by the required day, but the shipment was delayed and did not reach the buyer in the appointed time. The buyer rejected them, and Bloom sold the shoes elsewhere at a loss. In a suit against the railway, Bloom sought to recover the entire amount of his loss, which in his opinion was the difference between the contract price and the price for which he sold the shoes. The court said that this was not correct. Under part (a) of the Hadley rule, the railway was liable for the loss which would ordinarily be expected to result from delay. The result of such delay would usually be (the court thought) that the goods might be rejected and would have to be sold on the open market; and the loss should be the difference between the market value (not the contract price) at the time when delivery should have been made, and the market value at the time when they were sold. To this could be added the reasonable cost of finding another buyer.

To make this clear, assume that the market value of the shoes on the day they should have been delivered was $400.00 per case, and that the customer had promised to pay $450.00 per case. The actual loss to the seller (in his opinion) was fifty dollars per case; but if he sold them for four hundred dollars per case, his only recovery under the rule would be the cost of finding a buyer. He is not entitled to the profit which he claims he would have made by the delivery. If Bloom wished to charge the railway for more liability than this, he should have advised their agent of the peculiar contract under which the goods were sold. Had that been done, it would have been fair to assume that the railway should have expected more than an ordinary loss as a result of delay. The extra fifty dollars loss was really due to the special contract which Bloom had with his customer, but which was not known in detail to the railway company.

In another case, a seller of furniture took proper precautions. Brown agreed to deliver certain furniture to Green. Then, Brown, after notifying Black of the previous agreement with Green, entered into an agreement to purchase, and Black agreed to sell, the furniture to Brown. Black failed to deliver the goods to Brown, thus causing a breach of contract between Brown and Green. It was held by a court that Black must pay more than the difference between the price which Brown was to receive for the goods and the price for which he could get the furniture elsewhere; in addition to that amount, Black was compelled to repay to Brown the amount of damages which Brown was required to pay Green for Brown's breach of contract. The second amount was due only because it was fair for the court to assume that Black must have expected some such loss since Brown had told Black why he wanted the furniture.[15]

In a third case, Harvester Company agreed to deliver a threshing machine to Gray on a certain date. It was not delivered until thirty-one days after the stipulated time. In the meantime, the grain which Gray had expected to thresh had been damaged by wet weather. Some of it was spoiled, and the remainder could not be sold until it had been dried out. When it was ready to sell, the market had fallen off, and the grain was sold for substantially less per bushel that it would have brought earlier. In an action for breach of the contract, the court awarded damages to Gray for the loss of the grain which was wet and spoiled because this, under the first part of the rule, was naturally to be expected; but it refused to allow anything for the loss due to the falling market because, under the second branch of the rule, such a loss was not reasonably to be foreseen.[16] In many cases in which railway companies have unduly delayed livestock in transit, it has been held that they are liable for the difference between the market price when the delivery should have been made and the market price when it was made, in the event that the price has fallen during that time.

The point of chief importance in these cases is that whenever one makes a contract for some special purpose, he should advise

---

[15] This case is an application of the second branch of the rule of the case of *Hadley* versus *Baxendale*.

[16] So far as one could see at the time of the delay, the market might just as well have risen.

the other party of the peculiar circumstances. This will not only increase the damages if the contract should be broken, but it may also, in some cases, actually prevent a breach of the contract, as it probably would have done in the mill-shaft case.

This method of measuring damages is often quite unsatisfactory to the injured party; but that is because of the fact that the injured party believes that he would have made a profit if there had been no breach, and he thinks that the other party should pay him such profit. In some cases, this may be true; but the courts are very loathe to award any damages for loss of profits because they regard them as *speculative* (uncertain) and *remote* (not necessarily directly due to the breach of contract in question).

There have been many cases against telegraph companies for damages due to mistakes in delivering messages. Most of these cases have arisen in actions for breach of the contract by which the company agreed to transmit the messages for a payment. There are some contradictions in the decisions in such cases. One view is shown by a case in which Leonard ordered by telegram 5000 *sacks* of salt. The message was transmitted to read 5000 *casks* of salt. A *cask,* in the salt trade, meant 320 pounds of coarse salt, while a *sack* meant 14 pounds of fine salt. The recipient sent 5000 casks. Leonard was bound to buy it under the contract, but he could find no market for it at the time. He stored the salt and sold it at a loss of some $1500. It was held that the telegraph company was liable for this loss since this was the kind of loss which would naturally result from such an error. The company was liable for the loss, as well as for the costs of moving and storage. In another case, however, although a mistake in a cipher message caused a loss of about $20,000, the Supreme Court of the United States decided that such a loss (though it involved quantity, just as in the salt case) was not fairly contemplated by the company when it sent the message. These two cases are representative of the contradictions referred to at the beginning of this paragraph. Some states have tried to do away with the conflict by statutory regulation of the liabilities of telegraph companies for mistakes in transmitting messages. In some states, for example, in the usual case, the sender is entitled to recover only the amount he paid for the transmission of the message if it is mistakenly sent.[17]

In employment contracts which are broken by the employer, the damages are usually measured by the difference between the amount which the employee would have earned under the contract and the amount which he could have earned in other employment if he had exercised ordinary diligence to find other work of the same general kind. That is, the employee who is wrongfully discharged is not necessarily entitled to recover his full weekly or monthly pay. For example, Warner was to be employed in a cannery as foreman for a period of eight weeks at $30.00 per week. At the end of two weeks, he was discharged without a lawful reason. When he sued for six weeks' pay, it was shown that, had he exercised ordinary diligence, he could have gotten three weeks of similar work at $27.00 per week. He was therefore entitled to six times thirty dollars, *minus* three times twenty-seven dollars. This rule is sometimes called the rule of *mitigation* of damages. It is applied only in personal service contracts.[18]

There are so many uncertainties about the measure of damages for breach of contract[19] that the parties often include in their agreements provisions as to how damages are to be measured in case of breach. For example, there may be a provision in a building contract to the effect that, for each day's delay after a stated time, there shall be due a sum of one hundred dollars. Such stipulations are known as *liquidated* damages, which means merely that the amount is agreed on in advance of the breach. But the courts do not favor such arrangements. They are apt to construe provisions for liquidated damages as *penalties,* and there is a persistent antipathy on the part of the courts to penalties. If such a stipulation is held by a court to be a penalty, the damages will be meas-

---

[17] If a cipher telegram is not delivered at all, there is liability for the loss of the bargain if the failure to deliver is the direct cause of such loss.

[18] Parties to contracts may not do anything to increase damages, however. See **Rule 80.**

[19] There are some very difficult questions in connection with the measure of damages for breach of contracts to deliver goods in installments. The subject of such contracts is highly technical and cannot be satisfactorily dealt with in a general outline of commercial law.

ured by the application of the rules which have just been discussed. What a penalty is cannot be determined by definition because it is determined, in general, by local rules and by the attitude of the court which happens to have jurisdiction of a given suit for breach of contract. Provisions for liquidated damages are uncertain even when they are devised by expert counsel. The danger is probably less than it was some years ago, but there is still a real uncertainty in every case of this kind. This danger exists because of the risk that such provisions will be held invalid because they are regarded as penalties, and, as such, not enforceable.

QUESTIONS AND PROBLEMS

1. In general, when a dispute arises as to the meaning or effect of a contract which was made in one state and signed in another, by the law of which state will the dispute be settled? **Rule 352.**

2. What is the *parol evidence* rule? What precautions should be taken by parties to contracts to prevent the arising of disputes either as to what they agreed to do or as to the meaning of the language used in a document? **Rule 353.**

3. What is the general rule followed by the courts in determining the interpretation of words which might have more than one meaning? **Rule 354.**

4. If an agreement is ambiguous, or if some part of it contradicts some other part, are the courts inclined to regard the agreement as invalid for uncertainty, or are they inclined to try to iron out inconsistencies and give the agreement the effect which seems to have been intended when the instrument is considered as a whole? **Rules 356 and 359.**

5. For what purposes may one show the circumstances under which an agreement was made? **Rule 357.** State in brief the chief primary rules which are allowed to govern the interpretation of contracts.

6. What rule is followed when ambiguous language is encountered and when it is clear which party chose this particular language? **Rule 360.** Indicate a common illustration of this, in which one can be certain which party selected the language.

7. A builder of garages entered into a contract to erect a garage for Thompson. On the blank which was used to make the contract, there was a printed statement to the effect that the builder did not agree to install a driveway. It was agreed between the parties, however, as a part of the agreement, that a driveway would be installed and that the charge for it would be $200.00. Would the provision

about the driveway be regarded as a part of the agreement and enforcible if there were no mention of it on the document which was signed? See question 2. Suppose that before signing the document, the parties typed along the margin of it the words, "It is agreed that the party of the first part shall construct a driveway of cement, seven feet wide and five inches thick with suitable cinder foundation and drainage, to be included in the price named herein." Would the courts enforce such a provision in view of the printed statement referred to? **Rule 361.**

8. Suppose that in a certain instrument it is stated that the dimensions of a certain tract of land to be sold are one thousand feet by two hundred feet, while, at another place in the document, it is stated *in figures* that the total area of the piece to be sold is 20,000 square feet. Which of these would be given effect by a court? Or would a court declare it invalid for uncertainty? **Rule 362.**

9. Which rule would be applicable in case of ambiguous language in a corporation charter, **Rule 360** or **363**? Why?

10. Copy three times the ten rules printed in italics on page 303.

11. Write out in full the rule for determining the amount of damages recoverable for breach of contract in the case of *Hadley* v. *Baxendale.* Does the rule seem reasonable to you? Why, or why not?

12. Jones agreed to buy, and the F company agreed to sell to Jones, a piano on the installment plan. Jones made a down payment of five dollars and signed an agreement. The piano was to be delivered within a few days. Before it was delivered, Jones decided not to buy the piano and notified the F company not to deliver it. When they delivered it anyway, Jones refused to accept delivery. If the company decided to bring suit, could they recover anything at all from Jones? Why or why not? If they could recover anything at all, how would you estimate how much they could recover? See page 304.

13. Can the rules for the interpretation of contracts be used to escape the consequences of undesirable agreements or bad bargains? **Rule 363,** footnote [12].

14. Suppose, under the preliminary facts of question 12, that the piano company decided not to sell to Jones and offered to return his deposit. Would this relieve them from liability under the contract if Jones accepted the money? You may have to use your imagination on this question, but try it. If Jones refused to accept the return of the deposit, and if he wished to sue on the contract, how much do you think he could recover as damages for breach of the agreement? Pages 305 and 306. See also **Rule 93.**

15. How are damages measured, as a general rule, when a contract of employment is broken by the employer's discharge of an employee in violation of the agreement? Explain this carefully. Page 308.

West Virginia State Capitol, Charleston
Underwood & Underwood

New Hampshire State Capitol, Concord
Harold Orne Photo

Wisconsin State Capitol, Madison
Madison & Wisconsin Foundation

Wyoming State Capitol, Cheyenne
Underwood & Underwood

CHAPTER XIII

COUNTERFEIT MONEY[1]

Our economy is a money economy. This means that all of our property values and most of our commercial service values are evaluated in terms of a monetary unit called the dollar. As defined by the Congress in 1785 and subsequent enactments, the dollar was originally a metallic coin; but in the growing commerce of the nineteenth century, business demands for money became so great that it would have become very difficult, if not impossible, to coin enough metallic money to meet all of the demands of exchange and trade. Furthermore, large sums of coined money are extremely difficult and expensive to transport from place to place to make payments. To relieve the business community of these inconveniences, as well as to enable the Government of the United States (and other governments) to take advantage of government credit, the governments of the world have resorted to the issuance of paper currency. Our own present form of currency began with the Civil War, but its final form dates from the adoption of the Federal Reserve Act of 1913.

For all of the purposes of trade, private exchange, and government uses of money, paper currency is precisely as good and as safe as metallic coinage, so long as two conditions are maintained.

---

[1] The material in this chapter, including certain reproductions of portions of currency, is published by special permission of Henry Morgenthau, Jr., Secretary of the Treasury, in furtherance of the U. S. Secret Service program of Crime Prevention Through Education. Further reproduction of the illustrations, either in part or as a whole, is strictly forbidden.

The interested student may obtain further information on the subject of counterfeit money by writing to the U. S. Secret Service, Treasury Department, Washington, D. C. A simple request for information will be sufficient.

A 32-page illustrated booklet on counterfeit money, entitled *Know Your Money*, published by U. S. Secret Service, can be purchased from the Superintendent of Documents, Government Printing Office, Washington, D. C., for ten cents.

The first of these conditions is that the credit of the issuing government must remain sound. There has been no question on this score since the difficult times immediately following the Civil War. The second of these conditions is that all paper currency in circulation must be genuine; that is, every note must be an actual obligation of the government. If more than a very little counterfeit currency should be in circulation at any given time, people would find out about it and this would make some of them, at least, hesitant about taking even genuine money, for fear that it might be spurious. For this reason, our government has from the very beginning worked upon the sound principle that the discovery and punishment of every single counterfeiter is of the utmost importance. The enforcement of this branch of the law has been entrusted to the United States Secret Service, which is a unit of the Treasury Department.

During recent years, the United States Secret Service has gone beyond the mere detection and punishment of counterfeiters. It has developed a widespread program for the *prevention* of this type of crime. For the first time in history, a major law-enforcing agency has decided to rely upon public education as a preventive of crime. The farther this education can be spread, the less will be the danger of national and personal losses due to counterfeiting. For the counterfeiter must rely upon the ignorance of his victims; and if large numbers of clerks, shopkeepers and salespeople, as well as bank employees, know something about the characteristics of both good money and bad money, counterfeit money and the counterfeiter will soon practically disappear. In fact the results of the educational program are already astonishing, as the table of losses shows. The business of the counterfeiter is decidedly unprofitable, but the edu-

Year	Yearly Losses to Victims of Bogus Bills
1933-36 yearly average	$771,000
1937	519,000
1938	407,000
1939	294,000
1940	146,000
1941	91,000
1942	48,000

cational program must continue until the marks of good money are so widely known that no counterfeit money can circulate at all.

It is unlawful to reproduce facsimiles of either counterfeit or genuine money, but for convenience of reference an open diagram is produced (see Fig. 1), showing the general outline of the face of a Federal reserve note. The backs of all notes are printed entirely in green. It is just possible that one may encounter a gold certificate (called *yellow-back*), which should be turned in to the recipient's bank for other currency.

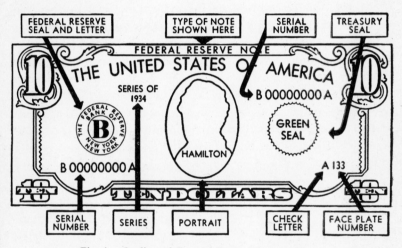

Fig. 1.   Outline of Face of Federal Reserve Note

This reproduction published by special permission of the Secretary of the Treasury in furtherance of the U. S. Secret Service program of Crime Prevention Through Education. Further reproduction in whole or in part is strictly forbidden.

In 1942 the Federal reserve banks released $660,000,000 in National Currency notes, series of 1929. This money had been stored in Treasury vaults and was issued to save paper and man-hours which would be expended by the production of an equivalent amount of new currency.

Study this chart carefully, noting where the different features appear. The signature of the Treasurer of the United States appears on the lower left side. Study a genuine Federal reserve note, comparing it carefully with this diagram.

There are four types of paper currency. Silver certificates are issued by the government, secured by actual silver; United States notes are issued by the Treasury as promissory notes of the Government of the United States; Federal reserve notes are issued by the Federal reserve banks, secured by gold and other collateral; and National Currency has been issued since December of 1942, by the Federal reserve banks. These four types of currency have certain features common to all of them, which are easy to note, and which the counterfeiter often overlooks.

Each type has its own color of seal and number. On Federal reserve notes, the Treasury seal and the serial number are printed in *green* ink; on the silver certificate, they are printed in *blue;* on United States notes, they are printed in *red;* and on the National Currency notes they are in *brown.* The type of note is designated at the top of the face of each note, as shown in the diagram.

Each denomination has a distinguishing portrait. No matter what the type of a particular bill is, if it is genuine its denomination will correspond with the proper portrait, as shown in Fig. 2.

Washington appears on all one-dollar bills.

Jefferson appears on all two-dollar bills.

Lincoln appears on all five-dollar bills.

Hamilton appears on all ten-dollar bills.

Jackson appears on all twenty-dollar bills.

Grant appears on all fifty-dollar bills.

Franklin appears on all one hundred-dollar bills.

The first five of these should be known instantly to every person who handles currency. Study them carefully and commit the list to memory.

Federal reserve notes are numbered and lettered by districts. There are twelve Federal reserve districts. In each district is a Federal reserve bank, authorized to issue Federal reserve notes under certain conditions prescribed by law. The notes, of course, are made in the Bureau of Engraving and Printing in Washington. Each Federal reserve district has a number and also a corresponding letter of the alphabet. Every Federal reserve note bears a regional seal, indicating the reserve city and showing in *black* the letter of the issuing bank's district, as indicated in the diagram on page 313; and on the face of each note (in four separate places on a genuine Federal reserve note) will be found the district number. If the name of the city, the number, and the letter do not correspond,

Fig. 2. Portraits on Genuine U. S. Currency

This reproduction published by special permission of the Secretary of the Treasury in furtherance of the U. S. Secret Service program of Crime Prevention Through Education. Further reproduction in whole or in part is strictly forbidden.

the bill is not genuine. The following table of Federal reserve cities will enable you to check this.

Federal Reserve Cities	Symbol Letter	District Number
Boston	A	1
New York	B	2
Philadelphia	C	3
Cleveland	D	4
Richmond	E	5
Atlanta	F	6
Chicago	G	7
St. Louis	H	8
Minneapolis	I	9
Kansas City, Mo.	J	10
Dallas	K	11
San Francisco	L	12

There are certain general indications of counterfeit money. Many counterfeiters of currency, of course, are thoroughly familiar with the characteristics of genuine money, and many of them do not make mistakes of the kinds already suggested. But they do make other mistakes and their work usually bears upon its face the signs by which it can be known for what it is; *bad money looks bad!* Study the bills you receive. Become familiar with the portraits and with the designs and workmanship you find on the bills. When you see a suspected bill, make the following comparisons with a bill known to be genuine:

PAPER—*Genuine* has a characteristic feeling which one learns by handling money. The colored fibers will not always show if the money is worn or very dirty.

Counterfeit usually has no colored fibers, though the threads are sometimes imitated by light ink lines. The *feel* of the paper may be wrong.

SEAL—*Genuine* is of proper color and saw-tooth points are even and sharp.

Counterfeit, even though of proper color, usually has points that are uneven or broken off, or both.

SERIAL NUMBERS—*Genuine* will be of same proper color as seal, and figures will be well-spaced and firmly and evenly printed.

Counterfeit, even though of proper color, may be poorly printed, badly spaced, and uneven in appearance.

PORTRAIT—*Genuine* background is fine screen of regular lines; eyes appear lifelike; whole picture seems to stand out from background clearly.

Counterfeit background is apt to be too dark, with lines uneven and broken; eyes are dull and often unmatched; portrait merges with background; whole picture is generally not lifelike.

BORDER—*Genuine* is made of fine lines, crossing and recrossing. All lines are clear, complete, distinct, and unbroken.

Counterfeit crossing lines are broken and uneven, indistinct and irregular.

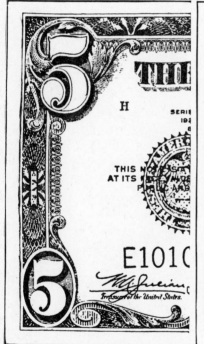

Fig. 3

In addition to this, the general appearance of many counterfeits is rather poor. The printing is often inferior and smudged, and letters and figures uneven. However, even imperfect counterfeits may pass one who does not know what to look for, or one who knows but does not look.

Figs. 3 and 4 are enlargements of portions of *counterfeit* bills. They show some of the differences between good money and bad money. Compare these enlargements with the same portions of five- and twenty-dollar bills. A magnifying glass will help you to make the comparison, but it is not necessary because, once you have studied good money carefully, you can usually detect counterfeits by defects which are visible to the naked eye.

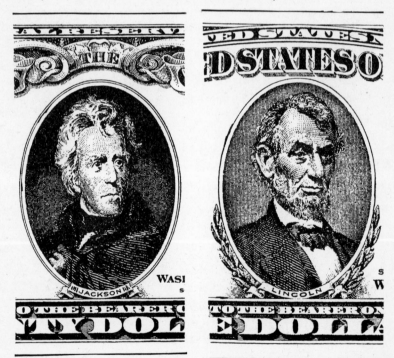

Fig. 4

This reproduction published by special permission of the Secretary of the Treasury in furtherance of the U. S. Secret Service program of Crime Prevention Through Education. Further reproduction in whole or in part is strictly forbidden.

In the corners, note the characters of the fish-net lines and the lines back of the figures. On good money, these lines are always sharp and clear, while on bad money they are often smeared, broken, or indistinct.

How to detect counterfeit coins. In some parts of the country, there is in circulation a larger proportion of coins than in others. This is especially true, of course, of silver dollars. The United States Secret Service recommends that, in dealing with suspected coins, the following points be observed:

First: Study genuine coins to become familiar with the expert workmanship found on them.

Second: Ring a suspected coin on a hard surface. Genuine coins have a distinct ring; counterfeits give out a dull sound.

Third: Counterfeits usually have a greasy feeling.

Fourth: Cut the edges with a knife. Genuine coins are hard to cut; counterfeits are usually soft and easy to cut.

Fifth: Notice the *reeding,* or *milling.* The ridges on genuine coins are sharp and clear, while those on counterfeits are apt to be irregular and not clear.

Sixth: Silver coins—dimes, quarters, half dollars, and dollars—can be tested with a silver-test solution which can be obtained for a few cents at a drugstore. The solution will not discolor genuine silver, but it will turn counterfeits black.

Nitrate of silver	10 grains
Nitric acid	1 cubic centimeter
Distilled water	30 cubic centimeters

What to do if counterfeit money is tendered you. The laws of the United States provide that if any person has knowledge of counterfeiting of the money of the United States and does not at once communicate such knowledge to the authorities, such person himself becomes a party to a crime and shall be fined not more than five hundred dollars or imprisoned for not more than three years, or both. The law also provides that if any counterfeit money of the United States (or of any other government) shall be found in the possession of any person without authority from the Secretary of the Treasury, such counterfeit shall be confiscated by an authorized agent of the Treasury Department; and that failure to surrender such counterfeit to an authorized agent, upon request, is also a crime, punishable by a fine of not more than one hundred dollars or imprisonment of one year, or both. The law further authorizes all banks to confiscate counterfeit money for surrender to the Treasury Department. Therefore, if you have in your possession any counterfeit money, it is your legal duty to inform the authorities (the Secret Service, local police, or banks), and to surrender the counterfeit. The government does not redeem counterfeit, but if genuine money has been altered, the original face value will usually be paid to an innocent holder. If someone offers you money which seems to be counterfeit, try to detain the passer by some excuse—to run out and get change, or some such device—while you call the police. In case the party walks out on you, note his description as best you can, and, if he is driving a car, note his license number.

Enemy counterfeiters are dangerous in time of war. The menace of the domestic counterfeiter has been reduced by about 93 per cent in the past few years. This is largely because of the fact that the Secret Service has conducted its widespread program of education of potential victims of counterfeiters. But there is still danger during wartime that some of our enemies will attempt to dump considerable quantities of counterfeits upon us. This may be done partly to try to finance the work of enemy agents, and partly to make our people suspicious of our own country's genuine money. This was attempted in China by the Japanese at least once between 1938 and 1942, when Chinese counterfeits were distributed in Manchukuo. To the informed person, however, most counterfeits are usually detectable because of certain faults similar to those which have been discussed in this chapter.

Know your money! Watch your money!

QUESTIONS AND PROBLEMS

1. Whose portrait is found on all bills of ten-dollar denomination? On two-dollar bills? On five-dollar bills? On one-dollar bills?

2. In how many colors are the seals on United States currency? What does each color signify?

3. What does the law require the possessor of counterfeit money to do with it as soon as he knows that it is counterfeit?

4. What are the distinguishing features of coined money with regard to which it is fairly easy to detect counterfeits?

5. Does the government treasury redeem counterfeit money?

6. What should one do if he is offered money which he suspects is counterfeit?

7. How does a Federal reserve note differ from a silver certificate? What difference can you detect instantly?

8. Name two places in which the engraving on a counterfeit is apt to be noticeably bad, and which can often be detected with the naked eye.

9. Of what branch of the government is the United States Secret Service a unit?

10. How many kinds of paper money are now in circulation as United States Currency? What is the easiest mark of distinction of each kind?

INDEX